HENRY CHRISTOPHE

and

THOMAS CLARKSON

A Correspondence

HENRY CHRISTOPHE

painted from life by Richard Evans

The painting was exhibited at the Royal Academy in 1818.
Reproduced by courtesy of Captain Bruce S. Ingram,
editor of the Illustrated London News.
This portrait is now on loan to the Birmingham Art Gallery.

HENRY CHRISTOPHE

THOMAS CLARKSON

A Correspondence

Edited by
EARL LESLIE GRIGGS
and
CLIFFORD H. PRATOR

GREENWOOD PRESS, PUBLISHERS
NEW YORK   1968

To
DR. ROBERT GLASS CLELAND

PREFACE

The British Museum possesses a large collection of manuscripts preserved by Thomas Clarkson, the English abolitionist. Among them are to be found his Haitian papers (Brit. Mus. Add. MS 41266), consisting of his correspondence with Henry Christophe, the Negro king of Haiti, as well as other letters and documents pertinent to Haitian affairs. Because much of the correspondence with Christophe was of an official nature, Clarkson considered it of the utmost importance and carefully preserved not only the letters he received from Haiti, but also copies of many of his replies. In great measure, therefore, both sides of the correspondence are still extant.

This material forms a valuable commentary upon the obscure history of Haiti, and it tends to modify the interpretations which legend and fiction have woven around the personality and activities of Christophe. Instead of the spectacular and savage despot so often found in books dealing with him, Christophe becomes a wise and farsighted monarch dedicated to the welfare of his people.

The letters of Christophe are, indeed, remarkable productions. Their brevity, conciseness, and coherence, and the temperate discussion of Haitian problems show the intelligence and energy of his mind. They would do credit, as the Emperor of Russia remarked to Clarkson, to the best-trained European statesmen.

Introduced by four letters from Christophe to his son, the main correspondence begins with a letter from Christophe to Clarkson in 1816 and continues down to the King's death four years later. Interspersed are several letters from Haitian officials. The correspondence concludes with a series of letters written after Christophe's death. They give a vivid, firsthand account of the King's paralysis, of the revolution which followed, of Christophe's suicide, and of the rapid disintegration of the kingdom.

Attention should also be drawn to the three official documents included in Part III. These decrees are of the utmost importance not only in evaluating the foresight and administrative genius of Christophe, but also in showing Clarkson's influence on Haitian domestic affairs.

Although the philanthropic labors of Thomas Clarkson are nowhere better exemplified than in this correspondence, in striking contrast to Christophe, he wrote at great length, to avoid any possibility of misunderstanding, and as a result his letters are repetitious and laborious. An Englishman, William Wilson, and an American Negro, Prince Sanders, who both resided for a time in Haiti, also wrote in a rambling and lengthy manner. In the interests of readability, therefore, certain omissions, varying from a few words to several pages, have been made in editing these letters, as well as those from Wilberforce and Sutherland. Each omission is clearly indicated in the text. Obvious misspellings, faulty punctuation, haphazard capitalization, and the indiscriminate use of italics have been silently corrected.

The letters are printed in chronological order, and since they are in the main self-explanatory, editorial comment has been kept as unobtrusive as possible. The Haitian letters and documents are in French, the official language of Haiti, but have been translated and only the English translations appear in this volume.

A brief historical survey dealing with the island from its discovery by Columbus in 1492 to the death of Christophe in 1820 has been included. From 1806 until 1820, Haiti was divided into two governments, one under Christophe in the north, the other under Pétion (and later Boyer) in the south. The account of these years, therefore, has been centered upon Henry Christophe, in order to place in its proper setting the correspondence which follows.

Mr. Prator transcribed the microfilm of the manuscripts and translated the French letters and documents. Mr. Griggs prepared the historical survey (Haiti, 1492–1820) which precedes the correspondence and edited the text of the letters and documents.

We are indebted to the University of Michigan and to the University of California for grants in aid of research; to Miss Mary Isabel Fry of the Huntington Library and to Miss Corinne Babcock for generous assistance; and to Dr. Edward Howard Griggs and Dr. Price-Mars for a careful reading of the historical introduction. We wish to acknowledge the courtesy of the Pan American Airways System in permitting us to reproduce photographs of the Citadel Henry and the Palace of Sans Souci.

E. L. G.

CONTENTS

PART THREE: DOCUMENTS *issued by King Henry and sent to Thomas Clarkson*

APPENDIX

SELECTED BIBLIOGRAPHY

INDEX

MAPS & ILLUSTRATIONS

HAITI, 1492-1820

HAITI, 1492-1820

INTRODUCTION

Out of the fertile island of Haiti have come some of the most fascinating stories of modern times. A confusing mixture of legend and fact, their central theme unfolds a mighty drama, in which half a million Negro slaves struck off their chains, expelled their white masters from the island, and set up rulers of their own race. The luxurious, tropical vegetation has obscured the evidence of battle and bloodshed, and the island today seems almost a sleeping Paradise; but as the equinoctial storms and recurrent hurricanes sweep across the peaceful landscape, so once the unruly passions of men and the wild outpourings of race prejudice turned Haiti into a maelstrom of destruction. Not even the ruin and havoc caused by the earthquakes which occasionally shake the island can match the devastation of fire and sword.

Among the Negroes who emerged into prominence during the interracial conflicts of a century and a half ago, Toussaint L'Ouverture, Jean-Jacques Dessalines, and Henry Christophe are the most spectacular. In spite of the degrading effects of the slavery of their youth, they rose to positions of absolute authority; but personal failure came to each man at the height of his power. Toussaint, who for a brief interval united the whole island under a single government and miraculously transformed it from anarchy and civil war to peaceful productivity, spent his last days in a French prison, a victim of Napoleon's treachery; Dessalines, who proclaimed Haitian independence and founded the first independent government in Haiti, was assassinated by his disgruntled subjects; and Christophe, who strove to raise the Haitians to a civilized level, committed suicide when his subjects revolted. Despite the tragic endings of their lives, they did not, however, work entirely in vain. It is true that their dream of a prosperous, self-respecting, and successful Negro state has not yet been fully realized and that chaos and instability have marked most of the governments of Haiti down to the early years of the present century, but it is likewise true that the island over which

3

they gained supremacy has remained, for better or for worse, under native control. Toussaint and Christophe were of heroic mold, and if the limitations and handicaps under which they labored are taken into consideration, they bear favorable comparison with the white leaders of their era.

Henry Christophe, the principal figure in this volume, has won fame as an absolute sovereign who, by sheer force of personality and strength of will, ruled despotically over his kingdom. His elaborate palace, Sans Souci, his magnificent and awe-inspiring fortress, the Citadel Henry,—which even in ruins stand among the wonders of the Western world,—and his grandiose and pompous court emphasize his love of power and ostentation; but the ruthless cruelty with which he carried out the stern measures he imposed upon his people for their ultimate improvement has cast a shadow over his reputation. Undoubtedly, the same titanic energy with which he opposed the French and, with his fellow leaders, drove them from Haitian soil, characterized his actions as a monarch. Human life was cheap in Haiti, and Christophe let nothing stand in the way of what he considered a desirable objective. Much, however, can be offered in extenuation of his conduct. There was little in his heritage to improve his character; almost every circumstance of his life until he came to power was calculated to foster only the most savage instincts, and he committed no act of cruelty which had not already been practiced by his white oppressors. He must be judged, then, not wholly by the *means* he employed to achieve his objectives, but also by the nobility and grandeur of his aims. Once he had assumed control of his kingdom, he dreamed of the future, of a time when the Haitians, raised from ignorance, indolence, and poverty to industry and self-respect, would take their place among the nations of the world. Driven by an insatiable ambition, Henry Christophe endeavored to accomplish for his black brothers in fourteen years what the white race had been centuries in achieving.

An understanding of Henry Christophe demands a glance backwards over the story of the island in which he ruled and an examination of the milieu in which he was reared. The history of Haiti, too complicated to be retold here *in extenso,* explains in great measure the contradictions of her people and especially of her rulers. If the biography of Christophe seems too fantastic for belief, the story of Haiti is equally so.

Haiti (the aboriginal name, meaning hilly land), or Hispaniola, is a West Indian island lying between Cuba and Porto Rico. It is bounded on the north by the Atlantic Ocean and on the south by the Caribbean Sea. Much of the island is mountainous. The tropical climate is mild and admirably suited to growing coffee and sugar cane, but generations of primitive methods of farming have seriously depleted the once rich and productive soil. Today Hispaniola contains two sovereign states. To the east lies the Dominican Republic, occupying about two-thirds of the island. To the west lies the Republic of Haiti, comprising an area of about ten thousand square miles and with a population of more than two and a half millions.

EARLY PERIOD

On the evening of December 6, 1492, Columbus first set foot in Haiti at what is now the Môle Saint-Nicolas, off the northwestern coast. Six days later, at the Baie des Moustiques, he erected a cross; and, taking possession of the island in the names of Ferdinand and Isabella, called it Española,[1] later Latinized as Hispaniola. On the island he found simple, friendly, and peace-loving aborigines, estimated by the Spanish to number a million persons. Believing he had landed in the Indies, he called the natives Indians.

Although Columbus considered Española "the Paradise of God," and wrote of living out his life there, those who followed him under the Spanish flag came not to settle in idyllic surroundings but to seek gold, and as fortune hunters they enslaved and exploited the natives of the island. It has been declared that by 1533 barely six hundred Indians had survived. Certainly today not one pure-blooded descendant of the aborigines remains. Thus began the tragic story of the second largest island in the Caribbean Sea.

During the seventeenth century, French buccaneers and freebooters settled in considerable numbers in the island, and though there were long struggles with the Spanish inhabitants, eventually, in 1697, Spain ceded the western portion of Española to France. The French called their colony *la partie française de Saint-Domingue.*[2] The rest of the island remained in Spanish hands and was known as Santo Domingo.[3]

Since the Indians were being rapidly exterminated by hard physical labor

---

[1] The Spanish later called the island Santo Domingo, and when the French gained control of the western third of the island, they called their territory Saint-Domingue. English and American writers of the nineteenth century often used Santo Domingo, St. Domingo, and San Domingo to designate the island. In order to avoid confusion, the United States Hydrographic Office has recently established Hispaniola as the official name of the whole island.

[2] Now the Republic of Haiti, although the area is today somewhat larger than in colonial times.

[3] Now the Dominican Republic.

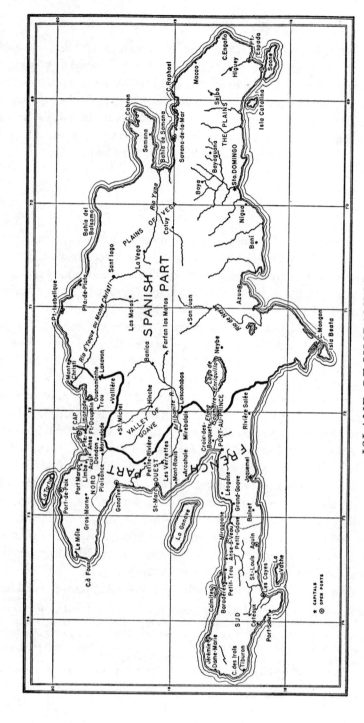

ISLAND OF HISPANIOLA

showing the French part (Saint-Domingue) and the Spanish part (Santo Domingo) in 1789

and the cruelty of their conquerors, the Spanish early began to import Negroes from Africa; and the French, on gaining possession of Saint-Domingue, continued the practice. Under French jurisdiction an economic transformation took place, and the colony soon rose to a high level of prosperity. Huge plantations, made productive by elaborate irrigation systems, dotted the countryside. Sugar mills and distilleries were built, and the ports, busy with commerce, were thriving centers of activity. By 1789 there were three thousand sugar plantations alone, as well as hundreds of coffee, cotton, and indigo plantations; and in that year the value of the colony's imports and exports amounted to $140,000,000. Small wonder that Saint-Domingue became known as the "pearl of the Antilles." The plantation owners lived like kings, entertained lavishly in the island, and when they visited France, spent their money with reckless abandon—"wealthy as a Creole" became a popular adage. Prosperous as Saint-Domingue had become, however, its economic system was founded on slavery.

Saint-Domingue was divided into three provinces for purposes of administration. The North Province, with its rich Plaine du Nord, had as its capital city Cap Français or Le Cap. The West Province, with the fertile valley of the Artibonite, was controlled by Port-au-Prince. The South Province, which extended far to the west, had Les Cayes as its principal town. The government of the colony was vested ultimately in the French minister of marine, representing the King, and his edicts were laws. He appointed the governor-general, who was the military authority, and the intendant, who controlled the civil and judiciary administration. This centralization of authority in Paris for the rule of the colony was ultimately to produce unbounded mischief.

Gradually there had grown up in the colony a confused and complicated social system, which by 1789 was as likely to lead to bloodshed as conditions in France itself. At the top was the white population, estimated at forty thousand persons, but it was by no means a homogeneous group. The opulent planters, the rich merchants, and the important civil authorities, known as the *grands blancs,* lived in the greatest luxury and enjoyed the prestige and power their wealth conferred upon them; while the small tradesmen, overseers, and minor officials, called the *petits blancs,* were in much the same position as the petty *bourgeoisie* in France.

Below the whites were the *gens de couleur,* sometimes known as the *affranchis,* or freedmen, numbering about twenty-eight thousand. This group, which included all *free* persons with any degree of African blood in their veins, was composed mainly of mulattoes. From the time slavery was introduced into the colony, miscegenation had been common between white masters and female slaves, and it became customary to free the progeny of such relationships and often, too, to manumit the mothers as well. The mulattoes married among themselves; but many of the mulatto women

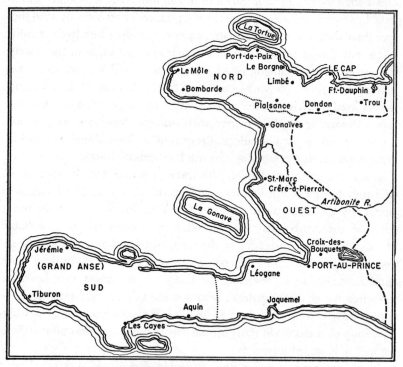

SAINT-DOMINGUE

became the mistresses of the white men. It should be noted, however, that the *gens de couleur* included a number of pure Negroes who had won their freedom through the generosity of their masters or who had been able to purchase it. These free Negroes were sometimes themselves slaveowners. The *gens de couleur* were permitted to own property and many of them were wealthy; in fact, some authorities claim that by 1791 they owned a third of all the land in the colony and a fourth of all the slaves. They were often persons of culture and some of them had been educated in France. At first, when they were a small group and offered no threat to the authority and mastery of the whites, they enjoyed full rights as French citizens; but as they grew in number and power, legislative measures were taken against them. They were gradually deprived of their political rights and debarred from social intercourse with the white population. They were denied the right to bear legal testimony against white men; they could not hold any responsible office, and most of the professions were closed to them. Segregated in the churches, theaters, and inns, forced to wear clothes different from those of the whites, and forbidden marriage with them, they were everywhere humiliated. Despite these discriminations against them, however, many of the *gens de couleur,* being slaveowners, were as relentless in preserving slavery as were the whites above them.

At the bottom of the social scale were the Negro slaves—nearly half a million of them. Although they outnumbered the whites and *gens de couleur* nearly seven to one, their potential strength was as yet unrecognized. They were treated, with few exceptions, with the most savage and inhuman cruelty. Subject to the slightest whim of their masters, they had no redress. Minor disobedience was punished with the severest penalties, and even a suspicion of insubordination or an attempt to escape brought mutilation or death. It was no uncommon occurrence for a slave to have his ears, arms, or legs cut off, or to be buried alive. On one plantation a slave was nailed to the wall and at the end of the day forced to eat his own amputated ears. On another all slaves had their tongues cut out. Apparently, unlimited and unrestricted power over the Negroes awakened only the most bestial and depraved instincts of their masters. Unheard and unregarded, the plantation slaves labored from daybreak to nightfall under the whips of the overseers, while the household Negroes were at the mercy of the base desires, the irascible moods, and the diabolic sadism of those whom they attended. Death, whether from fatigue, sickness, accident, or the deliberate brutality of the whites, often came as a relief.

Of such combustible materials was Saint-Domingue composed. Overbearing, dissipated, and pleasure-loving, the whites despised the *gens de couleur*—"a bastard and degenerate race," they called them—and treated them with the utmost contempt; rankling under the humiliation of their position, the *gens de couleur* were filled with an implacable hatred of the whites and awaited the day of retaliation; and the Negro slaves, brutalized and outraged by both groups, needed only the impetus of leadership to arouse them into savage and bloodthirsty fury. It was inevitable that such a system could not last, that Saint-Domingue, the richest colony in the world, would soon be swept by ruin and disaster.

REVOLUTION IN SAINT-DOMINGUE

By 1788 a group among the white planters in Saint-Domingue began to oppose the arbitrary authority of the governor-general and intendant; and when they learned that the French King had given consent to a meeting of the States-General in France, they at once asked for representation for Saint-Domingue. Their request was refused; but the more hotheaded and determined among them held irregular elections in the island against the advice of the more conservative planters. When the States-General met in May, 1789, after an interval of nearly two hundred years, thirty-seven deputies from Saint-Domingue presented themselves for admission. After two months' discussion, six only were permitted to join the Assembly. Once seated, the deputies outlined their grievances and demanded a measure of colonial self-government. Before anything conclusive could be adopted, the fall of the Bastille and the Declaration of the Rights of Man plunged France into a maelstrom of confusion; and the colonial party in France, including the six recently seated deputies and a good many planters residing in Paris, saw that they had been unwise in drawing the attention of all France to Saint-Domingue. Indeed, the *gens de couleur* living in France and the "Amis des Noirs," a French abolition society, began loudly to proclaim the abuses of the colonial system. Fearing that the National Assembly might apply the Declaration of the Rights of Man to Saint-Domingue and thus destroy the supremacy of the white planters there, the colonial group appealed to the minister of marine for permission to convoke a Colonial Assembly to deal with internal affairs in the colony but responsible to the King. The request was granted on September 27, 1789, and orders providing for an Assembly were dispatched to Saint-Domingue. The property qualifications for the franchise were so severe as to guarantee control by the rich planters.

The colonial group had acted none too soon. Within a few days the King and the National Assembly were forced by the mob to return to Paris and the Revolution was in full sway. Thenceforth the fate of Saint-Domingue and that of the mother country were inextricably interwoven, and the chaotic conditions in France were to be duplicated in the colony.

News of the fall of the Bastille and the Declaration of the Rights of Man threw all Saint-Domingue into an emotional furor. The *petits blancs*, long restive in their position of inequality with the wealthy white planters, embraced the Revolution, and the planter class, fearful of mob violence, was forced to include them in the election of deputies to the Colonial Assembly. The Assembly met at Saint-Marc on April 14, 1790; but instead of presenting recommendations for the future internal status of the island, this body, fired by the principles of the Revolution, and representing not merely the wealthy planters but the whole white population, arrogated to itself the supreme authority of the colony and promulgated a constitution. Actually the Assembly rendered the royal authority impotent by ignoring the governor-general and other officials in the island, but it also alienated the support of the National Assembly in Paris by acknowledging allegiance to the King. Thus its position was wholly anomalous. Since the Colonial Assembly seized the control from the wealthy planters, the whites in the colony were quickly divided into contending factions.

The *gens de couleur* saw in the Declaration of the Rights of Man an opportunity to gain for themselves the status of French citizens and immediately began overt agitation on their own behalf. Nobody even dreamed of applying the Rights of Man to the hordes of Negro slaves, but they, too, were fired by the course of events. The low beat of the voodoo drums sounded across the countryside and the Negroes met in secret gatherings deep in the forests; the mighty strength of half a million slaves was slowly awakening.

The Declaration of the Rights of Man placed France in an embarrassing position in relation to Saint-Domingue, for to carry out its provisions would be to destroy the whole social and political structure of the colony. As matters turned out, the colonial policy of the mother country succeeded only in intensifying the quarrel between the *gens de couleur* and the whites and undermining French authority among all classes in the colony. Preoccupied with domestic affairs, subject to pressure from the colonial interests on the one hand and from the more radical advocates of equality on the other, and often ignorant of the changing conditions in Saint-Domingue, the National Assembly temporized by issuing a series of highly contradictory decrees for the colony. Attempting to mollify the whites, it first invited the colony to make known its wishes by means of local assemblies, but left ambiguous the status of the *gens de couleur;* next, trying to appease the *gens de couleur,* it provided for the admission of all free men to the rights of French citizenship; then, yielding to the protests of the whites, it placed the status of both the *gens de couleur* and the slaves in the hands of the Colonial Assemblies; finally, under the radicalism of the Jacobins, it reinstated the political equality of the *gens de couleur* and sent troops to enforce its wishes. Out of such vacillation came the inevitable—civil war in Saint-Domingue.

The first serious resort to arms by the *gens de couleur* broke out in the autumn of 1790. The revolt was led by Vincent Ogé, a mulatto who had gone to France during the early days of the Revolution in order to forward the cause of the *gens de couleur,* but who had despaired of decisive action by the French Government and had returned to Saint-Domingue. Under Ogé a band of several hundred of the *gens de couleur* in the North Province attempted to win their rights by force. They were no match for the troops sent against them and were utterly defeated. Ogé and his fellow leader, Jean-Baptiste Chavannes, fled to Spanish Santo Domingo but were soon returned to the civil authority in Saint-Domingue. Half in anger, half in sheer barbarity, the magistrates determined to make an example of them, and they were condemned:

whilst alive to have their arms, legs, thighs and spines broken; and afterward to be placed on a wheel, their faces toward Heaven, and there to stay as long as it would please God to preserve their lives; and when dead, their heads were to be cut off and exposed on poles.[4]

So read the death sentence, and on February 25, 1791, it was carried out in a public square in Cap Français, amidst the jeering taunts of the white spectators.

Ogé had not died in vain, however, and his death awakened a wave of indignation in France. The National Assembly in Paris on May 15, 1791, passed a decisive decree:

The National Assembly decrees that it will never deliberate upon the political status of the people of color *who are not born of free father and mother* without the previous free and spontaneous desire of the colonies; that the Colonial Assemblies actually existing shall continue; but that the people of color born of free father and mother shall be admitted to all the future parish and Colonial Assemblies, if in other respects possessed of the required qualifications.[5]

When news of this action was received in Saint-Domingue, it shook the colony to its foundations. The white population were united in their determination to resist it by every means in their power and even "resolved on secession if the mother country attempts to enforce this decree." The governor-general of the colony, equally stunned by the edict, wrote the minister of marine not only condemning it but absolutely refusing to enforce it.

---

[4] J. N. Léger, *Haiti: Her History and Her Detractors* (New York, 1907), p. 46.
[5] T. Lothrop Stoddard, *The French Revolution in San Domingo* (Boston and New York, 1914), p. 122.

The *gens de couleur,* inspired by French approval and smoldering with bitterness over the martyrdom of Ogé, were as strongly determined to carry into effect the provisions of the decree. As soon as they saw the reaction of the whites, they secretly prepared for an armed revolt and in late August, 1791, began an uprising in the West Province.

Almost concurrent with this interracial struggle came a mighty insurrection of the slaves in the North Province. Gaining momentum as it spread from district to district, it soon engulfed the whole province like a great tidal wave. The rich plantations were laid waste and the white inhabitants were slaughtered by the hundreds. The whites offered what resistance they could; and though they hunted down and killed Boukman, one of the instigators of the uprising, and other leaders, their efforts were unavailing. The vast hordes swept on, until what had been the most prosperous part of Saint-Domingue was turned into a shambles. Ruin and anarchy prevailed over the whole North Province and thousands of whites cowered in the city of Cap Français, which was surrounded by ditches and palisades.

In the West Province, the *gens de couleur* and the whites, fearful lest the Negro insurrection overwhelm the whole colony, drew up peace terms, promising observance of the May 15 decree and guaranteeing to the *gens de couleur* a share in civil and military affairs. While rancor and bitterness remained, some compromise might have been effected; but the French Government, changeful and wavering as ever, reversed its earlier stand and issued an edict returning to the Colonial Assembly the power of determining the status of both the *gens de couleur* and the slaves. The National Assembly went even further: "in order to take this question out of politics, the decree was declared an unalterable article of the French Constitution."

The arrival of news of this decree destroyed all hope of further reconciliation between the whites and the *gens de couleur.* The latter lost faith in France, while the whites, smarting under the humiliating treaty forced upon them by the victories of the *gens de couleur,* used the decree as an excuse to abrogate their agreement. Hostilities recommenced and a race war, almost as bloody and inhuman as the Negro insurrection in the North Province, brought disaster to the west. The South Province, too, was now aflame with an uprising of the *gens de couleur,* under the leadership of André Rigaud.

The slave insurrection in the north likewise might have been settled, for late in 1791 the Negro leaders made overtures to the whites, who were still entrenched at Cap Français. Their terms were simple: in return for amnesty and freedom for themselves, the four hundred leaders promised to quell the uprising and return the hundred thousand insurgent Negroes to work on the plantations. The whites, however, were as blind to the power of the Negroes as they were to their own ultimate fate, and they haughtily rejected the proposal. Toussaint, one of the Negro emissaries, reported to the insurgents that reconciliation was hopeless, and the slaves continued their depredations.

In April, 1792, the Jacobins having gained control of France, the new National Assembly took a firm stand on the situation in Saint-Domingue, not only enfranchising the *gens de couleur* and giving them the right to hold political office, but also sending out three commissioners, to whom dictatorial powers were given, and six thousand troops to ensure establishment of order and the observance of its will. These Jacobin measures were regarded by the whites in the colony as "a virtual sentence of death." The commissioners, indeed, possessed neither tact nor perspicacity. Soon after their arrival on September 18, 1792, they asserted their superiority over the governor-general and disbanded the Colonial Assembly, establishing in its place a body composed of six whites and six *gens de couleur*. When the city of Port-au-Prince in the West Province refused to acknowledge their authority, the commissioners, enlisting the aid of the *gens de couleur,* subdued the town in a bloody battle. As if to humiliate the whites still further, they placed the *gens de couleur* in the highest positions of trust both in the army and in civil offices. So flagrant was the partiality to this group, who became insolent and overbearing towards the whites, that even the colonial troops refused to obey the commissioners.

In May, 1793, Galbaud, the newly appointed governor-general, arrived at Cap Français. His qualifications were challenged by the commissioners, and he was ordered to depart. Before he sailed, however, the commissioners renewed their mistreatment of the whites in the town, and even the French sailors on shore leave were insulted and mistreated by the *gens de couleur* soldiery. Yielding to the pleas of the white population, Galbaud again landed, placed himself at the head of an army composed of sailors and the white troops who manned the harbor defenses, and soon occupied most of the town. The commissioners now called upon the Negro insurgents of the Plaine du Nord to attack Cap Français, offering them liberty and permission to pillage. Galbaud and his forces were driven to the water front, and the town was soon a blazing ruin. The next day, accompanied by ten thousand despairing white refugees, he embarked for the United States.

In February, 1793, England had gone to war with France. Spain followed a month later. Many of the whites who remained in Saint-Domingue now openly disavowed all allegiance to France and asked for intervention by English troops. When English soldiers landed in the ports of the island, they were welcomed as liberators by the white population. From Santo Domingo, too, Spanish troops poured across the border into the colony. Fearing the loss of the whole of Saint-Domingue, the frantic commissioners began arming the Negro slaves and promising freedom to all who fought for the Republic; thereby alienating the *gens de couleur* whom they had so recently favored. Finally, in a last desperate effort to save the colony for France, they proclaimed the abolition of slavery in the summer of 1793, and in the following February the Government in France confirmed their action. In June, 1794, the commissioners, complying with a mandate to appear for trial before the French Convention, embarked for France.

Thus had the perversity of race hatred, abetted by the vacillations of the French Government, turned the rich colony of Saint-Domingue into chaos and anarchy; but neither the whites nor the *gens de couleur* had emerged triumphant. Only the Negro slaves had won a victory—their emancipation. That out of such confusion the Negroes, untutored in the ways of modern war and only a step from the African jungles, should have gained supremacy seems miraculous; but that such Negro leaders as Toussaint and Christophe should have arisen to lead their people seems almost to indicate the hand of destiny.

THE RISE OF TOUSSAINT L'OUVERTURE

By 1794 the fortunes of the French Republic in Saint-Domingue were at their lowest ebb. England and Spain held most of the seacoast and a large portion of the interior. In the north, hemmed in on all sides, Laveaux, a white French general, and a handful of starving troops were in danger of annihilation; in the south, the mulatto leader, André Rigaud, supporting the French cause, held a portion of territory, including the port of Les Cayes. At this time, however, Toussaint L'Ouverture emerged as the strongest man in Saint-Domingue. Born a slave about 1743, he showed such natural intelligence as a boy that his kindly master gave him less arduous tasks and allowed him leisure to develop his mind. In 1791 he became one of the leaders of the Negro insurgents and was among the intermediaries who proposed a cessation of the slave uprising. In 1793 he joined the Spanish in Santo Domingo. There he gained a good knowledge of the principles of warfare and rose to a position of considerable importance. From the onset of the Negro insurrection, Toussaint thought of himself as selected by Providence to lead his people. "From the first rise of the troubles in St. Domingo," he was sometimes heard to say,

I felt myself destined to great things; and when I first received this divine annunciation I was fifty-four years old.... The Revolution went on. I saw that the

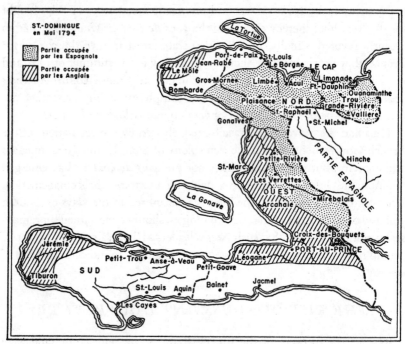

SAINT-DOMINGUE
showing the areas occupied by the Spanish and the British in 1794

whites could not hold out because they were divided among themselves, and likely to be overwhelmed by the numbers of the blacks, and for the first time I felicitated myself for being a black. I felt that the time had come for me to begin my career, and I fled to the Spanish territory, where protection and an asylum were offered to those of my color. This enterprise however ended in nothing.... The French republic was at the height of its power, and had already proclaimed liberty to the blacks. A secret voice told me, "since the blacks are free they will want a leader. It is I who am to be this leader—the chief foretold by Raynal." Gladdened by this hope I returned to the service of France, and the voice of God has not deceived me.[6]

---

[6] J. Brown, M.D., *The History and Present Condition of St. Domingo*, 2 vols. (Philadelphia, 1837), Vol. II, p. 26.

Thus recognizing that his opportunity lay in Saint-Domingue, he threw in his lot with the French Republic, and in May, 1794, marched across the border at the head of four thousand well-disciplined Negro troops. The French general, Laveaux, who had sought his aid, welcomed him with open arms.

At the time of his espousal of the French cause in 1794, Toussaint acted in the capacity of a French subject, and for a time, nominally at least, he acknowledged the jurisdiction of the Republic. He received his first commission, *général de brigade,* from General Laveaux. In 1796, the mulattoes in the north having thrown Laveaux into jail, Toussaint rushed to his assistance and set him free. In appreciation, Laveaux, having himself become Governor-General of Saint-Domingue, appointed Toussaint Lieutenant-Governor, even going so far as to refer publicly to Toussaint as "that black Spartacus prophesied by Raynal, whose destiny is to avenge the outrages upon his race."

Toussaint's campaigns against the Spanish and the British have become legendary. Within a year he had driven the Spanish invaders from Saint-Domingue and had released Laveaux from his desperate predicament. The struggles against the English were more prolonged; but by 1796, English power in the island was broken, and though they held on in isolated spots for two more years, they steadily lost ground. In 1798 Toussaint and the English commander, General Maitland, arranged for the evacuation of the one or two strongholds still in English possession, and signed a secret agreement of friendship and trade, ignoring General Hédouville, whom the French Government had sent out in the early spring of 1798 to reëstablish French authority in the island. Thus an English occupation of five years, during which, it is reported, forty thousand men perished and a sum of twenty million pounds was expended, had come to an ignominious close.

Since the commerce of Saint-Domingue, from the Negro insurrection of 1791 to the banishment of the English in 1798, played so important a part in the history of the island, a brief review of its course will be pertinent here. The United States had long participated in the lucrative trade with Saint-Domingue, which by 1790 was second only to her commerce with Great Britain. During the Negro uprisings from 1791 to 1793, the desperate plight of the French colonials forced them to turn still further to America for supplies and munitions; but the beginning of the European war in February, 1793, and the occupation of most of Saint-Domingue by Spain and England a few months later placed the United States in a difficult position.

Despite her 1778 French treaty, which had guaranteed French possessions in the West Indies forever, the United States adopted a policy of neutrality, and American merchants endeavored to trade at all ports in the island. Both England and France sought supplies from the United States, each attempting at the same time to restrict the commerce of the other and seizing American ships bound for ports held by the enemy. Late in 1794, Jay's treaty between England and the United States cemented Anglo-American commercial relations. France was so incensed at what she considered her betrayal by the United States that Franco-American relations degenerated to the breaking point. Depredations on American shipping to the West Indies on the part of both belligerents continued, however, to such a degree that the United States would have been justified in going to war as much with one as with the other. The famous XYZ affair, in which French statesmen demanded bribes from American envoys, turned the scale against France and provoked bitter resentment. In the early summer of 1798 Congress passed a series of warlike measures, among them the abrogation of the 1778 treaty of alliance and suspension of commerce with all places acknowledging the authority of France. The quasi war of 1798–1800 followed.

With the ejection of the British from Saint-Domingue in August, 1798, Toussaint appealed to the United States for a resumption of commerce. The American Government also took the initiative on learning of the departure of the principal French agent, Hédouville, and made Toussaint an offer of trade in a letter which crossed the one from Saint-Domingue. While these arrangements were developing, news of the secret agreement of General Maitland came to light, and American statesmen persuaded England to include the United States in the commercial pact with Toussaint. Throughout these negotiations France, whose sovereignty Toussaint only tacitly acknowledged, was utterly ignored, and a lucrative trade developed between the island and the two countries now at war with France.

Peace in Saint-Domingue did not follow, for the mulattoes[7] in the West and South Provinces were unwilling to acknowledge the authority of a former Negro slave. During the war against the English, it is true, the mulattoes fought them with the same energy as did the Negroes; but once

---

[7] With the abolition of slavery in Saint-Domingue, the term *gens de couleur* (meaning free persons with any degree of African blood) ceases to have significance, and *mulatto* (meaning a person of mixed blood) has been adopted for the remainder of this narrative. While the word *mulatto* (*mulâtre*) is not used in Haiti today, it clearly defines the group which clashed with the Negroes after the French lost control of the island.

foreign foes were driven out, the old racial problem flared anew. Recognizing that civil war was inevitable, Toussaint struck with sudden fury. The United States and Great Britain now openly espoused the Negro cause, and when hostilities broke out, blockaded the ports held by André Rigaud, the mulatto leader. Toussaint's triumph quickly followed, and by July, 1800, the mulattoes were crushed. Rigaud and those who were able to do so fled from the island; those who remained had no choice but to accept the domination of Toussaint. Foreign intervention had not only helped to bring about Rigaud's downfall but had also encouraged Toussaint to further defiance of French authority.

Soon after Rigaud's defeat, the quasi war between France and the United States ended with the signing of the Treaty of Morfontaine on September 30, 1800. While France looked with suspicion on Toussaint's growing spirit of independence, she permitted American commerce with Saint-Domingue to continue.

It was during the struggles against the English and the mulattoes that Jean-Jacques Dessalines and Henry Christophe rose to positions of power in the island. Both of them, like Toussaint, were former Negro slaves; like him both were endowed with mental agility, self-confidence, and the qualities of military leadership. Toussaint seems to have estimated the value of his fellow Negroes with the same uncanny judgment with which he took the measure of his foes, and he chose the two Negroes most capable of protecting Saint-Domingue against her enemies. After the defeat of Rigaud, he made Dessalines the governor of the South Province. In order to gain control, Dessalines—"a ferocious brute from the Congo," one historian calls him—methodically massacred ten thousand mulattoes. Christophe, on the other hand, was chosen to supervise the return of the Negroes to agricultural labor, to restore the ravaged plantations and the coastal towns, and to organize and discipline the troops. Enjoying Toussaint's full confidence, Christophe profited by this opportunity to gain the knowledge and experience which proved so useful in later years. His administrative responsibilities also brought him into contact with the foreigners in the North Province, where he was the military commandant, and he developed a great admiration for the English, who attended his banquets and were much impressed by his gentlemanly courtesy.

Toussaint, in control of the whole of Saint-Domingue, now turned his attention to Spanish Santo Domingo, for he was well aware that Napoleon, who had become First Consul and absolute master of France, would seize the first opportunity to attack the island. The Treaty of Basle in 1795 had provided for the cession of Spanish Santo Domingo to France, but it was expressly agreed that the Spanish were to retain possession until France was in a position to occupy and defend the territory. In the spring of 1796 it was placed under the authority of the French commissioner Roume. Feeling that he could offer a better defense if the whole island were under his authority, Toussaint won reluctant permission from Roume to occupy Santo Domingo; and in January, 1801, two armies marched across this part of the island. After a brief skirmish the Spanish capitulated. All Hispaniola now acknowledged the authority of Toussaint.

Much has been written of Toussaint. Some authors consider him the savior of Saint-Domingue and the greatest leader of the Negroes. Others describe him as a crafty opportunist, interested only in his own aggrandizement. Probably both points of view contain elements of truth; but the fact remains that Toussaint succeeded in bringing peace to the island. Tolerant, wise, and patient, he followed the course of expediency. When action was demanded, he struck with the suddenness of lightning; when he was confronted with deceit and treachery, he was capable of dissimulation and deception. The secret of his power—and as he said, he alone could control the Negro hordes—lay in the magnetic and almost hypnotic quality of his personality. Not only did his troops follow him with fanatic devotion, but at his command, his people, after years of pillage and banditry, docilely returned to labor on the plantations. Toussaint may have been all his detractors assert; his protestations of loyalty to France and his appearance of deep religious piety may have been only sham and duplicity; nevertheless, under his brief "rule," his people settled down to agricultural pursuits and prosperity returned.

Whatever may have been Toussaint's earlier views, it was undoubtedly the honors heaped upon him by General Laveaux that marked the beginning of his open disregard for French authority. Not only did he return Laveaux himself to France by the simple expedient of getting him elected a deputy from Saint-Domingue, but on occasion he warned the French of the folly of attempting to interfere in the island, where he alone held mastery over the Negroes. It was to Toussaint that the British surrendered, not to General Hédouville, the authorized French representative. In 1798 Toussaint signed a secret treaty with Great Britain, still at war with France, granting her special commercial privileges, and in 1799 he resumed trade with the United States, although all commerce between that country and

France had been discontinued. When Franco-American hostilities ceased with the end of the quasi war in September, 1800, Toussaint continued to trade directly with the United States, but he thereupon closed certain ports to American shipping and imposed severe regulations on American merchants in the island.[8] He also invited the French *émigrés* to return to their plantations, though he was expressly forbidden to do so by the French Government, which considered them traitors to France.

Nor did Toussaint hesitate to defy the authority of Napoleon, who became First Consul in 1799. In 1801, as we have seen, he mastered Spanish Santo Domingo, but against the explicit orders of Napoleon that the island was not to be unified under one command. In the summer of the same year, he promulgated a constitution which made him Governor-General for life, with the power of designating his successor. This constitution reaffirmed the freedom of the Negroes, it provided only an empty acknowledgment of the sovereignty of France, and placed the control of the island entirely in Toussaint's hands. Although the constitution was immediately put into effect, Toussaint dispatched it to France for Napoleon's approval— a hollow and defiant gesture. The "first of the blacks," as he styled himself, had thus chosen a dangerous course; and though he had earlier sent conciliatory messages to France and in elaborate and formal terms had pretended a respect for French authority, he now declared a virtual independence for the island. But the day of reckoning was at hand.

THE INVASION OF HISPANIOLA

With the preliminaries of the Treaty of Amiens settled on October first, 1801, Napoleon, who had watched with bitter resentment the rise of Toussaint and his open flouting of orders, was at last free to deal with Hispaniola, and he set about the conquest of the island with his usual thoroughness. He assembled twenty thousand veterans of the European wars, placed them under the command of his brother-in-law, General Leclerc, and dispatched them, along with a huge armada, to the island. His orders were explicit and drastic. The campaign was to be divided into

---

[8] Such restrictions, however, did not curtail American commerce with Toussaint, "a commerce in which from five hundred to six hundred ships averaging one hundred and fifty tons were annually employed." R. W. Logan, *The Diplomatic Relations of the United States with Haiti, 1776-1891* (Chapel Hill, N.C., 1941), pp. 126–127. This book contains an excellent analysis of the commercial relations between the United States and Haiti.

three phases. Leclerc was first to occupy the coastal towns. During this period Toussaint and the black generals were to be flattered, loaded with honors, and allowed to keep their rank, provided they submitted voluntarily to the French. In the second period Leclerc was to smash all organized resistance in the island. If after fifteen days from the arrival of the French, Toussaint and the Negro generals had not surrendered, they were to be proclaimed traitors, and when captured, summarily shot. During the third period any remaining rebel bands in the mountains were to be hunted down, and with the island wholly subdued, the Negroes were to be put back to work. During this period, too, those Negro leaders who had voluntarily submitted were to be sent, with as little commotion as possible, to France. In the meantime, all officers above the rank of captain were also to be deported. Napoleon wanted no half measures, and to see that his wishes were performed, he equipped the largest and most costly expedition yet sent out to the New World.

Toussaint, too, had made his plans. Resistance was everywhere to be offered. Anticipating the very invasion now under way, he had bought enormous quantities of muskets and war matériel in the United States, and twenty thousand soldiers stood armed and ready. Many of the agricultural laborers, too, had been armed and awaited only a signal to become guerrilla fighters. Under his command three powerful generals divided the defense of the island. In the South and West Provinces, Dessalines held full charge; in Spanish Santo Domingo, the mulatto Clervaux, assisted by Paul L'Ouverture, had four thousand soldiers in battle array; and in the North Province, Henry Christophe prepared to resist invasion at Cap Français. Toussaint's orders to his generals were to burn the towns, destroy the countryside so that the invaders would find only ruin and ashes, and retreat to the mountains.

There were, however, several weaknesses in Toussaint's position. Although he had showered every privilege on the French whites whom he had freed from foreign control or whom he had induced to return to Saint-Domingue, they were not really loyal to him and welcomed an expedition from France. The mulattoes, too, awaited an opportunity to renounce the authority of a Negro. Finally, his plan of defense distributed his troops at too many points, and hence there was no single force strong enough to repel a determined assault.

When, on January 29, 1802, the French armada was sighted off Cape Samaná, on the eastern coast of the island, Toussaint was hastily sum-

moned. Gazing on the vast flotilla, he was filled with melancholy fore-
bodings. "We must perish," he said, "all France has come to St.-Domingue."
But he did not swerve from the path he had chosen.

A few days later, on February 3, 1802, Leclerc appeared with half his fleet
in the harbor of Cap Français and at once demanded permission to land;
but Christophe refused it on the plea that he must first have the acquiescence
of Toussaint. The messages between Leclerc and Christophe reveal the
highhanded disdain of the one and the steadfast courage and dignity of the
other. "I learn with indignation, Citizen General," first wrote Leclerc:

> that you refuse to receive the French squadron, and the French army that I com-
> mand, under the pretext that you have received no orders from the Governor-
> General.
>
> France has concluded a peace with England, and its government sends to St.
> Domingo, forces capable of subduing the rebels; at least if any are to be found at
> St. Domingo. As to you, General, I confess it will grieve me to account you
> among them.
>
> I give you notice, that if you have not in the course of this day surrendered the
> Forts Picolet and Belair, with all the batteries on the coast, tomorrow, at day
> break, fifteen thousand troops shall be disembarked.
>
> Four thousand men are, at this moment, landing at Fort Liberté; eight thou-
> sand more at Fort Republican.
>
> Herewith you will receive my Proclamation[9] which expresses the intentions
> of the French Government; but recollect, whatever individual esteem your con-
> duct in the colony may have inspired me with, I hold you responsible for what
> may happen.[10]

Christophe's answer is remarkably forthright:

> Your Aid-de-camp, General, has delivered to me your letter of this day; I have
> the honour to inform you that I could not deliver up the forts and post confided
> to my command, without previous orders from the Governor-General, Toussaint
> Louverture, my immediate chief, from whom I hold the powers with which I am
> invested. I am fully persuaded that I have to do with Frenchmen, and that you

---

[9] Napoleon had issued a grandiose document: "Whatever be your origin or your colour, you
are all Frenchmen, *you are all free and all equal before God, and before the Republic.* . . . All
nations have embraced the French, and sworn to them peace and amity. . . . Come you, likewise,
to throw yourselves into the arms of France. . . . The government sends you the Captain-General
Leclerc; he takes with him a numerous force for your protection against your enemies. . . .
Should any one whisper in your ear, *'These forces are destined to despoil you of your liberty';*
answer, *'It is the Republic that has given us liberty; the Republic will never suffer it to be rav-
ished from us.'*

"Rally around the Captain-General; he brings you back peace and plenty. . . . Whoso dares
to separate himself from the Captain-General shall be accounted a traitor to his country, and
the wrath of the Republic shall devour him as fire devours your parched sugar canes." Prince
Sanders, *Haytian Papers* (London, 1816), pp. 1–3.

[10] *Ibid.*, pp. 4–5.

are the chief of the armament called the expedition; but I wait the orders of the Governor, to whom I have dispatched one of my Aid-de-camps, to apprize him of your arrival, and that of the French army, and cannot permit you to land until I have received his answer. If you put in force your threats of hostility, I shall make the resistance which becomes a general officer; and, should the chance of war be yours, you shall not enter Cape Town till it be reduced to ashes; nay, even in the ruins will I renew the combat.

You say that the French Government has sent to St. Domingo forces capable of subduing the rebels, if any such be found; it is your coming, and the hostile intentions you manifest, that alone could create them among a peaceable people, in perfect submission to France. The very mention of rebellion is an argument for our resistance.

As to the troops which you say are this moment landing, I consider them as so many pieces of cards which the least breath of wind will dissipate.

How can you hold me responsible for the event? You are not my Chief; I know you not, and can therefore make no account of you till you are recognised by Governor Toussaint.

For the loss of your esteem, General, I assure you that I desire not to earn it at the price that you set upon it, since to purchase it I must be guilty of a breach of duty.[11]

Infuriated at such insolence, Leclerc landed his troops on February 5; but, as he had been warned, he found Cap Français "reduced to ashes." Tradition has it that Christophe, as an example to his men, first set a flaming torch to his own luxuriously furnished house, thereby destroying all his worldly possessions. Then, taking a considerable number of whites with him as hostages, he fled with his army to the protection of the hinterland.

The French landings were uniformly successful. Spanish Santo Domingo surrendered on February 2, and thenceforth recognized the sovereignty of France. Port-au-Prince was captured on February 5. Two days later the South Province submitted to French control. Everywhere the forces of Toussaint were reeling before the blows of Leclerc, but strong centers of resistance remained. Some of the Negro leaders had already gone over to the French, but Toussaint had no thought of surrendering. Accordingly, on February 17, Leclerc declared him and Christophe to be outlaws.

During the next phase of his conquest, Leclerc was equally successful, but only after a series of sanguinary campaigns. In a few weeks he had subdued the North Province and the one or two almost impregnable fortresses of the interior. Toussaint's power seemed definitely broken.

By April, Christophe decided to abandon the hopeless cause of Toussaint

---

[11] *Ibid.*, pp. 6–8.

and throw in his lot with the French. With Leclerc's forces in possession of most of the island, brigandage in the mountains—a course chosen by some of the lesser chieftains—was the only alternative. Leclerc, for his part, was in no position to enforce the proclamation of outlawry against Christophe and was compelled to take a conciliatory attitude. He had lost five thousand men in the bloody battles accompanying his conquest, five thousand more lay in hospitals, and he could ill depend upon the loyalty of the Negroes whom he had enlisted under his command. He promised, therefore, amnesty to Christophe and his troops. He hoped, too, to use Christophe as a means of capturing Toussaint. "I will keep," he wrote:

the promises which have been made you; but, if it is your intention to submit to the Republic, think on the essential service you could render her by furnishing the means to secure the person of General Toussaint.[12]

Christophe, though ready to submit to Leclerc's authority, did not intend to do so in a servile and treacherous manner, and he refused to betray Toussaint:

You propose to me, Citizen General, to furnish you with the means of securing the person of General Toussaint Louverture. It would be perfidy and treason in me to do so, and a proposition so degrading to me, is, in my opinion, a mark of your invincible repugnance to believe me susceptible of the smallest sentiment of delicacy and honour. He is my commander, and my friend. Is friendship, Citizen General, compatible with such monstrous baseness?[13]

At the same time, Christophe outlined the one condition necessary for his capitulation.

I wait only for a proof which must convince me of the intention to procure the liberty and equality of the population of this colony. The laws which ... the mother country, without doubt, has enacted, will carry to my heart this conviction. ... On obtaining this desired proof, by being made acquainted with these laws, I shall submit immediately. ...

The laws which I have just mentioned, have been promised us by the mother country. ... Fulfil this maternal promise, by unfolding to our view the code which contains it, and you will soon behold all her children rushing into the arms of that beneficent mother, and amongst them General Toussaint Louverture, who, thus undeceived, like the rest, will hasten to correct his error. It is only when this error shall have been so dispelled, that, if he persist in spite of evidence, he can fairly be regarded as criminal.[14]

---

[12] *Ibid.*, p. 9.
[13] *Ibid.*, pp. 10–11.
[14] *Ibid.*, pp. 10-12

When Leclerc indicated that he would "take pleasure in finding myself deceived" in regard to Toussaint, whom he had not believed "to be actuated by such loyal views as yourself," Christophe wrote even more pointedly:

I am flattered with the opinion you entertain of my loyalty; but regret that you still persist in thinking General Toussaint uninspired by that estimable feeling; give me leave to say that you are deceived with regard to him. I have no apprehensions of finding myself deceived, when I assure you, that the confirmation of civilized liberty and equality will make him throw himself into the arms of the Republic.[15]

Although his desperate plight undoubtedly made Christophe receptive to Leclerc's proposals for surrender—"I expect to receive every day the blow that will annihilate me," he had written to one of the French generals—he conducted himself with honor and integrity throughout the negotiations. The first overtures were made by the French, and he refused to consider any proposal for his capitulation unless Leclerc guaranteed the freedom and security of the Negroes. Nor did he falter in the face of threats. "Calculate my means, and your chances of successful resistance," Leclerc wrote to him; to which he replied, "It is hopeless to enter upon any calculation of our respective means; the resolution to be a man, and a freeman, is the unit of my arithmetic." Since Christophe repeatedly demanded that he be furnished with the code of laws confirming liberty and equality to the people of the colony, Leclerc, acting upon Napoleon's orders to flatter and deceive the black leaders, assured him that the "code is not completed: I am engaged upon it at this moment"; and he went on to add:

I declare to you in the presence of the colony, I protest before the Supreme Being, whose assistance is never invoked in vain, that the bases of this code are, liberty and equality; [and] that the Negroes shall be free.... If this declaration is insufficient, it will be to me a convincing proof that you have no wish to submit to the Republic.[16]

Christophe apparently believed the assurances of Leclerc; "the word of a French General is, in my estimation, too sacred and inviolable to be denied belief." Thus, with "the hope of seeing...peace, and prosperity return to this too-long agitated colony, under the auspices of liberty and equality," Christophe came to terms with Leclerc. He entered the French army, retaining his commission and the command of twelve hundred soldiers who

---

[15] *Ibid.*, p. 18.
[16] *Ibid.*, pp. 14–15.

followed him. It is significant that several of his officers refused to surrender their posts to the French until he personally prevailed upon them to do so.[17]

Leclerc wrote to Christophe that the commandant, Lafleur,

> would not consent to surrender his post without having seen you. It appears that the same thing has taken place on the side of the landing-place of Limbé. . . . As soon as you have completed the arrangements on the side of Grande Rivière, proceed to the crossway of Limbé, where you will find General Salme, who commands the arrondissement. . . . Take measures, . . . so that he may forthwith occupy the military posts at present in charge of your troops, and give orders that the rustic militia retire immediately to their habitations.[18]

Perhaps the strongest evidence of Christophe's belief in the sincerity of the French was his action regarding his eldest son, Ferdinand, then nine years of age. Desirous that the child should enjoy the privileges of French training, Christophe placed him under the care of General Boudet, who was returning to France, and provided ample funds for the boy's education and maintenance. His trust was misplaced. His son was soon thrown into an orphan asylum in Paris, where he later died, neglected and in want.

Christophe's capitulation was followed in early May, 1802, by the submission of Toussaint and Dessalines. The former was allowed to retire with a small following to one of his estates, while Dessalines, like Christophe, entered the French service. Leclerc was overjoyed at having won over Toussaint and the leading Negro generals; but though he had succeeded in crushing organized resistance, he realized that the Negroes were subdued, not broken; and he did not dare proceed with the next step in the conquest of Saint-Domingue—the deportation of the leaders, the disarming of the population, and the destruction of the bands of Negroes in the mountains.

Had Toussaint, Dessalines, and Christophe held out a month longer, however, they might have smashed Leclerc's power; for in the middle of May, yellow fever—a foe destined to be far more deadly than the Negroes—broke out among the French troops. The epidemic, reaching the proportions of a plague, proved to be the most virulent ever encountered, and it raged on unabated until the end of the year. The military power of Leclerc melted away, and he found himself more and more dependent upon his Negro soldiers, who were immune to the fever. Fearing that they would renounce his authority at the first sign of weakness, he wrote in desperation to

---

[17] Authorities differ markedly on the circumstances of Christophe's surrender. The résumé given above is drawn from a series of letters between Christophe and Generals Leclerc, Hardy, and Vilton. There seems to be no reason to question their authenticity. *Ibid.*, pp. 9–54.

[18] *Ibid.*, pp. 19–20.

Napoleon for new troops—a request to be repeated with monotonous regularity in every succeeding letter.

Toussaint, on his plantation at Ennery, watched with ill-concealed satisfaction the decimation of the armies of his enemy. Surrounded by his faithful soldiers, now temporarily transformed into "cultivators," but ready to take up arms in a moment, he was a constant threat to Leclerc. Warnings from Christophe and Dessalines that Toussaint might seize upon the scourge of yellow fever as an opportunity to regain his power, as well as written evidence that he was actually plotting a new uprising, convinced Leclerc that he must act. Since a direct attack upon Toussaint might invite a general insurrection among the Negroes, Leclerc determined to obtain possession of the person of the Negro by treachery. Toussaint was, therefore, invited to a conference on the pretense of seeking his advice concerning the French troops which had been deliberately stationed near Ennery and which, he protested, were alarming the plantation workers. Unwisely he accepted the absolute pledge of one of the French generals, who gave his word as an officer and a gentleman for safe-conduct, and on June 7 came unarmed with only two or three followers to the French headquarters. At a prearranged signal he was surrounded by French soldiers and carried prisoner aboard a French frigate lying in the harbor. As he embarked, he uttered a prophetic warning:

In overthrowing me, they have felled in Saint-Domingue only the trunk of the tree of Negro liberty; it will shoot forth from the roots, because they are deep and numerous.

Even though Toussaint was in captivity and on his way to France, Leclerc still feared him. Warning Napoleon that the blacks regarded their betrayed leader with religious fanaticism, Leclerc recommended confinement far from the sea, to prevent Toussaint from finding a means of returning to Saint-Domingue. And Napoleon, who had a score to settle with him, complied. When Toussaint reached the French coast, he was hurried, under strong guard, to the Fort de Joux near the Swiss border. There, in a dank, unhealthy dungeon, deprived of all but the barest necessities, Toussaint L'Ouverture died of consumption on April 7, 1803. Saint-Domingue had lost one of her ablest defenders.

Although the treacherous removal of Toussaint did not cause the widespread disturbances which Leclerc had anticipated, he was, nevertheless, in no position to follow the plans of Napoleon in ridding himself of the other

Negro leaders. Instead, he was forced to seek their aid in accomplishing another purpose—the disarming of the Negro hordes. The undertaking promised to be difficult, for they had not forgotten the oft-repeated exhortation of Toussaint. "This is your liberty!" he had warned, holding aloft a musket; and they were not likely to yield their arms without a struggle. In the South and West Provinces, however, the work went forward; but in the north, where the first Negro insurrection had begun and where there continued to be the strongest resistance to French authority from the Negro bands in the mountains, the disarming of the Negroes was only partially successful.

Early in April, 1802, Napoleon had sent an expedition for the conquest of Guadeloupe. That island had been quickly subdued, and he gave orders for the restoration of slavery there. Since the population had been "winnowed like wheat" and more than three thousand persons deported, the reintroduction of slavery and the reëstablishment of all the old discriminations against the mulattoes were easily accomplished. Added to this, Napoleon officially sanctioned the resumption of the slave trade for all the French colonies.

News of the subjugation of the Negroes in Guadeloupe soon reached Saint-Domingue and set the entire North Province aflame with insurrections. The Negroes and mulattoes alike were convinced that Napoleon was playing a perfidious game and that his ultimate goal was the return to the old colonial system of slavery and color distinction. Leclerc was caught in a trap. Again and again he had solemnly promised that slavery would not be restored, but thenceforth he could no longer convince anyone in the island that Napoleon would refrain from doing so. "My position," he wrote to Napoleon on August 6, 1802,

grows trying and may well become worse. Here it is: disease had made such frightful ravages among my troops that when I wished to disarm the negroes an insurrection broke out. . . . Our first attacks drove the insurgents, but they scattered into other cantons. In the present insurrection there is a veritable fanaticism. These men may be killed, but will not surrender. They laugh at death;—and it is the same with the women. I begged you, Citizen Consul, to do nothing to make these people fear for their liberty till the moment when I should be prepared. Suddenly there came the law authorizing the [slave] Trade, and on top of that General Richepanse has just decreed the restoration of slavery in Guadeloupe. With this state of things, Citizen Consul, the moral force I had here acquired is destroyed. . . . I can only use force,—and force I have none.

At present, Citizen Consul, now that your colonial plans are perfectly well known, if you wish to preserve San Domingo send a new army,—and especially send money. I declare positively that if you abandon us to ourselves as you have so far done, this colony is lost;—and, once lost, you will never get it back again.[19]

For a time, however, the insurrections were led by the lesser Negro chieftains, and such Negro generals as Christophe and Dessalines still supported the French. On September 16, Leclerc reported to Napoleon:

Here is the state of my black generals. Maurepas is a dangerous rascal, but I dare not arrest him at this moment, since this would surely entail the defection of all his troops. Christophe has so maltreated the negroes that he is hated by them, and is therefore not to be feared. Dessalines is at present the butcher of the negroes; it is through him that I execute all my odious measures. I shall keep him as long as I need him. He has already begged me not to leave him at San Domingo when I return home. Laplume, Clervaux, and Paul Louverture are three imbeciles whom I shall get rid of at will. Charles Belair has been tried and shot.[20]

A fuller understanding of the sincerity with which Christophe had espoused the French cause comes from a conversation he had with General Lacroix. "You are young and a European," he said,

you have always served in Europe and cannot know the prejudices about slavery. The revolt increases because confidence is lost; and if you were yourself black you would not perhaps rest in tranquillity as I do, who am about sending my son to be educated in France. The brigands who lead the insurrection are nothing— the danger is not in that direction, but it lies in the convictions of the blacks. They are alarmed at the decree of the 30th of April for the maintenance of slavery in St. Domingo, and at the attempts of the First Consul to restore the ancient regime, and they are exerting themselves against it. If I did not confide in Gen. Leclerc, I should not be among you. Sans Souci is a brigand, base and cruel, who does not hesitate to murder all whom he suspects. He knows when to fly and when to cover his flight by leaving a desert behind him. He is doing better than we did when you landed. If instead of fighting we had fled before you, and alarmed the negroes of the country, you would never have succeeded over us. Toussaint ceased not to say what no one would believe—"We have arms in our hands—pride alone makes us use them"; and now these new insurgents have arisen up to follow that very system; and if they continue their warfare we shall find it difficult to subdue them.[21]

With the continued depletion of his troops from yellow fever, Leclerc instituted a veritable reign of terror. "We must destroy all the mountain negroes, men and women," he wrote to Napoleon on October 7, 1802,

sparing only children under twelve years of age. We must destroy half the ne-

---

[19] T. Lothrop Stoddard, *op. cit.*, pp. 335–336.
[20] *Ibid.*, p. 339.
[21] J. Brown, *op. cit.*, Vol. II, p. 122.

groes of the plains, and not allow in the colony a single man who has worn an epaulette.[22]

This was Leclerc's "last will and testament," for on November 2, 1802, he died a victim of the yellow fever which had reduced his armies to a shadow.

Even before his death it was finally becoming clear to the leading mulatto and Negro generals that they were being used as mere tools and would be disposed of by the French at the first favorable opportunity. They were quick to act. A serious revolt occurred on October 12, when the mulatto general, Clervaux, stormed Cap Français with ten thousand rebel troops. Although he was unsuccessful in capturing the town, he made good his escape. The next day Christophe broke into open rebellion, to be followed shortly by Dessalines. For the first time, the Negroes and mulattoes were united, fighting not only for their personal freedom but for the independence of Saint-Domingue as well.

Leclerc's successor was General Rochambeau. No worse choice could have been made. Leclerc had cautioned Napoleon that although "Rochambeau [is] a brave soldier and a good fighter, [he] has not an ounce of tact or policy. Furthermore, he has no moral character and is easily led." Rochambeau considered the Negroes lower than animals, and on the assumption of supreme command, he began a systematic slaughtering of the whole population. Men and women were put to the sword, shot, or hanged. Others were crowded into ships, taken out to sea, and drowned. Savage hunting dogs were imported from Cuba, not only to track down the Negroes but to feed upon them as well. Rochambeau had begun a war of extermination; little did he anticipate that within another year the Negroes would exact a vengeance upon the whites as brutal and far-reaching as the atrocities he initiated.

The slow recuperation from yellow fever of the remnants of his armies and the timely arrival of reinforcements from France enabled Rochambeau, by the beginning of 1803, to wrest a large portion of Saint-Domingue from the insurgents; but his sucesses only increased the fanatic resistance of the Negroes and mulattoes, now unified under Dessalines, their commander-in-chief. In May, 1803, however, a new disaster befell the French in Saint-Domingue, for in that month the uneasy peace between France and England came to a close and a blockade was thrown around the island. Without hope of further replacements from France, Rochambeau was soon in desperate straits. Quickly Dessalines won back the South and West Provinces,

---

[22] T. Lothrop Stoddard, *op. cit.*, p. 342.

and by autumn he was assailing the North Province as well. By November the French held only Cap Français and the Môle Saint-Nicolas. Faced with annihilation, Rochambeau signed on November 19 a truce with Dessalines, whereby he agreed to evacuate Cap Français. "General Rochambeau," wrote Miss Hassal[23] to Aaron Burr, then Vice-President of the United States:

after having made a shameful capitulation with the negroes, has evacuated the Cape. He presented his superb horses to Dessalines, and then embarked with his suite, and all the inhabitants who chose to follow him, intending to fight his way through the British ships.

Soon afterwards, he surrendered to the British fleet lying offshore.

With the surrender of the French garrison at the Môle Saint-Nicolas a few days later, Saint-Domingue was at last entirely free. The Negro and mulatto uprisings of 1791, which began merely as desperate attempts to throw off the unbearable tyranny of the whites, with no thought of future independence, ended with the destruction of the French armies and the loss of the colony to France forever. Negro supremacy in Saint-Domingue had begun.

The cost of Napoleon's ill-starred attempt to repossess Saint-Domingue had been tremendous. In addition to the enormous expenses attendant upon an undertaking of such proportions, the waste of human life was staggering. Out of fifty thousand troops sent out during the two-year period only a few thousand survived to return to France. Nobody knows how many Negroes lost their lives, but historians estimate that the black colonial population of nearly half a million had dwindled by 1804 to three hundred and fifty thousand.

It is, perhaps, worth remarking that the United States had good reason to look with great concern upon Napoleon's venture. Although the quasi war between France and the United States had ended in September, 1800, President Jefferson learned not long afterward that Spain had secretly ceded the Louisiana territory to France. Added to this disconcerting news, came information about the projected conquest of Hispaniola. Nor was this all. On December 30, 1801, the American minister in Paris warned "that the armament destined in the first instance for Hispaniola is to proceed to Louisiana provided Toussaint makes no opposition."[24] *Provided Toussaint*

---

[23] Miss Hassal, an American woman whose sister was married to an officer in the French invasion force, published in 1808: *Secret History; or the Horrors of St. Domingo, in a Series of Letters, Written by a Lady at Cape François to Colonel Burr, Late Vice-President of the United States, Principally During the Command of General Rochambeau.* This work was published anonymously.

[24] Ludwell L. Montague, *Haiti and the United States, 1714–1938* (Durham, N.C., 1940), p. 43.

makes no opposition: ominous words! Fortunately the Negroes resisted until the inevitability of a new European war made the fulfillment of Napoleon's grandiose plans impossible. On April 11, 1803, on the eve of the renewal of hostilities on the Continent, the American minister to France was astonished to find his offer to buy New Orleans met with a proposal by Talleyrand to sell the whole of Louisiana to the United States. The grim resistance of Toussaint and the Negroes, played, then, an important part in extinguishing Napoleon's ambition to extend his empire to America, and along with the European war, led him to relinquish the vast Louisiana territory to the United States.

Throughout the conflict, the United States followed a policy of uneasy neutrality and endeavored to preserve friendly relations with France, although the avowed intentions of Napoleon made Toussaint the first line of defense. Soon after his arrival in Saint-Domingue, Leclerc preëmpted the cargoes of American merchants, went on to declare a blockade of the ports not yet in his hands, and demanded that the United States stop all commerce with the rebellious Negroes. Jefferson merely advised the French minister that he was powerless to order Americans to refrain from such trade and pointed out that if they persisted in ignoring the blockade they did so at their own risk. The United States did nothing to coöperate with France; meanwhile Leclerc battled against hopeless odds until his death, and Rochambeau fared no better. Even the sale of Louisiana failed to change the policy of the American Government and active help was not forthcoming. Indeed, as the Negroes wrested the ports from the French, American merchants resumed trade, their ships sailing in armed convoys for protection against French privateers.

JEAN-JACQUES DESSALINES

On New Year's Day, 1804, at Gonaïves, where Toussaint, after being treacherously betrayed by Leclerc, embarked for France, the independence of Saint-Domingue was proclaimed at a conclave of all the leading generals, amidst a huge crowd of soldiers and citizens. It is reported that the night before the ceremonies, one of Dessalines' secretaries, having composed a document inspired by the American Declaration of Independence, read it aloud. Dessalines thought it lukewarm. Suddenly one of his men shouted, "To set down the Act of Independence there are necessary the skin of a white man for a parchment, his skull for a writing desk, his blood for ink, and a bayonet for a pen." Such views appealed to Dessalines. He charged the speaker "to express my sentiments with regard to the whites," and a new manifesto was drawn up.

The independence ceremonies began with a reading of the proclamation, which was signed by Dessalines. It fairly seethed with hatred of the French and demanded vengeance. It reminded the people that almost every one of them had a close relative, a brother, a father, a son, a sister, or even a mother, who had been murdered by French assassins. "Frighten all those who dare to attempt to take away [freedom] from us still," it affirmed. "Let us begin with the French; let them shudder at approaching our shores. . . . Peace to our neighbors! But anathema to the French name! Hatred eternal to France! Here is our outcry!"

Following this bloodcurdling proclamation, the Act of Independence signed by Dessalines and the leading generals was read: "Before posterity, before the entire universe, . . . [we swear] to renounce France forever and to die rather than to live under her domination." Dessalines was then declared Governor-General for life, with the power of choosing his successor, and the generals swore "to obey blindly the laws emanating from his authority." To obliterate all traces of French domination, Dessalines gave to Saint-Domingue its ancient Indian name of Haiti. Thus was established the second independent nation and the first Negro government in the New World. And to this day, the first of January remains for the Haitian people their Day of Independence and is so celebrated.

Whatever may have been Dessalines' military abilities—and some authorities consider him a better tactician than Toussaint—he was utterly unfitted for the Herculean task ahead. During colonial days he had been the slave of a Negro, the most degraded position that even a slave could occupy. Following the Negro insurrection, he joined the troops of Toussaint and was soon elevated to a high place of leadership. He was, of course, wholly uneducated. He had no particular intellectual endowments, and he was vain and sullen. Ferocious, audacious, and cunning, he emerged as the strongest man in Haiti solely because of his military prowess. Where brute force was needed, Dessalines was the man of the hour. Possessing an innate sense of drama, he dominated the scene. He it was who tore the white band from the French tricolor flag as a visible symbol of the extinction of white power. He it was who boomed, "Liberty or Death!" at the independence ceremonies. But for the problems of civil administration, for the means of welding his people into a unified nation, he had neither talent nor leadership.

Haiti was now in a deplorable state. The plantations were devastated and many of the towns destroyed. The population, after twelve years of warfare, had lost all habits of industry. Fears of a new French invasion and internal disorders made imperative the maintenance of a large standing army. There was no state treasury, no civil authority, no educational system. A strong hand was needed, to be sure, for only force could produce order out of such chaotic conditions; but a wise head, too, was necessary. Dessalines, who was accustomed only to cruelty and military power, was an unfortunate choice.

Dessalines turned almost at once to the extermination of the French population in Haiti. At the time of Rochambeau's capitulation, he, Clervaux, and Christophe had issued on November 29, 1803, a proclamation promising safety and protection to all French proprietors who "have adjured their ancient errors, renounced their foolish pretensions, and recognized the justice of the cause for which we have been shedding our blood for the last twelve years," but woe to "anyone who dares speak to us of slavery." Many Frenchmen who had fled to near-by islands thereupon returned to Haiti. Their property and all their possessions were there, and they hoped to find a haven under Dessalines as they had earlier enjoyed under Toussaint. Dessalines' proclamation of January 1, 1804, however, had been calculated to arouse his people against the whites, and he later issued a downright order for the massacre of all the French in Haiti. He personally supervised its execution, for many of his generals, notably Christophe, were horrified by this fiendishness. In a few weeks he had slaughtered almost all the French residents, including the women and children. Only a few priests and professional men were spared. Dessalines had exacted a frightful retaliation for the atrocities of General Rochambeau.

In October, 1804, in imitation of Napoleon, Dessalines had himself crowned Emperor Jacques the First of Haiti. He created no nobility; "Moi seul, je suis noble," he declared. He did not establish an hereditary empire but retained the right to nominate his successor. The new constitution abolished slavery forever. It renounced the word *Negro* and chose the term *black* to describe all the inhabitants of Haiti, regardless of their color. It decreed that no white man should ever set foot in Haiti as a landowner and provided that all French property in the island should be confiscated to the state to constitute a national domain. Dessalines instituted a military dicta-

torship, with two classes of men, soldiers and-laborers. The latter were reduced to serfdom and put back to work on the plantations under the most
stringent regulations.

It was, of course, necessary for Dessalines to establish commercial arrangements with the outside world, a world startled by the spectacle of a
mass of ex-slaves declaring their independence and setting up a Negro
government. American merchants had already opened trade with Haitian
ports; the British had blockaded the island and had asked for exclusive
trading privileges. Dessalines, who had come to distrust all whites, believed,
however,—and with justice—that the United States would eventually accede
to Napoleon's demand for the cessation of all trade with the assassins of the
French;[25] yet he was afraid to bind himself to Great Britain. He determined,
therefore, to trade with England, the United States, and other nations under
severe restrictions set by himself. The ports at which foreign ships might
enter were specified. When a ship arrived, it was placed in the charge of a
Negro consignee chosen by Dessalines, and its cargo disposed of. If the
foreign merchant did not have confidence in the official consignee, he was
under no obligation to sell, but was prohibited thenceforth from trading
anywhere in the island. Such a system encouraged irregularity, dishonesty,
and smuggling.[26]

There were many other problems too. When Rochambeau surrendered
in November, 1803, the French general Ferrand and a small detachment of
troops held the town of Monte Christi across the border in what had been
Spanish Santo Domingo. When attacked by Dessalines, the French troops
fled across the island to the city of Santo Domingo. Instead of pursuing
them and gaining control of all Hispaniola as Toussaint had done, Dessalines temporarily delayed the campaign. In 1805, however, he determined
to resume his conquest. Several armies marched across the border and soon
the city of Santo Domingo was under siege. Almost at the moment of victory, French ships were sighted in the harbor of the besieged city. Then
came false rumors that French ships were also threatening the shores of
Haiti. Dessalines abandoned his military operations and rushed precipi-
tately back to the west. Thus Spanish Santo Domingo remained in French
hands.

---

[25] The United States endeavored to avoid conflict with either England or France, both of
whom were preying on her trade, first, in March, 1805, by prohibiting armed merchantmen
from selling munitions in the West Indies, and second, early in 1806, by prohibiting trade with
any part of Hispaniola denying the sovereignty of France. See R. W. Logan, *op. cit.*, pp. 170–
177.

[26] James G. Leyburn, *The Haitian People* (New Haven, 1941), pp. 250–252.

The fear of another French invasion was an obsession with Dessalines, as it was with most of his countrymen, for the atrocities of Leclerc and Rochambeau were not to be forgotten. A scheme for repelling any new attack was, therefore, designed. Since experience had proved that the coastal towns could not be held against the guns of an attacking fleet, they were to be burned and abandoned. The population meanwhile was to retire to the hinterland. Resistance was to be concentrated in the interior, where the Negroes could take advantage of the rugged terrain and the jungles to harass and eliminate the enemy, and Dessalines ordered the construction of a series of fortresses designed to withstand sustained attacks by superior forces.

Despite, however, the unity of the generals in preparations for the defense of Haiti, all was not well. From the beginning, the mulattoes had resented the ascendancy of a Negro. Dessalines, for his part, recognized no color or social distinctions. After the wholesale slaughter of the French, he had told Pétion, one of the mulatto leaders, that he had often been unable to distinguish the lighter mulattoes from the whites, indicating that a good many mulattoes had suffered the same fate as the French. Nor was Dessalines less cruel and despotic in his treatment of the Negroes. Everywhere throughout his kingdom Negroes and mulattoes alike opposed his increasing tyranny, and as time went on, resentment burst into open hostility. On his way to crush an uprising in the South Province, he fell into an ambush not far from Port-au-Prince, and on October 17, 1806, was brutally murdered. So violent were the feelings of his assassins that his body was horribly mutilated. That night the mangled remains of the former emperor were gathered into a sack by a half-mad old Negress, named Défilée, and carried to a cemetery. Later, when bitterness against him had receded, a modest tomb was erected, with the simple inscription, "Here lies Dessalines, dead at forty-eight years."

Present-day Haitians look to Dessalines as the founder of their independence. As the indomitable general-in-chief against the French, he deserves to be eulogized; the tragedy is that he should have undertaken to govern the island he had freed. He failed to bring about a spirit of unity and concord, and at the time of his death, only a year and ten months after the proclamation of independence, the island was divided into rival factions.

HENRY CHRISTOPHE

Although Dessalines failed to nominate a successor, Henry Christophe, the commander-in-chief of the army and the last of the three great Negro leaders produced by the slave insurrection, was proclaimed provisional head of the state. The circumstances and place of his birth remain obscure. According to an official document published by his own order, he was born on October 6, 1767, in the British island of Grenada. Some historians, however, give his birthplace as the British island of St. Kitts, formerly St. Christopher, thus offering an explanation of his name. Some authorities claim that he was born of free Negroes; others assert that he was the son of slave parents. At all events, he was a pure-blooded Negro, he was certainly a slave during his childhood, and he found his way to Saint-Domingue as a boy. Charles Mackenzie, who became British Consul-General to Haiti in 1826, says that Christophe "was the slave of a French gentleman, whose daughter resided there when I was at the Cap, to whom the former domestic was kind and attentive in his prosperity"; but it is not clear whether the "French gentleman" was his master before or after Christophe came to Saint-Domingue. He became the property of a French naval officer, whom he served as bootblack and messboy and whom he accompanied to Savannah, Georgia, during the American Revolution. He was later sold to a free Negro owner of an inn at Cap Français. Serving first as a stableboy and afterward as a waiter, he came into contact with white men; and though he had received no education, his natural powers of observation and his sagacity gave him firsthand information about the French and particularly about the new political ideas emanating from France—revolutionary ideas, which, as later events proved, had been eagerly absorbed by the listening Negro slaves. In 1793, apparently having purchased his freedom, he married Marie-Louise Coidavid, the daughter of his Negro master. During the rise of Toussaint he became a formidable leader.

Christophe was tall, strong, and handsome, with bright, flashing eyes— "a fine portly looking man," as a British naval officer who visited Haiti in 1818 describes him. "He is now growing stout," the officer continues, "and on horseback, where he certainly looks his best, has much the appearance of old George.... He is quite black, with a manner and countenance, when in good humour (and I have never seen him in any other) very intelligent, pleasant, and expressive."[27] He had risen to power by dint of his indefatigable

---

[27] R. Coupland, *Wilberforce, a Narrative* (Oxford, 1923), p. 467.

energy and his dominating personality. He was a man of action and demanded unhesitating obedience. He had little inclination to pity. Impetuous, irascible, and headstrong, he permitted no opposition to his will, and the fury of his anger knew no bounds. Yet he was gifted with social graces. White men who visited him report that his conversation was entertaining and his manners charming. He was ostentatious and delighted in pomp and ceremony. He possessed an exceptional memory, and he seems to have understood both French and English. It has been reported that he conducted his conferences with English officers in French in order that he might gather his thoughts while the translations were being made and that he might test the loyalty of his interpreter. On one occasion he used his English to rebuke an American captain who was brought before him for some infraction of the law. Muttering that he wished he had "the sable king at Charleston," the indignant American was appalled when Christophe quietly asked in perfect English, "How much do you think I should fetch?"

Proud and ambitious, Christophe was well equipped to lead his people; but he had no illusions concerning self-government, and he believed that only arbitrary power could bring order and prosperity to the devastated island. He realized, with almost tragic clarity, that the Haitians must be protected against themselves—from sloth, from apathy, and from ignorance. They had fought their enslavers until at last they were free, yet for tradition and race culture they had only voodoo worship, the vestiges of their African background, and the degradation of slavery. Proud though they were of their freedom, won by blood and pain, they were as yet untouched by any desire for self-improvement. But Henry Christophe, fired by a magnificent ambition, determined to transform them overnight into an orderly, hard-working, and self-respecting nation.

Christophe was opposed by Alexandre Pétion, the leader of the mulattoes. Born in Port-au-Prince, the son of a Negro mother and a white French jeweler, Pétion was educated in a French military academy in Paris. At the time of the mulatto struggle against Toussaint in 1800, he was Rigaud's favorite lieutenant, and with Rigaud he fled to France when Toussaint mastered the South Province. He accompanied Leclerc's expedition against the Negroes in 1802. Napoleon's reinstitution of the colonial discriminations against the mulattoes turned Pétion into the camp of the Negroes, and he recognized that the future of the mulattoes lay in the independence of Haiti. He participated in the declaration of Haitian independence at Gonaïves, took the oath of allegiance to Dessalines, and was made general in command at Port-au-Prince. Mild-tempered and conciliatory, he was slow to action. As a military man he preferred the siege to the shifting battle, for he was an artilleryman, not a campaigner like Christophe. His gentle manners were combined with a genuine desire for the good of his country.

Two men of such widely different temperaments as the Negro Christophe and the mulatto Pétion were naturally in disagreement on political policy. Christophe believed in an iron rule. Pétion felt that the Haitian people ought to be given full liberty and that force should be abandoned. Conflict between the two was inevitable.

It was generally agreed, after the despotism of Emperor Dessalines, that the monarchical form of government should be modified, and Christophe as the provisional leader ordered the election of representatives to a Constituent Assembly, which was to meet in Port-au-Prince for the purpose of establishing a republican government. He did not, of course, envisage the creation of a democratic state; rather he expected the Assembly to frame a government which would concentrate the executive, legislative, and military power in a president, and he felt sure that he would be elected to that office. Since the thirty-three electors from the North Province and the Artibonite formed a majority and since Christophe could dominate them, he remained aloof at Cap Haïtien (formerly Cap Français), confident that the Assembly would do his bidding. Pétion, however, circumvented him. By increasing the number of deputies from the West and South Provinces, he succeeded in gaining a majority of forty-one to thirty-three in the Assembly. Despite the protests of the members from the north at this illegal proceeding, the Assembly set to work, and on December 27, 1806, a constitution, mainly inspired by Pétion, was approved. Democratic in form, it reduced the office of president to that of a mere figurehead and placed the legislative power, the control over the army, and the right to appoint ministers in the hands of a Senate of twenty-four members. The next day, the Assembly, having denuded the presidency of all real authority and made of it only an honorary distinction, elected Christophe President for a four-year term.

When Christophe learned of these transactions, he was infuriated, and he spurned the proffer of so empty an honor, which, as one of his delegates declared, demoted him to the authority of a mere corporal. Instead, he determined to make himself military master of Haiti, and thus be able to impose a government of his own upon the country. He quickly assembled his troops and marched towards Port-au-Prince. A few miles from the town he was opposed by an army led by Pétion, who had hastily prepared to resist the assault. On January 1, 1807, the two armies met. The superior forces of Christophe were completely successful, and Pétion, his army shattered, barely escaped with his life. On January 6, Christophe launched an attack upon Port-au-Prince itself; but the forces of Pétion having been augmented by reinforcements from the south, stood their ground and Christophe was defeated. Two days later he withdrew with his army to the north.

At the end of January, the new Senate at Port-au-Prince declared Christophe to be an outlaw and the presidency to be vacant. On March 9, after considerable bickering, the Senate elected General Pétion President of the Republic of Haiti for four years. The turn of events now ironically placed him in the very office he had so carefully divested of all power, and before long he found it necessary to abrogate many provisions of the new constitution. In the end he vested himself with all the powers he had been so unwilling to grant to Christophe.

In the meantime, Christophe set about drafting a constitution for the area he controlled. On February 17, 1807, it was approved by delegates of his own choosing, and he was elected President and generalissimo of the land and sea forces for life.

Thus, by 1807, only three years after the proclamation of independence, Haiti was divided into two governments, the State of Haiti under Christophe and the Republic of Haiti under Pétion. Christophe controlled the North Province and the valley of the Artibonite in the West Province. Pétion held sway over the remaining part of the west and the province in the south. Christophe located his government at Cap Haïtien, while Port-au-Prince was the seat of Pétion's regime. Although the territory of Christophe was somewhat larger, the population of the two domains was about equal.

Perhaps Christophe should have accepted the presidency which was offered to him in 1806 and then gone on to annul the provisions of the constitution, as Pétion was later to do. He was too headstrong, too impetuous, to follow such a course. But his action in creating a separate state in the north plunged Haiti into a civil war destined to last six years and divided it into two governments for fourteen years.

Between 1807 and 1810, Pétion made a series of incursions, both by sea and by land, into the realm of Christophe. Although Pétion achieved some initial successes, Christophe's armies were ultimately victorious. In the end

Christophe had not only driven out the invaders, but he had cleared the entire North Province of pockets of resistance to his authority.

Although Pétion was able to launch four separate campaigns against his rival, there was much dissension in his own territory. The South Province especially resented his authority, and after the return in 1810 of Rigaud, the old mulatto enemy of Toussaint, broke into open rebellion.[28] The death of Rigaud in 1811 brought an end to the schism. Meanwhile Christophe was highly distressed by innumerable defections among his adherents, which he attributed to Pétion's insidious influence, and in 1812 he launched a full-scale attack upon the West Province with twenty thousand soldiers. His armies soon captured the outposts protecting Port-au-Prince and placed the city under siege. For more than two months he battered the city's defenses, but instead of pushing his attack to its conclusion, he suddenly raised the siege and withdrew, thus bringing to an end not only his campaign but open warfare between him and Pétion. Thenceforth a sort of armed truce existed and no further military operations were undertaken.

During the years between 1807 and 1811, Christophe seems to have clung to the belief that unity of the whole of Haiti might be achieved, and he awaited the expiration of Pétion's four-year term of office in the vain hope that the new election would place himself and not Pétion in the presidency of the whole island. The reëlection of Pétion by the Senate on March 9, 1811, indicated clearly the determination of the West and South Provinces to ignore him. Accordingly, on March 28, he was proclaimed King Henry the First.

The rapidity with which Christophe announced the hereditary monarchy, promulgated a constitution, and set up a nobility offers irrefutable evidence that he had long planned to abandon the farce of a republican government in his territory. The creation of an hereditary nobility was his first concern. Whereas Dessalines had refused to permit the establishment of an aristocracy, Christophe believed it a necessary adjunct to his government. At the top was the royal family, including the King himself, Queen Marie-Louise, the Prince, Jacques-Victor-Henry, the two Princesses, Frances-Améthiste and Ann-Athénaïre, and several others. Next in order were the grand officers of the kingdom, the ministers of the four general departments of government, and the grand civil officers of the crown. There were created

---

[28] At the end of 1810, three separate spheres of authority existed in Pétion's domain. Pétion held sway in the west; Rigaud in the south; and in the extreme southwest a band of maroon Negroes in the mountains, under the chief Gomar (or Goman), defied all efforts of either Pétion or Rigaud to subdue them.

eight dukes, twenty-two counts, thirty-seven barons, and fourteen chevaliers. Christophe also founded the Royal and Military Order of St. Henry. His court, patterned after that of England, was to be as lavish and formal as any in Europe, and the minutest details of dress and etiquette were strictly prescribed.

In preparation for the coronation Christophe ordered the construction of a cathedral. In two months several hundred laborers, regimented and formed into brigades, produced a building two hundred and fifty feet square and eighty feet high; and "furnished with a throne, galleries for the great ladies of the court, chapels, oratories, an orchestra, and all the arrangements necessary for the august ceremony." The formal coronation was held on June 2, 1811. The new archbishop of Haiti consecrated Christophe King Henry the First, with the stately splendor so dear to the King's heart. The festivities consumed "eight days of rejoicing." Several British and American guests were invited to attend an official banquet, at which the new king, in acknowledgment of a toast proposed by Captain Douglas of the English frigate *Reindeer,* responded by toasting, "My dear brother, George! May his life be preserved by the Great Ruler of the Universe, and may he oppose an invincible obstacle to the unbridled ambition of Napoleon and remain always the constant friend of Hayti!"[29]

Christophe was a shrewd and farsighted man who judged himself as well as others. He had dreamed his dream of the future of his race; but having had no formal education, he gathered around him a group of men who advised him in the administration of his kingdom, taught him the history of other nations, and read to him from the important journals of the day. Thus he came to know a good deal about political science and civil and military organization and kept himself conversant with the stormy events of Napoleon's career. He particularly reverenced the genius of Frederick the Great. His administrative experience under Toussaint, too, had given him some practical knowledge of government; but the gigantic task of framing a code of laws suited to the Haitian people and yet capable of transforming them into hard-working and law-abiding citizens required the assistance of others. The ambitious plans were his own; but for their realization he depended upon those more fortunate than himself. "It is *his* mind and his alone that governs all," said an English visitor to Haiti; "he has the ablest men of his kingdom employed about his person, but they are the mere executors of his will."

---

[29] R. Coupland, *op. cit.,* p. 463.

To Julien Prévost, the Comte de Limonade,[30] Christophe assigned the important posts of secretary of state and minister of foreign affairs. A mulatto who had been educated in France, Limonade was intelligent and well informed. Mild and temperate, he was wholly attached to the cause of the monarchy and worked with unflagging energy for the best interests of the state. In 1811, as an official propagandist of the King, he published an account of Christophe's rise to the throne.[31] He carried on much of the foreign correspondence and composed many of the edicts and proclamations issued during Christophe's reign. He was one of the most cultured and distinguished of Christophe's close associates.

Second in importance was Pompée Valentin, Baron de Vastey, another mulatto who had been educated in France. Christophe gave him the office of private secretary and appointed him to the Privy Council. Vastey possessed a wide range of historical and political information, and he was among the chief defenders of the Kingdom of Haiti.[32] He had been one of Dessalines' secretaries. Fierce and passionate, he hated the whites and wished to exterminate them; "in short," says one authority, "he was the very counterpart of Dessalines,—an assemblage of all that was mean, and savage, and diabolical."[33] Yet he was fanatically devoted to Christophe and placed the results of his wide reading at the disposal of his king. Made secretary of the commission which drew up a code of laws for the kingdom, he was no mere amanuensis, but in the fullest sense, Christophe's friend and adviser. He was entrusted, too, with the duty of superintending the education of the Prince Royal.

The third of Christophe's advisers was Baron Dupuy, also a mulatto. Born about 1780, he had been a subaltern under Dessalines, but had not risen to a position of any importance. Despising Dessalines, he migrated to Philadelphia, where he is said to have made a fortune. The reign of Christophe seemingly presaging peace and opportunity, he returned to Haiti. Dupuy was a man of great natural talent and was well versed in history

---

[30] This title and that of the Duc de Marmelade were derived from French names given to areas in the North Province of Haiti.

[31] *Relation des glorieux événemens qui ont porté leurs Majestés Royales sur le trône d'Hayti; suivie de l'histoire du couronnement et du sacre du Roy Henry I*er*, et de la Reine Marie-Louise* (Cap Henry, 1811).

[32] See Baron de Vastey, *Le Système colonial dévoilé* (Cap Henry, 1814); *Réflexions sur les noirs et les blancs* (Cap Henry, 1816); *Réflexions politiques sur quelques ouvrages et journaux français concernant Hayti* (Sans Souci, 1817); *Essai sur les causes de la révolution et des guerres civiles d'Hayti, ...* (Sans Souci, 1819).

[33] W. W. Harvey, *Sketches of Hayti; from the Expulsion of the French, to the Death of Christophe* (London, 1827), p. 224.

and politics. He became Christophe's secretary and interpreter and was able to be of assistance in the practical administration of the kingdom. But, as was the case with Limonade and Vastey, Dupuy did not create the dreams of Christophe; he merely brought to bear on the ambitious schemes of his sovereign a mind tempered by successful competition among American businessmen.

Mention should be made of Prince Sanders (also spelled Saunders). An American Negro, he was born in New England and attended Moor's Charity School at Dartmouth College in 1807 and 1808. Sanders' activities on behalf of the less fortunate members of his own race won him the friendship of several influential Americans, who sent him to England with numerous letters of recommendation. At the suggestion of the English abolitionists, he came to Haiti to assist in organizing the schools and to forward the cause of Protestantism. He became almost at once a rabid follower of Christophe, and determined to make known the integrity of the King's character and the enlightened nature of the government. In 1816 he published *Haytian Papers* in London and two years later reissued the book in Boston. It is said that Sanders introduced vaccination into Haiti and personally vaccinated Christophe's children.

Within a few months of his coronation, Christophe issued the Code Henry, a comprehensive series of laws regulating commerce, civil proceedings, the police, agriculture, and the military. The Code Rural, however, was in many ways the most original part of the Code Henry. While Christophe had a precedent in the policies enforced by Toussaint, nevertheless his formal codification of the rules and regulations concerning agriculture represents a new venture in statecraft. This code covered such diverse matters as the duties of plantation owners and the laborers, the policing of the plantations, and the cultivation of the major crops. Sir Joseph Banks once said, "It is worthy to be written in letters of gold; nothing that I have ever seen which was written for the same purposes by white men is worthy to be compared to it." The laborers were bound to the plantations and were not allowed to leave their work without permission. The workday, too, was regulated. One article reads:

The following hours of labour are irrevocably established. Work shall commence with the day-light, and be continued uninterruptedly till eight o'clock:— one hour is allotted to the labourer for breakfast on the spot where employed; at nine work recommences until noon, when two hours repose are granted them: at two exactly they recommence work, and shall not leave off before night-fall.[34]

---

[34] Prince Sanders, *op. cit.,* p. xiii.

There were provisions for medical care—though unfortunately the lack of physicians or even trained nurses prevented their full realization—and for the protection of the laborer against exploitation. Evening prayers were required, marriage was encouraged, and it was decreed that the "peasantry who shall bring up the greatest number of legitimate children in a reputable manner, shall be distinguished and encouraged by the government itself." Christophe wanted no beggars or idle persons:

Mendicity and female licentiousness are severely reprobated; all beggars on the highway, prostitutes, and stragglers shall be arrested, and such as have no legal settlement placed by the proper authorities, in their discretion, to labour for their livelihood. His Majesty's governors and lieutenants are strictly ordered to enforce these regulations, and the good and faithful subjects invited to denounce the delinquents.[35]

He taught his people self-respect by requiring them to appear in the towns dressed in neat and clean clothing. He inculcated honesty in them by setting the severest penalties for theft. He even went so far as to have pieces of jewelry planted where they might easily be found. Woe to the Negro who did not immediately report his finding of one of these items and turn it over to the nearest official.

When Christophe came to power much of the land belonged to the state and was divided into plantations of hundreds of acres, an inheritance from the colonial system. At first he kept the estates intact and leased the national domain in large blocks to members of the nobility and others, who held their land only so long as they enjoyed his favor. To increase productivity, he had the irrigation systems rebuilt and he gave great care to the raising of sugar. Inspectors were appointed to every district to see that cultivation was maintained on schedule, and under their supervision production reached a very high level. The Code Rural required that one-fourth of the annual crop be paid to the state, thus greatly enriching the treasury. On every plantation one-fourth of the total crop was payable to the workers as wages. In addition, each family was allotted a garden plot where the laborers were required to raise food crops for their personal consumption. Since they received an adequate income and since on Saturday afternoons and Sundays they were not required to work, they could go to the villages and spend their money as they pleased. They were assigned to the plantations, where they worked under a routine as strict as that of a school. In many ways they were mere serfs, but they were infinitely better off than they had been under slavery.

Later in his reign, Christophe took advantage of "the tranquillity we at present enjoy," to sell off much of the national domain, to "augment the number of property owners" and to give every Haitian, whatever his rank or station in life, a right to purchase land.[36] Special attention was paid to "heads of families and to the most laborious and deserving tillers of the soil." To prevent a decline in production, however, he provided for the fullest supervision of these new proprietors. Thus under Christophe practically every acre of fertile soil was put under cultivation.

Knowing that the welfare of Haiti depended primarily upon agriculture, Christophe restored the devastated plantations at the earliest possible moment and maintained production by the most efficient means. A benevolent despotism was the result. He ruled with absolute authority, deprived his subjects of initiative, and punished without pity those who attempted to thwart his plans; nevertheless, under his guiding hand, his country soon attained prosperity.

Christophe had a passion for monuments, and he built a number of sumptuous palaces, of which his favorite was Sans Souci. From its windows he could see the ocean far in the distance and the wide expanse of the Plaine du Nord. Lying nestled among the mountains twelve miles inland from Cap Haïtien, which was renamed Cap Henry,[37] and rising four stories above a majestic staircase, it dominated the whole countryside. Emphasis was placed on spaciousness and grandeur, both in the large apartments within and in the stately gardens surrounding the palace. Here, indeed, was the proper setting for the levees and state affairs which Christophe demanded of his people, and it became the center of the life of his kingdom.

Sans Souci, perhaps the most magnificent building in the West Indies, now lies in ruins. Its rich tapestries and paintings, its extensive library, and its exquisite furnishings have long since disappeared. Tropical storms have discolored its once gaily painted walls, and the mountain stream, which underneath the large reception rooms brought coolness to a perspiring court, has eaten its way into the foundations. Yet even today the gaunt and lonely structure is an imposing and impressive sight.

---

[36] In 1819, Christophe made still further inroads on the public domain by gifts of land to his soldiers of all ranks. For an account of this action see page 67, and for the text of the edict of the King providing for these concessions of land see Part III, Document 3, pp. 268–271.

[37] Throughout the Introduction, Cap Henry (rather than the English form Cape Henry) has been used to correspond with Cap Français, the French colonial name of the town, and Cap Haïtien, which Dessalines named it and which is the appellation used from Christophe's death to the present.

Among the white persons who came to Christophe's court were two ladies from Philadelphia. They were to have charge of the education of his two daughters. "We embarked," recounts one of these teachers, "at Philadelphia, and in fifteen days reached Cape François. We landed much debilitated by the illness we had suffered during the passage." The Queen on their arrival sent for them to call at Sans Souci. But let them tell their own story.

At the appointed time, an elegant London-built chariot, drawn by four greys, was sent to convey us to the palace. We set off on one of those soft and beautiful mornings . . . and during the ride, we thought nothing comparable to the beauty, the freshness, and the loveliness of a morning's excursion in a tropical winter. We were accompanied by the baron de Dupuy, who amused us as much by his inquiries and remarks respecting America, where he had lived sometime, as he pleased us by his polite and gentlemanly manners. On reaching Sans Souci, we alighted at prince John's, the king's nephew. His wife, a stout, fat, well-looking mulatto, was awaiting our arrival; by whom we were ushered into a saloon, where we were immediately surrounded by a crowd of visitors. . . . Some of them had never seen white ladies before; and their repeated exclamation of *"Gueté femme blanche la qu'elle belle!"* amused us exceedingly. After taking coffee, we retired. . . .

About 11 o'clock we were summoned to the palace, and conducted into the library, where the count de Limonade, the secretary for foreign affairs, was awaiting us. After handing us chairs, he remained some minutes in silence. . . . In about a quarter of an hour, we heard a bustle in the adjoining passage,—the door opened,—and Christophe, preceded by six young negroes, as pages, and accompanied by some of his nobles, made his appearance. We rose and made a profound *salut:* he desired us to be seated: we knew better, and stood while he remained; not in the least intimidated by the appearance or manners of his sable majesty. He said little to us, but turning to baron de Dupuy, he enquired if our house at the Cape was in readiness; and finding it was not so, he said, "Oh, these ladies can come here and instruct my daughters"; and immediately left us to prepare them for our reception.

We were now conducted to another part of the palace, and shown into a spacious saloon, furnished with great magnificence and taste. We were scarcely seated when the large folding doors . . . again opened, and Christophe, with the queen, the prince royal, and the princesses appeared, dressed most handsomely, and with a degree of elegance which we had not expected. The queen was exceedingly obliging and affable; she made kind inquiries respecting our passage and health; she expressed her hope that we should be perfectly happy as long as we should remain with them; and she assured us that she would be always ready to assist us;—and her evident sincerity convinced us that she had a kind and affectionate heart. Her daughters were equally polite; and appeared quite pleased at the idea of our coming to reside in the palace. On the whole we were much pleased and satisfied with the interview.

The breakfast hour approaching, we retired to another apartment, where we partook of an elegant *déjeuné,* in company with the king's niece, and the officers of the household, black and yellow barons.... They were very attentive to us, and the conversation, though on common-place topics, we thought more interesting than could have been expected....

It was five weeks before the necessary arrangements were made for our residence at the palace; which time we spent most agreeably in the town, where every possible attention was shown us. The apartments in the palace with which we were at length furnished, were sufficiently large for our purpose; and as soon as we were comfortably settled, we commenced instructing our royal pupils. They studied English, French, composition and drawing; and the hours we were engaged with them were from between seven and eight till ten, in the morning; and from three to five in the afternoon. The princesses differed much in their abilities and dispositions.... Yet the progress of both was considerable; and the queen, and we believe the king also, felt perfectly satisfied with our endeavours....

We occasionally dined with the queen; our pupils also sometimes stopped after the hours of instruction for conversation, or we accompanied them to the gardens; but we felt, in a great measure, excluded from society.... If we used the carriage which was at our service, we could ride only to a prescribed distance; and we were perpetually annoyed by the guard, if we ventured on a ramble, inquiring who we were, and whither we were going. The etiquette of the court was intolerably irksome.... We had come from America; and the confinement, restraint, and ceremony, we had been quite unaccustomed to, and could not suffer.... We determined at length to resign our charge, and to quit the place. But though our stay was shorter than we originally intended, we can never recollect our residence in Hayti but with feelings of deep and lasting interest.[38]

From the time of his assumption of authority, Christophe not only maintained a large standing army but attempted to transform his soldiers, accustomed to predatory warfare, into an orderly fighting force. The morale of an army, he insisted, lay in the respect of the men for their leaders and in their pride in themselves; and he knew that the scrupulous observance of military regulations provided the key to the efficient coördination of his troops. Thus he imposed the harshest discipline on his men. They were drilled constantly, carried out difficult maneuvers, and were frequently required to participate in formal reviews. On the parade ground the most meticulous attention to details of dress, posture, and formality was required. The uniforms of the officers were extravagantly colorful. Christophe took pleasure in reviewing his troops; and his giant stature, his manly and dignified bearing, and his powerful personality lent impressiveness to the

---

[38] W. W. Harvey, *op. cit.,* pp. 226–232.

scene. He created a noteworthy military machine, and during the last years of his reign his army won the approval of visiting Englishmen, for whom he was proud to exhibit the discipline and skill of the Negro soldiers.

Realizing that he could not entirely trust the maintenance of order and the preservation of his power to the Negro troops who had witnessed his rise to supreme authority, who had seen the fall of Dessalines through intrigue among the generals, and whose loyalty was often fickle and insecure, Christophe made arrangements with foreign merchants for the transportation of twenty thousand Negroes from Africa. Carefully selected and given the most rigorous training, they not only served as his bodyguard, but acted as an internal police force, and to them was assigned the surveillance of the entire kingdom. Placed in every village and district, they provided him with an intimate knowledge of the actual condition of his realm and gave him a potent means of imposing his will upon the people. The Royal Dahomets, so named from the area in Africa from which they had come, were well clothed and accoutered. Better trained, more efficient, and disciplined to a higher degree than the regular Haitian soldiers, they were personally responsible to the King and enjoyed his royal favor. Through them he was able to maintain order, to suppress crime, and to require obedience to the exacting provisions of the Code Henry.

From Dessalines, Christophe inherited a plan for the defense of the island against French aggression. He, too, intended to offer no resistance along the coast, to burn the towns as they were abandoned, and to meet the armies of the invader deep in the mountains of the island. Under Dessalines, indeed, he had begun the construction of a great fortress atop Le Pic des Ferrières (La Ferrière),[39] a mountain rising to a height of three thousand feet, and he made the completion of this citadel his greatest ambition. The difficulties were almost insuperable. The mountaintop lay high above the plains. Thick, tropical foliage barred the way. But Christophe was not to be frustrated. He assembled vast hordes of laborers—virtual slaves—and put them to work. Soon they began to drag the stones and mortar, the cannon and military supplies, up the steep sides of the mountain. On the summit hundreds of masons were kept busily at work. There was no respite for anyone. Whips cracked over the toiling laborers' heads. Those dropping from exhaustion were passed by, their groans and complaints going unheeded, but the construction went on. Christophe's ambition had become an obsession. It is said that many lives were sacrificed in the building of this fortress.

---

[39] Cf. Vergniaud Leconte, *Henri Christophe dans l'histoire d'Haïti* (Paris, 1931), p. 351.

Slowly, a great citadel, known in Christophe's time as the Citadel Henry, rose to meet the sky. It is today, despite the action of time and neglect, a wondrous thing to behold. As the traveler exploring the island toils up the mountain, he can see nothing except the thick, overhanging jungle; but as he reaches the top of the trail, all at once the mighty fortress, breath-taking and awesome in its sheer immensity, bursts into view. Pointing north, it rises in solemn strength to a height of one hundred and thirty feet. In outline it resembles the hull of a ship, with a massive prow that seems to grow out of the mountain on which it rests. Inside, the Citadel is a maze of passages and galleries. Deep down below are murky dungeons, where Christophe incarcerated those who dared to defy him. There are supply rooms still filled with gunpowder. In the midst of the courtyard stands a little, rectangular building, the tomb of Christophe. To one side are the apartments of the King; to the other the barracks, capable, it is said, of housing ten thousand soldiers. Within their embrasures, the cannon lie useless on their rotten wooden carriages, while all around are piles of cannon balls. There are the vast cisterns, built to store the rain water for use in case of siege. The walls of this fortress are from twenty to thirty feet thick. And from the flat roof, if the day happen to be clear, the island of Tortuga and the stretches of the ocean can be seen in the distance, while nearer at hand are the rolling plains and woodlands and a countryside dotted with plantations.

The Citadel was never used for military purposes, and Christophe did not live to bring it to completion. An earthquake has caused an ugly rent, now moss- and foliage-lined, and rich orchid and mimosa blossoms soften the ravages of time. Even in ruin, however, it rivals the Egyptian Pyramids and offers a testimony to its creator. Age may crumble its walls, but the Citadel Henry, born of suffering and hope, is a living symbol of the magnificent dream of Henry Christophe.

In order to develop commerce with the outside world, Christophe had sent, as early as November, 1806, a manifesto to all neutral nations. Wishing to allay the distrust which the policies of Dessalines had produced, he promised to remove the stupid and vexatious restrictions of his predecessor. The storehouses, he pointed out, were overflowing with the rich produce of the island, and he indicated the mutual advantages in an exchange of goods. He offered, too, protection to foreign merchants entering his ports or desiring to settle in Haiti. Thus he initiated commercial relations with trading nations, and before long Cap Henry became a busy center of activity.

Christophe's favorite customer was Great Britain, and he did everything in his power to create friendly relations with her. Article IX of his first constitution (1807) made his intentions clear:

The government of Hayti declares to those powers who have colonies in its neighbourhood, its fixed determination to give no disturbance to the government of these colonies. The people of Hayti make no conquests out of their own island; and they confine themselves to the preservation of their own territory.[40]

Almost at once an opportunity arose to demonstrate his good will. In southern Haiti an incipient plot was brewing for an uprising among the slaves of Jamaica. When Christophe heard of the conspiracy, he "professed a burning zeal to defeat the meditated movement" and immediately arrested some of the accomplices. In recognition of his action, the British ministry issued an order conferring important commercial advantages upon Christophe and directing English ships to trade at all Haitian ports under his authority. In 1808 and 1809, Christophe coöperated with the English, who launched an attack against the French forces in Spanish Santo Domingo, by sending arms to the Spanish insurgents;[41] and in 1810, English naval units helped him to wipe out a pocket of resistance at the Môle Saint-Nicolas. Two years later, when some of the sailors in Christophe's infant navy revolted and went over to Pétion's government, the crew of one of the ships, *L'Améthyste,* was foolhardy enough to offer battle against an English frigate under Sir James Lucas Yeo. Quickly subdued by the superior English fire, the revolting seamen were made prisoners and returned to Christophe for punishment. Christophe and the British, as one historian remarks, were almost in open alliance.

Christophe did not fare so well in his commercial dealings with the United States. During the reign of Dessalines, the American Congress had passed a law (February 28, 1806) prohibiting trade with any portion of Hispaniola not acknowledging French authority, partly to assuage Napoleon, who demanded in no uncertain terms that all commerce with the Negroes be stopped, and partly because of the effect an independent Negro state might have on the slave system in the United States. This act was renewed in 1807 and continued until 1809. At the onset of his career, therefore, Christophe had no official trade with the United States. Even when commerce was renewed in 1810, there was no great increase in trade, for

---

[40] Sir James Basket, *History of the Island of St. Domingo from Its First Discovery by Columbus* ... (New York, 1824), p. 241.

[41] In 1809, the French having been driven out of Spanish Santo Domingo, it reverted to Spanish control, and at the Treaty of Paris in 1814, it was formally ceded to Spain.

American merchants found that Englishmen were enjoying a fifty per cent reduction in duties. Nor did Christophe improve matters. In 1811, finding himself unable to recover large sums entrusted to the firm of Von Kapff and Brune of Baltimore for the purchase of goods, he seized property valued at about $125,000 from American traders in Haiti, and in answer to their protests, told them to obtain redress from the Baltimore firm, if they were able. Thus his American commerce dwindled.

Christophe made good his promise to protect foreign merchants residing in Haiti, most of whom lived at Cap Henry. They were given every encouragement and courtesy. An English naval officer who visited Christophe's kingdom in 1814 received the most favorable reports from the white residents. "We conceive," they told him,

> our persons and property under the protection of the King to be as safe as in Kingston unless the French land an expedition. Nor could I hear of one act of injustice that could fairly be attributed to the King. He is sharp in his dealings and in making them fulfil their contracts. But it is almost needless to mention how far a merchant adventurer will go for gain and how necessary it is to watch them.[42]

A number of distinguished foreigners visited Haiti, and Christophe was always honored to have them attend his weekly levees at the palace. He received them in a gracious and polished manner. Among the Englishmen who occasionally came to visit him was Sir Home Riggs Popham, commander-in-chief on the Jamaica Station. He was shown the utmost hospitality. A luxurious house at Cap Henry was placed at his service, and every Haitian, from the King to the lowliest subject, was solicitous for his comfort. He was invited to inspect the schools and hospitals and professed himself amazed at the proficiency of the students and the high level of medical care. Christophe received him in royal splendor at Sans Souci, regaled him at a sumptuous banquet, and proudly marched the royal troops in formal review before him. Popham was greatly impressed with what he saw.

Christophe's purpose in establishing amicable relations with the English was not merely to gain economic advantages and to win foreign approval of his kingdom, but also to further his self-education. Just as he had sought the advice of mulattoes and Negroes alike in the administration of the state, so he went out of his way to form intimate friendships with the whites. Painfully conscious of his own limitations—it is said that he re-

[42] R. Coupland, *op. cit.*, pp. 466–467.

gretted most of all his lack of education—he delighted in conversation with white men. Perhaps his closest white friend was Duncan Stewart, a Scotsman who served not only as his personal physician but as his intimate adviser as well. Another friend was M. J. Moore of London, "mathematician and _bon vivant._" Often the three men sat for hours, talking over the affairs of the world and the plans Christophe had made for the civilization of Haiti.

Although Christophe made every effort to win foreign approval of his government, he did, nevertheless, impose very severe restrictions upon all foreigners. Upon arrival at the ports of Haiti all persons were required to surrender any letters or papers in their possession for examination by a government official. No foreign resident, moreover, was allowed to go more than three miles into the interior, and late in Christophe's reign it was decreed that foreigners were not, after sundown, to leave the vicinity of Cap Henry. On one occasion, two Englishmen decided to ascend a mountain not far from the town. They were stopped by the soldiers and spent the night in jail. The next day they were brought before Christophe; and though they had the temerity to tell him they considered the restrictions absurd and a reflection on English honor, he dismissed them with a stern warning to "beware how they treated, in future, that or any other regulation which he thought proper to establish." Christophe was particularly careful to guard the secrets of the Citadel Henry, and no foreigner ever approached even the environs of that fortress. As a matter of fact, an Englishman visiting Haiti nearly a decade after Christophe's death found it impossible to prevail on the guards, who had been trained under Christophe, to let him make more than a cursory examination of the Citadel.

The whites were not the only ones who felt the severity of Christophe's demands. Ever vigilant, he seemed to be everywhere and personally to supervise every activity in his kingdom. He was accustomed to wander about his domain accompanied by a single attendant and decorated with only the Star of the Order of St. Henry to distinguish him from his subjects. A laborer careless in his work or idling when he was supposed to be employed was likely to find the King standing over him, and the direst punishment often followed. Nor did a grandiose title and a glittering uniform make a man immune to Christophe's displeasure. Once Richard, Duc de Marmelade, the military governor of Cap Henry, was charged with an important commission. In carrying out his orders he found it expedient to vary the details, though he performed his duty. Christophe was highly incensed and condemned the Duke to hard labor for several months.

However much the Haitians disliked the rigid discipline imposed upon them and resented their loss of personal liberty, the will of their unrelenting king prevailed, and under his guiding hand the country prospered. Produce of every kind poured in from the plantations, a small navy patrolled the coasts, and a profitable commerce was developed with other nations. The state coffers were filled to overflowing—the annual revenue amounting to three and a half million dollars,—the nobility and landowners became wealthy, and want and hunger disappeared, the rural laborers enjoying one-fourth of the crops. The schools flourished, a printing press was established at Sans Souci, and a theater was built near Cap Henry. Indeed, in prosperity and in grandeur the Kingdom of Haiti was beginning to rival the old colony of Saint-Domingue.

In Pétion's territory, on the other hand, the public treasury was empty. Although the inhabitants had their heart's content of freedom and were spared the forced labor of Christophe's subjects, there was a complete neglect of the public welfare. The soldiers and the population were ragged. Petty theft and crime increased enormously. The plantations were untilled. If the tyrannical policies of Christophe were too harsh for the population to endure, Pétion's laxness left his people a prey to indolence and disorder.

Since some writers have highly extolled Pétion's administrative measures, a brief summary of them may be given. He began by favoring the mulattoes, first restoring to them their estates, many of which Dessalines had confiscated, then abolishing the tax of one-fourth of the annual crop, and finally paying subsidies to the proprietors in bad years; the two latter measures depleted the state revenue. Later Pétion gave away land from the national domain to his unpaid soldiery, allotting fifteen acres to the common soldiers and proportionally higher acreage to the officers. Finally, he turned his attention to the mass of the population and placed the public lands on sale at such low prices that thousands of poor Haitians were able to purchase small plots. Many of them, indeed, did not bother to make any payment but acquired land simply by "squatting" on it. At the same time, Pétion abolished the system of farm inspectors, whose duty since the time of Toussaint had been to keep crop production at a high level. This was a calamitous blunder, for the Haitians, who had always worked under coercion and strict supervision and had not acquired habits of industry or self-direction, were unprepared for absolute freedom. They refused to work on the plantations, lapsing instead into indolence and only cultivating their plots sufficiently to provide a bare subsistence. The proprietors of the estates, unable to secure the necessary laborers, were forced to abandon sugar cultivation; instead, they leased out their lands in subdivisions, thus getting what income they could from the wild coffee crop. Under Pétion and his successor, who continued his policies, the Republic of Haiti rapidly degenerated, as one modern author pertinently remarks, "from great estates to tiny plots; from carefully tilled fields to small gardens in a wilderness; from financial prosperity to debt; [and] from directed enterprise to sloth."[48] Pétion was probably motivated by the best intentions and he did raise his people from serfs to peasants, but in parceling the land and abandoning the system of compulsory labor, he unwittingly laid the basis for much of Haiti's subsequent difficulty.

Separation from France had been a *fait accompli* since 1804, but Haiti was still regarded by her as a colonial possession. Thus Christophe was never wholly free from the fear of a new attempt to repossess Haiti, and it was necessary for him to be always on the alert, with hundreds of men under arms who could have been more profitably engaged in agriculture.

Christophe had followed with the greatest concern the long and exhausting war which culminated in the defeat of Napoleon and his abdication on March 31, 1814, but the accession of Louis XVIII threw him into an agony of suspense. Since the armies of France, now freed from war in Europe, were in a position to deal with the former colony of Saint-Domingue, and since Christophe had no way of knowing what action the new French king and his advisers might take, he presented the position of Haiti to France, to his subjects, and to the nations of the world by means of three public announcements. First, his foreign minister, the Comte de Limonade, sent a congratulatory address to an agent in London with instructions to publish it in the French journals. The message expressed a friendly disposition toward the French royal family, evinced satisfaction at the defeat of Napoleon, and announced Christophe's willingness to resume commercial relations with France as long as the laws of Haiti were observed. Rather shrewdly it was pointed out that Christophe possessed a large military establishment ready for any emergency, but that these warlike preparations had been made in anticipation of a new assault by Napoleon. Next Christophe published a proclamation to his people on August 15, 1814. He congratulated them upon the downfall of Napoleon, an event removing the fear of reënslavement under which they had lived so long. If, he declared, the French Government is favorably disposed to the Haitians, then the way

---

[48] James G. Leyburn, *op. cit.*, p. 86.

is open for a commercial treaty advantageous to France and honorable to Haiti; if, on the contrary, "our implacable enemies, the French colonists," persuade the French to send another expedition, "we will show to the nations of the earth what a warlike people can accomplish, who are in arms for the best of causes—the defence of their homes, their wives, their children, their liberty, and their independence." As his final effort during this period of uncertainty, Christophe issued on September 18, 1814, a manifesto "to justify, before the tribunal of nations, the legitimacy of our independence." Reviewing the events in Haiti from the time of the abolition of slavery in 1793, he showed that the Haitians were loyal to France until Leclerc made it evident that Napoleon intended to restore slavery. He appealed "to all the Sovereigns of the world, to the brave and loyal British nation, . . . to mankind at large, to the whole universe," to witness the determination of the Haitians to remain free, and declared "that we will never become a party to any treaty, to any condition, that may compromise the honour, the liberty, or the independence of the Haytian people."

Christophe, indeed, was justified in his fear and suspicion of France. No sooner was Louis XVIII on the throne than the old colonial party raised a clamor for the recovery of Saint-Domingue, a demand with which Pierre-Victor Malouet, a former proprietor in the colony and now Minister of Marine, was in full agreement. It was decided, however, to postpone military intervention and to send out a commission for the purpose of ascertaining the actual state of affairs in Haiti. The secret instructions to the commissioners offer another example of French tactics. The commissioners were to present themselves in Haiti as merchants or as agents of some mercantile establishment, and to reveal their true identity only after they had made preliminary observations. They were first to communicate with Pétion, to whom they were to promise "a perfect assimilation to the whites, and a participation in all their advantages of fortune and honour." They were to persuade him that the Negroes ought to be returned to slavery or at least forced labor on the plantations, and that the former white proprietors should again take possession of their estates. The French believed that Pétion would agree to such an arrangement for his own safety and benefit. Should he hesitate, the commissioners were to declare that the King "will make the full weight of his power to be felt." Concerning Christophe the French were less certain, but it was pointed out that he could easily be subdued once Pétion acceded to their plans. It is evident that France had a twofold project in view: to facilitate the conquest of Haiti by widening the breach between Pétion and Christophe, and to restore slavery and the old colonial system.

Late in August, 1814, the three French commissioners, Lavaysse, Medina, and Dravermann, arrived in Jamaica. After gaining what information they could from the ex-colonists residing there, Lavaysse wrote to Pétion, who invited him to come to Port-au-Prince. In the subsequent correspondence Lavaysse indicated the willingness of the French King to welcome back the former colony to France and pointed out that it would be better for Pétion and the mulatto leaders to enjoy rights as French citizens "than to be treated as barbarous savages, or hunted as maroon Negroes." Apparently believing the protestations of good will on the part of Lavaysse, Pétion carried on extensive negotiations.

Christophe's conduct stands in sharp contrast to that of Pétion. On October 1, 1814, Lavaysse dispatched a letter to Christophe through Montorsier, who had long enjoyed Christophe's confidence and was one of the few Frenchmen permitted to remain in Haiti. When Montorsier returned to Haiti from Jamaica, his papers, along with the letter from Lavaysse, were turned over to Dupuy, Christophe's secretary. The letter was highly insulting. Christophe was offered French citizenship and a title in return for his acknowledgment of the sovereignty of Louis XVIII. Lavaysse warned Christophe that the European governments, including Great Britain, intended "to unite their forces if necessary ... to overthrow all the governments that have arisen out of the French revolution, whether in Europe or the new world." Should the Haitians resist, they would be annihilated. Lavaysse concluded his letter by announcing that he was sending Medina to negotiate with Christophe.

When Montorsier surrendered Lavaysse's communication, he demanded an audience with Christophe, which was finally granted. In the conference Montorsier enlarged upon the contents of Lavaysse's letter. Christophe, if he preferred, could have the sovereignty of the island of Tortuga, or he could retire to France, to the United States, or wherever he might choose to go. "I set no value upon my throne or crown," Christophe replied, "but what will my general officers, members of council, ministers, and secretaries, say to this?" To which Montorsier answered, "Destroy those who embarrass you; you must rid yourself of them as soon as possible." Christophe then called in the members of the Privy Council, which had been convened to deliberate upon the contents of Lavaysse's dispatch, and revealed what Montorsier had said. The first impulse of the Council was to kill the Frenchman on the spot, but Christophe insisted that Montorsier be allowed to leave unscathed.

In November, the French commissioner Agoustino Franco de Medina, who had formerly been a plantation owner in Spanish Santo Domingo, left Jamaica for Monte Christi, where he stopped to inspect his estates. When he crossed the border into Haiti, Christophe, having been forewarned, was ready for him. He was proclaimed to be a spy and his papers were seized. Thus Christophe came into possession of the secret instructions issued to the commissioners by the French cabinet and a full knowledge of the duplicity of the French. Medina was called before a military tribunal and interrogated. He not only confirmed the information in his instructions, but boldly revealed that plans were actually under way in France for the invasion of Haiti. He was found guilty of treason and imprisoned. Then Christophe sent the secret instructions and a full account of Medina's trial to Pétion, in order that the latter might be put upon his guard.

Pétion now brought his temporizing with Lavaysse to a close. Whatever may have been his motives in dealing with the commissioner, it was now unmistakably clear to him that the French could not be trusted and that Haiti must be prepared to defend her independence by force of arms. In his last letter to Lavaysse, Pétion asserted, on the authority of "the generals and the magistrates of the Republic of Hayti," that the recognition of Haitian independence would be "a source of everlasting glory" to Louis XVIII. Unfortunately for the future welfare of Haiti, Pétion went on to indicate a willingness to pay an indemnity to the French for the loss of their plantations and their slaves.

Lavaysse returned to France in January, 1815, and was officially rebuked for having exceeded his authority. The French, nevertheless, went on with their preparations for an invasion of Haiti. Before they were ready, however, Napoleon's unexpected return from Elba, in March, 1815, and the precipitate flight of Louis XVIII plunged Europe anew into war and put an end to their plans for the conquest of Haiti.

Christophe employed the year 1815 in feverish activity. He not only greatly increased the size of his army but placed on a military footing all of the population capable of bearing arms. He made ready his inland fortresses, particularly the Citadel Henry, and assembled guns and ammunition. Pétion, too, prepared for an assault. So great was the fear of France that relations between the rival governments seem to have become more amicable. Christophe went a step farther and proposed a union of the whole country. Nothing came of this scheme; but it shows that the threat of a French invasion tended to unite the contending factions in Haiti.

Louis XVIII regained his throne after the Battle of Waterloo, but it was not until a year later that the monarchy was able to turn its attention to Haiti. In 1816, two commissioners, Vicomte de Fontanges and Esmangart, were dispatched to take over the civil and military administration of the island. This time Pétion refused to enter into negotiations unless Haitian independence were recognized. Christophe's summary treatment of the French agent Medina in 1814 was well known, and the new commissioners did not dare to land in his realm. Instead they prevailed upon the captain of an American ship to deliver their communications. These letters were presented to the governor of Cap Henry, the Duc de Marmelade. When he saw that they were addressed "To Monsieur General Christophe, at Cap Français," he returned them unopened to the American captain, with a severe rebuke for being a party to this insult to the King, and ordered him to quit the harbor forthwith. Later, the French agents intercepted a brig off Gonaïves on the western coast of the island, and taking this opportunity to transmit their letters in a packet addressed to the commandant of that port, they were able to bring them to Christophe's attention. Taking no cognizance whatever of his kingdom, the communications refer to the colony of Saint-Domingue, and express the wish of the French King to extend to it "the blessings he has bestowed on France.... His majesty's only design in sending commissioners ... is to consolidate and legalize all that can exist without derogating from what is due to the dignity of his crown."[44] Enraged at this new affront, Christophe issued a declaration on November 20, 1816, asserting that he would not negotiate with France "on any other footing than that of power with power, and sovereign with sovereign," and that the preliminary basis of negotiation must be a recognition of the independence of Haiti—not only the kingdom but Pétion's domain as well. Christophe insisted that "no definitive treaty shall be concluded with this government without having previously obtained the good offices and mediation of a great maritime power which will guarantee the faith of the treaty from being ever broken by the French.... Neither the French flag nor individuals of that nation shall be admitted within any of the ports of the kingdom, until the independence of Hayti has been defini-

---

[44] For a detailed account of the two French commissions, see Baron de Vastey, *An Essay on the Causes of the Revolution and Civil Wars of Hayti,* ... translated from the French by W. H. M. B. (Exeter, 1823), pp. 138–247, and Appendix, pp. xiii–cvi.

tively recognised by the French government."[45] This positive statement put an end to all further attempts of the French Government to gain supremacy over Christophe.

The two insidious attempts by the French to regain control of Haiti caused Christophe more than ever to seek the friendship of England. He knew only too well that his country could not stand in isolation, and he believed that his hope of winning a place in the community of nations lay with Great Britain. Then, too, he had always admired "the institution of King, Lords, and Commons as in England; but how can I," he added, "have such a constitution among an unenlightened people? My subjects have all been slaves." He determined to eradicate the last vestiges of French culture, and, as far as possible, to imitate English civilization; and he announced his intention of making English rather than French the official language of his kingdom and of changing the state religion from Roman Catholic to Protestant.

Christophe's attempts to demonstrate to the world that the Negroes were capable of creating and maintaining a stable and efficient government had not achieved much success; for though law and order prevailed throughout his dominion and his propagandists had written books defending him, in general people in other lands were either ignorant of the facts or inclined to laugh at his pretensions. The French journals in particular carried on a regular campaign of slander and mockery. He was presented as a vain and despotic savage. His monarchy, his hereditary nobility, his formal and elaborate court—all were held up to ridicule; while his positive achievements were deliberately ignored.

The Treaty of Paris of 1814, Christophe pathetically remarked in one of his proclamations, did not even mention Haiti, thereby tacitly assuming that the French were welcome to reoccupy the island, if they could. The delegates, moreover, in response to a demand from France, permitted her, along with Spain and Portugal, to continue the slave trade for another five years. Although Napoleon, immediately following his triumphal reëntry into France in 1815, abolished the slave trade by decree, and Louis XVIII, after the Battle of Waterloo, issued a royal order to the same effect, it was clear to Christophe that however carefully they remade the map of Europe, the statesmen were utterly indifferent to Haiti.

Christophe needed friends abroad, friends who would advise him concerning the internal and external affairs of his kingdom, who would

---

[45] For the text of this declaration, see *ibid.*, Appendix, pp. lxxxv–xcvi.

recognize his achievements and publicly announce them to the world, and who would present his case to the European powers. Quite naturally he turned to members of the African Institution, an English society dedicated to the cause of the Negro, and in 1814 he entered into a correspondence with William Wilberforce, the parliamentary leader of the abolitionists.[46]

Wilberforce saw in the Haitian correspondence an opportunity "Providence has thrown in our way . . . of sowing the seeds of civilization, and still more of Christian faith," and he took up the labor with religious fervor—"I know that not a day has passed that I have not prayed for Christophe." He was so enthusiastic over the attempt of Christophe to civilize the Negroes in Haiti that he awakened similar feelings among his friends. "Were I five and twenty," wrote Sir Joseph Banks, erstwhile member of Captain Cook's expedition, "I am very sure I should not lose a day in embarking for Hayti. To see a set of human beings emerging from slavery, and making most rapid strides towards the perfection of civilization, must I think be the most delightful of all food for contemplation." Wilberforce himself held similar views. "Oh how I wish I was not too old," he wrote to Zachary Macaulay, "and you not too busy to go. It would be a noble undertaking to be sowing in such a soil the seeds of Christian and moral improvement, and to be laying also the foundation of all kinds of social and domestic institutions, habits, and manners." Nor did Wilberforce limit his influence to such humanitarian associates as Zachary Macaulay and Archdeacon Wrangham, but he also brought Haitian affairs to the attention of such statesmen as Castlereagh and Liverpool.

Wishing to develop his schools, to found a Royal College, and to introduce modern medicine, Christophe requested Wilberforce to send out "seven schoolmasters, a tutor for his son, and seven different professors; . . . amongst these . . . a classical professor, a medical, a surgical, a mathematical, and a pharmaceutical chemist." Christophe also asked for farmers, that he might introduce English methods of agriculture. Wilberforce not only sent the ploughmen, but the ploughs as well. With the greatest care, he examined applicants from every walk of life before dispatching them to Haiti. Christophe's confidence in him was unbounded, and £6,000 was sent to him for advancing salaries.

---

[46] The first letter from Haiti weighed eighty-five ounces, with a carrying charge of £37/10.

CHRISTOPHE AND THOMAS CLARKSON

Not long after he sought the assistance of Wilberforce, Christophe applied to Thomas Clarkson. "In 1815," wrote Clarkson in his unpublished Autobiography,

I entered into a correspondence with Henry Christophe, King of Hayti.... The King wrote me a letter in which he was pleased to say that "he had heard of my exertions to abolish the Slave Trade, for which, he, in common with those of his race, could not feel too thankful; that he had a just abhorrence of it; and would do all he could to suppress it, either by subscription to the society [the African Institution] in London, or by anything he could do at home; that he should for ever love the English Nation for their generosity towards Africa; and that he would endeavour, by degrees, to introduce their laws and constitution into Hayti."

Thus began the correspondence which forms the main portion of this book.

Born at Wisbech in 1760, Thomas Clarkson became interested in the cause of abolition while still a student at Cambridge. In 1785, he competed for a University prize, the subject being *Anne liceat invitos in servitutem dare?* ("Is it right to make men slaves against their will?"). As he worked over the problem, he gradually became acquainted with a story which shocked every decent and Christian feeling. A great passion was awakened within him, and thenceforth he dedicated his life to the antislavery cause. When the Committee for the Abolition of the Slave Trade was organized in 1787, as one of the original members, he became almost at once the society's field representative, and his documented evidence gave Wilberforce and the abolitionists in Parliament factual materials to present before the House of Commons.[47]

Christophe could not have chosen a more willing and devoted adviser. Clarkson "seems formed by Providence for the purpose,... and you may depend upon his being in earnest," Wilberforce wrote of him. Samuel Taylor Coleridge once called him "the moral Steam-Engine, or the Giant

[47] Victory crowned the efforts of the Abolition Committee in 1807, when the slave trade under the British flag was prohibited by an act of Parliament. Clarkson, indefatigable as ever, became an unofficial guardian of the new law, quick to notice and report violations. The British Parliament passed the Emancipation Act of 1833, which provided for gradual manumission of all slaves throughout the British Empire, and when he died in 1846, after sixty-one years' labor for the Negro cause, Clarkson was working with the British and Foreign Anti-Slavery Society for the abolition of slavery in the United States, which had abolished the slave trade in 1807. Few humanitarians have been privileged to witness the realization of so great a share of their philanthropic endeavors.

with one idea." He was a painstaking and tireless worker. No task was too irksome, too onerous, for him. He was filled with an almost fanatic devotion to the cause of the oppressed Africans.

Two more dissimilar men than Clarkson and Christophe can hardly be imagined. The Englishman was calm, steady, and methodical; Christophe was impetuous, domineering, and ruthless. Clarkson knew that civilization advances slowly. Christophe wished to accomplish in a generation the work of centuries. Clarkson sought the attainment of his objectives through the orderly processes of law. Christophe created new laws to suit the occasion. Yet these two men, so far apart in race, in character, and in culture, had in common their interest in the Negro, for whose improvement each was willing to sacrifice himself.

No one knew better than Christophe the contempt with which the Negroes were regarded, and he possessed an overwhelming ambition to lift his people to a civilized level. Public instruction had long been close to his heart, and in one of his earliest letters to Clarkson, he wrote:

My subjects inherit the ignorance and prejudice that belong to slavery. At this moment they have made but very little progress in knowledge. Where could they acquire it, for, in gaining their liberty, they have seen nothing but camps and war? They must be educated. Every child born into the world must receive a proper education, before I can realize my plans.[48]

From his English friends he had learned of the Lancasterian system of education and of its efficacy in teaching the rudiments of knowledge; and in 1815 he made application for assistance to the British and Foreign School Society, an organization devoted to the Lancasterian plan. Through this society and with the coöperation of Wilberforce and Clarkson, six teachers were sent to Haiti, and in 1816 and 1817 schools were established at Sans Souci and in the principal ports of the kingdom, Cap Henry, Port-de-Paix, Gonaïves, and Saint-Marc. Soon nearly two thousand pupils were in attendance. Christophe spared no effort or expense. Buildings were constructed, books and equipment were provided, and the teachers were liberally remunerated. About the same time, a Royal College was founded, to afford students with special aptitudes an opportunity to pursue a more advanced curriculum, and at Sans Sauci "a school of drawing and painting" was established, with the English artist, Richard Evans, in charge.

So gratified was Christophe by the success achieved under the Lancas-

---

[48] This quotation is taken from Clarkson's unpublished Autobiography. The letter is not among the Clarkson papers in the British Museum.

terian system and by the abilities of the English teachers that he determined to make education available to all Haitian children throughout the kingdom, and to place it under a uniform organization. With his usual emphasis on the concentration of administrative power, he appointed a Royal Chamber of Public Instruction to "systematize by means of regulations and surveillance" all efforts hitherto made for education. The Chamber was composed of sixteen members and included the most able men in the government.

To implement his designs, he issued on November 20, 1818, an ordonnance[49] carefully outlining the multifarious duties of this Royal Chamber. It was especially charged with establishing "primary schools in the parishes where none exist and academies and secondary schools throughout the Kingdom, wherever they may be needed," and with the direction and supervision of these schools and all other institutions of learning, including private schools then in operation. It was entrusted with the maintenance of order, morality, and the quality of teaching. All licenses for teachers (and no teacher was to conduct classes without one) were to be issued by the Chamber; and it was to appoint three supervisors for each school, as well as special inspectors, who were to make frequent tours of the institutions. Nor did Christophe merely delegate his authority. Every six months the Chamber was to "inform the King concerning the general progress of public instruction," and he was to be furnished with the names of the masters who had distinguished themselves and the scholars who had shown the greatest zeal for knowledge.

Although measures were now being instituted for the education of the rising generation of males, no provision seems to have been made for that of females. One writer states that with the exception of the mulatto and Negro girls attending two private schools at Cap Henry, the female population was entirely uneducated. The ordonnance makes no specific mention of females; it would appear, however, that Christophe had something in mind, for one article of the document reads, "Children of opposite sexes shall never be brought together in the same school."

On January 1, 1819, Christophe issued a second ordonnance.[50] Just as the first one instituted a Royal Chamber of Public Instruction and outlined its duties, so the second laid down the most rigid regulations for the parents, the schoolmasters, supervisors, and inspectors, and the pupils and monitors.

---

[49] For the text of this ordonnance see Part III, Document 1, pp. 257–260.
[50] For this ordonnance, see Part III, Document 2, pp. 261–267.

Exacting in every detail, it provided for admission of children from six to fifteen years of age, each child to present a doctor's certificate of good health. The parents were obligated to "lodge, nourish, and clothe" their children. School hours were clearly defined:

On the long days of the year, morning classes shall be in session from six o'clock until eleven o'clock, and afternoon classes from two to six; on short days the hours shall be from seven to eleven, and from two until five.

Absence from classes was not to be tolerated except on specified days of rest and the national holidays decreed by law, and on Sundays and feast days the pupils were required to attend prayers and a religious discourse.

The section of the ordonnance dealing with punishments was most severe. "Discipline shall be inculcated among the pupils by means of the rod or whip, or, in serious cases, by imprisonment on bread and water." Disobedience, absence from classes, and taking the name of God in vain, for example, were punishable by one to two weeks' imprisonment on bread and water, and monitors who failed to fulfill their duties were to be given double punishment.

Instruction in all schools was to be given in both English and French and "according to the English system." The elementary pupils were to be taught "to read, to write, and to figure." In the academies, instruction was to include grammar, history, geography, arithmetic, and the Latin, English, and French languages.

These two ordonnances, so comprehensive in their provisions, demonstrate equally with the Code Henry Christophe's capacity for leadership, and his project for universal education was fast being realized. New schools were rapidly established, and not only were the elementary and secondary schools thriving, but in the Royal College a number of students were progressing so satisfactorily that they were nearly ready to become themselves teachers of mathematics, chemistry, and literature. A medical school under the supervision of the King's physician was also going steadily ahead. Foreign visitors who inspected the schools brought back to England glowing reports of the aptitude and knowledge of the students and declared that the Haitain pupils equaled in learning English children of similar age.

Clarkson, who received copies of these ordonnances, was delighted to find the King so earnestly striving to better the condition of his subjects. Anxious to assist Christophe in every possible way, he acceded to a request for two professors of English and French for the Royal College by employing two talented young Englishmen, William Wilson and George Clarke, and sending them to Haiti under seven-year contracts. On their arrival, Christophe installed Wilson as tutor to the Prince Royal and Clarke as professor in the college. When Clarkson learned that Wilson had been made the Prince's tutor, he wrote a long letter in which he urged Wilson to give the future king the most careful training in both history and religion.[51]

Whereas Wilberforce served Christophe principally in bringing Haiti to the attention of influential persons and in providing qualified teachers, physicians, and farmers for service in the island, Clarkson became Christophe's European adviser. As the King's foreign agent he sent immediate and accurate information concerning the state of English and French public opinion, the attitude of the foreign powers toward Haiti, and the likelihood of any attempts by France, either diplomatic or military, to subdue her. Clarkson gave his advice freely and at length. Nor was the correspondence between the two men limited to a discussion of foreign affairs; many of the letters relate to the internal administration of the kingdom.

Clarkson was greatly disturbed over the size of Christophe's standing army, though he was well aware of the necessity for preparedness. In one of his letters he explained the advantages of organizing the soldiers into a militia as in England, thereby releasing one-third or one-half of them from full-time military service. He went on to suggest that the disbanded troops be given grants of land. A few months later Christophe replied that he was bringing this advice to the attention of the Privy Council; and within a year, reassured "that the French would not undertake any hostile action against Haiti," he issued an edict giving portions of the public domain to his soldiers of all ranks.[52] This edict is a further tribute to Christophe's perspicacity. Although the concessions of land were made irrevocably and the new owners were at liberty to sell or dispose of their holdings as they

---

[51] Since Clarkson's lengthy and laborious letter arrived in Haiti after the deaths of both Christophe and the Prince, it has not been included in this volume. The conclusion reads: "And now after all this long writing of two sheets what have I recommended to you? Only a few things—a little Latin, ancient and modern history combined with chronology, astronomy, and the Old and New Testaments. To assist you in this I have recommended to you Eutropius, Justin, Stackhouse's *History of the Bible*, Tytler's *Elements of General History*, Russell's *History of Modern Europe*, Priestley's *Lectures on History*, Bonnycastle's *Astronomy*, Paley's *Natural Theology*, Robinson's *Scripture Characters*, Gregory's *Letters on the Evidences of the Christian Religion*, Williams's *Letters on Political Liberty*, Telemachus, and Anacharsis. By this very night's post I shall write to my bookseller to procure them all, and to direct them to the King, ... and I shall tell the King that they are for your use."

[52] For the full text of this edict, see Part III, Document 3, pp. 268–271.

pleased, the rigorous regulations of the Code Rural were enforced upon those who retained their property.

All who receive concessions will be expected to produce various foodstuffs on their land, according to the nature of the soil, and to observe all present and future laws governing the possession of property.

Christophe wrote that he planned "to familiarize the troops with the transition from the soldier's life to that of the farmer by giving them leave, a group at a time, to go and cultivate their land for brief periods," and that when he could do so with complete security, he would embrace in its entirety the plan for maintaining a militia.

When Clarkson heard, from an American friend, of a project to send free people of color from the United States to Haiti, he saw another opportunity to be of service. He pointed out to Christophe the substantial advantages of increasing his population by these emigrants from the United States. They would assist materially in introducing the English language into the Kingdom of Haiti, and since many of them were skilled workers, they would prove useful by their example. Clarkson also wrote to Richard Peters, the president of the Triennial Convention (a congress of various abolition societies in the United States), urging him to send delegates to Haiti for the purpose of investigating conditions there. Nor was this all. He suggested that the United States might be prevailed upon to purchase Spanish Santo Domingo as an asylum for free American Negroes and then to cede it to Christophe. Such an arrangement would both enlarge Christophe's territory and enhance his reputation abroad.

Nothing came of Clarkson's hopes. A revolution in Spain put an end to any chance of selling Santo Domingo; but it is extremely unlikely that the United States would have considered such an arrangement. Yet Christophe received Clarkson's suggestions and wrote through Limonade to American abolitionists, offering to defray the costs of transportation for the Negro emigrants, whom he was willing to receive without any stipulation regarding the Spanish part of the island. There were many thousands of the free people of color who wished to go to Haiti, but the death of Christophe prevented the signing of an agreement, whereby he was to provide a vessel to transport them and to advance "twenty-five thousand dollars as a first donation towards incidental expenses."[53]

Clarkson constantly reiterated to Christophe the necessity of avoiding any contention with the Republic of Haiti, and his advice apparently bore fruit.

---

[53] See Letters 48 and 58 of this collection.

At the time of Pétion's death[54] in 1818, Christophe had urged, by means of a proclamation to the Haitians of the Republic and a letter to their generals and magistrates, that the country unite with his kingdom, an offer which was scornfully rejected. In 1820, however, Sir Home Riggs Popham of the Jamaica Station undertook the good offices of mediator between the rival governments, probably at the instigation of Christophe. He first went to Port-au-Prince to confer with President Boyer, Pétion's successor, whom he found quite willing to arrange a pact with the King for their mutual defense. He then communicated Boyer's proposals to Christophe. Finally, on the eve of his departure for England in the early summer of 1820, he wrote Boyer, advising him that the treaty ought to have for its principal objects the establishment of concord between the subjects of the two states and an agreement to unite their forces in case of a French attack, and warned him:

> Don't plan ever to make war; don't try to advance beyond your frontiers, because if you do I shall consider you as the aggressor, and you will be held responsible in the eyes of the whole world.

He assured Boyer that Christophe was "sincerely disposed to enter into an agreement of the most perfect amity" and that the delegates whom Boyer apparently intended to send into the north would be guaranteed absolute security.[55] Unfortunately, no formal treaty materialized before Christophe died in October, 1820, but it is significant that he should have made a complete *volte-face* between the years 1818 and 1820 and abandoned all ambition to unite Haiti under his authority.

Haitian foreign policy, however, is the most important and constant subject of discussion in the correspondence. In his first letters Christophe emphasizes the necessity of guaranteeing the safety of the Haitians before turning to their moral and cultural improvement. He begs his friend "to continue to impart to me those observations which your experience with the policy of the European cabinets may suggest to you," and implores him "to give me timely notice of any machinations which our enemies may devise against us." The collaboration between the two men offers a remarkable example of mutual understanding and good faith.

---

[54] Although Pétion was reëlected President of the Republic of Haiti for life in 1815, his last years were clouded by a profound melancholy. He had given his people personal freedom, but his experiment in self-government had been a disillusioning failure and his domain was one vast mass of indolence. Though he was beloved by his countrymen, in the last few months he lost all desire to live. Just before he died on March 29, 1818, he named the mulatto general, Jean-Pierre Boyer, to succeed him.

[55] Cf. Vergniaud Leconte, *op. cit.,* pp. 408–415.

To discuss in detail the many aspects of Haitian foreign policy treated by Christophe and Clarkson would be to anticipate the correspondence which follows. Clarkson warned Christophe to maintain the strictest neutrality with his Caribbean neighbors, and outlined for him the state of French opinion toward Haiti and the improbability of any warlike proceeding against her. Christophe, on the other hand, wrote longingly of his hope that England might recognize Haitian independence, though Clarkson clearly showed how impossible such action would be in the face of French resentment. Christophe dispatched for Clarkson's judgment several letters from France, which were obviously designed to effect some sort of understanding preliminary to a commercial treaty. "I need your advice and the wisdom of your experience," he wrote, "and shall await them with the anxiety which the seriousness of the subject justifies."

The extent to which Clarkson carried his assistance is almost incredible, and he devoted himself to the welfare of Haiti with unremitting labor and intense sincerity. He journeyed to the Congress at Aix-la-Chapelle to forward the Haitian cause. He mastered information on a wide diversity of subjects. He wrote voluminous letters. Nearly sixty years of age, he might have shifted the burden to younger shoulders; but instead he preferred to devote his entire energy to Christophe.

One example of the harmonious relations between the two men may be cited. Ever anxious to have Christophe's character and aspirations known by the highest potentates in Europe, Clarkson suggested that Christophe write directly to Emperor Alexander of Russia. Christophe at first questioned the propriety of doing so without some preparation. At Aix-la-Chapelle Clarkson had a most satisfactory conference with the Emperor, an account of which he transmitted in one of his letters. At this conference he lent one of Christophe's letters to Alexander, "who was so much struck with it, that he carried it to the Emperor of Austria and the King of Prussia for their perusal, and they pronounced it to be as good a letter as any of their own Cabinet-Ministers could have written on the occasion." Having been properly introduced, Christophe thereupon wrote a magnificent letter to Emperor Alexander. The letter was sent unsealed to Clarkson; "if you judge that it may be sent on to him, I beg of you to forward it to its destination." It begins with a tactful acknowledgment of the Emperor's "universal benevolence" and his "humane and beneficent disposition . . . towards the unfortunate Africans and their descendants, the Haytians," and then summarizes briefly the tragic story of the years preceding the declaration of independence in 1804. Christophe adds a brief account of his own efforts "to give my fellow citizens a code of laws suited to their wants and to their morals." Then follows a noble defense of the Negro:

Too long has the African race been unjustly calumniated. Too long has it been represented as deprived of intellectual faculties, as scarcely susceptible of civilization or government by regular and established laws: these false assertions spring from the avarice and injustice of men who have had the impiety to degrade the finest work of the Creator, as if mankind had not one common origin. These persons attribute to difference of colour that which is only the result of civilization and knowledge.

In concluding the letter, Christophe tells how he had hoped that after Napoleon's defeat the new French Government "would have been directed by principles of moderation, justice, and humanity, and that... [the King] would have acknowledged the independence of the people of Hayti." Since Louis XVIII *"openly showed* his disposition to make use of the same system of duplicity and perfidy" as had formerly been employed, Christophe hopes that Alexander will grant his "powerful and generous protection, and benevolence to the cause of the unfortunate, oppressed Africans, and of the good and interesting people of Hayti."

Clarkson had become a good-will ambassador for Christophe, and the latter, ever quick to estimate the character of others, determined to use his English friend in an official capacity. Clarkson, he knew, was a man of the highest integrity and one well versed in European politics and intimately acquainted with many of the leaders in England and France. Christophe had long realized that his own position was precarious and that his aspirations for the Haitians could not be achieved until Haiti was recognized as an independent nation. Such recognition must come first, however, from France. Yet where was he to begin? He had indignantly driven off the French agents who came in 1814 and again in 1816, and in the early months of 1819, in reply to repeated French overtures made through General de Vincent, for a commercial treaty, he had boldly asserted that the preliminary basis must be a recognition of Haitian independence. He determined, nevertheless, to take the initiative, and on November 20, 1819, he appointed Clarkson his delegate to France. He accompanied the appointment with a letter of instructions, and dispatched £6,000 to cover the expenses of the mission. In acknowledging the independence of Haiti, France was not to expect more than a share of Haitian commerce; the treaty was to contain no provision for any indemnification of the former colonists; and any agreement must be for the whole of Haiti and take no cognizance of the existing disunity there.

Clarkson must have been astounded by Christophe's arbitrary terms, which in return for the recognition of Haitian independence by France, provided only for a share of Haitian commerce and neutrality in time of war. He had earlier advised Christophe to consider paying France an indemnification to reimburse the ex-colonists for the loss of their land; but despite Christophe's uncompromising attitude, he accepted the trust placed in him and in two detailed letters outlined the course of action he pursued. In the first letter, he said he had taken up the matter with Wilberforce and others in England, and all were agreed that the present unsettled state of France and the new administration of Ultra Royalists—all enemies to Christophe—made any immediate proposal unwise. Unless Christophe were to offer some tangible advantage to France, "all hope of a treaty then is at an end," and he was advised "to continue as you are." Clarkson, however, proposed to go to France in a private capacity to sound out French opinion; nevertheless, he intended to take the official papers with him, to be ready to act as Haitian envoy, should an unexpected occasion arise.

The second letter reports the results of Clarkson's French journey. He ferreted out information which he summarized under three headings: "Will France ever fit out an Expedition for the Conquest of Hayti? Will France ever acknowledge the Independence of Hayti? Upon what terms will France consent to acknowledge such Independence?" The answer to the first question was an unequivocal No. Not only was France in no position to undertake so costly a venture, but the very suggestion of an expedition to Haiti would meet with unanimous disapproval by the military—"as hopeless and disastrous as the Expedition of Leclerc" had become a proverbial expression—and Clarkson found the general opinion to be that no French regiment would consent to go there. The answer to the second question was that Christophe could gain a favorable treaty if he would "acknowledge the King of France as your nominal Sovereign," but that if the French recognized the independence of Haiti, they *"would make you pay very dearly for it."* The answer to the third question was more complicated. Clarkson dealt first with the terms which the Ultra-Royalist ministry would be likely to demand in making a treaty with Haiti; he then outlined the somewhat milder terms the Liberals might propose, should they come into power.

The letter is filled with temperate counsel. Among other things Clarkson advised Christophe to have Baron de Vastey compose a "little work" to refute the charge that "yours was no Government, it was a mere Despotism." He pointed out that "the French Cabinet are much better disposed to...[the Republic] than to yourself." He also suggested that in case France, "contrary to all human reason and...contrary to all human expectation, ... should ever meditate an attack upon Hayti," Christophe ought to authorize his friends in England "to dispatch a light and quick sailing vessel to Hayti to make known to you such intention."

When this letter, which was written on July 10, 1820, arrived in Haiti, Christophe was no longer alive, and as Clarkson remarks in his autobiography, "my labours for him and the people of Hayti were all in vain."

THE DEATH OF HENRY CHRISTOPHE

Disaster came to Christophe in the midst of his labors. On August 15, 1820, he was seized with a fit of apoplexy while attending mass at the Queen's fête at Belle-Vue. He consulted with his physician, Duncan Stewart, who informed him that his whole right side was paralyzed, and that while the seizure probably would not prove fatal, his active days were over. Christophe received this disastrous news with stoical composure, and as soon as he was able to travel, had himself conveyed to Sans Souci.

No longer overawed by their king, the people began to talk among themselves of open revolt. Nor were they without provocation. Although at the onset of his career Christophe governed in a tolerant manner and conducted his administration with a view to establishing order and discipline in a nation long unused to them, towards the end of his reign he became more and more overbearing and tyrannical. He gave way to uncontrolled fits of temper and savage cruelty. He had learned to govern others but not himself. He spared no one, and the nobles and Royal Dahomet troops were as likely to become the victims of his wrath as the common field workers. In the dungeons of the Citadel Henry those who had incurred the King's displeasure languished and died. He continued to supervise everything. Early in 1820 he had ordered the rebuilding of Cap Henry, which had never been fully restored since the time of Leclerc's invasion. Daily he appeared on the scene of construction, exhorting the workers and punishing the idlers. During the last seven months preceding his stroke, he was more than usually active; he seemed to be everywhere, and his irascibility knew no bounds. He had turned from a benevolent sovereign into a tyrant and made enemies throughout the length and breadth of his kingdom.

Many of the acts of cruelty attributed to Christophe, however, were committed by his subordinates and without his knowledge or approval. The unrest in his kingdom, too, was as much due to the intrigues and machinations of those in important positions as to his tyranny. These unscrupulous men—members of the aristocracy, officials in the government, and army officers—had become jealous of his power and secretly awaited an opportunity to overthrow the government. Although they owed their positions and wealth to him, they resented his ascendancy over them and believed that they rather than he should rule the country.

The Queen, indeed, was uneasy over the intrigues being practiced at the court, but even if she had understood their serious nature, she was powerless to do anything. Christophe also seems to have had apprehensions of disaster during the weeks following his seizure, and to have indulged in moments of self-questioning. He told Stewart, who was in constant attendance upon him, that he was conscious of having been unnecessarily harsh in governing his people and illiberal in his treatment of the soldiers. He still kept the reins of government firmly in his control, however, and he greeted with a wild outburst of wrath the suggestion of some of his more temperate advisers that a provisional government be established with the Prince Royal at its head. "Every order, every disposition emanated as before from his proper person. His son was deputed only to preside over its execution."

At Cap Henry, the Duc de Marmelade, whom Christophe had publicly humiliated, and other high officers had been secretly plotting since the beginning of the King's illness to destroy the monarchy and establish a republic in its place. Baron Dupuy, one of the King's most loyal supporters, probably knew something of this scheme, but he did not communicate his suspicions to Christophe because of "his firm conviction that no measure of the King's could change his destiny." Before Marmelade's plans were perfected, however, a revolt against the King burst forth in an unexpected quarter. The garrison at Saint-Marc on the western coast, infuriated at the punishment of one of their officers by Christophe, revolted on October 1, killed their commander, and, wishing to unite with the republic of the south, sent a conciliatory message to President Boyer. To thwart this secession, General Romain, Christophe's Minister of War, who was then in the Artibonite, hurriedly assembled what troops were available in the vicinity, hastened to Saint-Marc, and placed it under siege.

Learning of this uprising, Christophe acted promptly, and on October 6 commanded the soldiers at Cap Henry to march against Saint-Marc; but instead of obeying his order, they flouted his authority and themselves broke into open revolt. So widespread was this spontaneous insurrection, that Marmelade, the royal governor at the Cape, and his fellow conspirators, whose own *coup d'état* was thus anticipated, took charge of the insurgent army. To indicate their hatred of the King, the generals tore from their uniforms the crosses of the Order of St. Henry and trampled them in the dust. The cry from every throat was "Down with the King!"; and after a night of rioting and dancing at Cap Henry, the troops with Marmelade at their head, on Saturday, October 7, began their march to Haut-du-Cap, a hamlet three miles away on the road to Sans Souci.

Stunned by the news of another rebellion, Christophe hesitated for the first time in his life. All day October 7 he kept to his private quarters at the Palace of Sans Souci, but his indomitable will had not deserted him, and at last, about four o'clock in the afternoon, he determined to act. Unable to mount his horse and ride at the head of his soldiers, he ordered his household troops to pass in review before him, for he knew only too well how much his power depended upon his personal bearing. Leaning heavily on the arm of a domestic, who supported his right side, and brandishing a pistol in his left hand, he harangued the palace guard, directed that four dollars be paid to each man, and ordered them to attack the oncoming insurgents.

In the meantime, the rebels from Cap Henry arrived at Haut-du-Cap, nine miles from Sans Souci, where they threw up hasty defenses. Here, on Sunday, October 8, Christophe's troops under the command of Prince Joachim opposed the insurgents; but instead of obeying the order to attack, they joined with the enemy. Prince Joachim, who alone remained faithful to his king, turned and fled to the palace.

Christophe, who was anxiously awaiting the outcome, received news at eight-thirty the same evening that even his personal troops had abandoned him. He called his family to him, and exhorting them to show courage and resignation, bade them an affectionate farewell. Turning to Dupuy, he said, "Save yourself, my time is finished." A few minutes later, having asked his attendants to leave him, he shot himself through the heart.

That same night Dupuy and Queen Marie-Louise, accompanied by the two princesses and several others, secretly carried the King's body from the palace, just in time to escape the bloodthirsty mob now almost at the gates of San Souci. Slowly they bore the corpse up the steep mountain trail to the Citadel, where they arrived about midnight. There in an open lime kiln they dropped the body of the first and only King of Haiti. Fittingly, and perhaps by his own order, Christophe had become a part of his most extravagant work. His death and interment had been as spectacular and dramatic as his rise to power.

On learning that the troops at Cap Henry were in revolt, General Romain, who had been in connivance with Marmelade's conspiracy, abandoned the siege of Saint-Marc and hurried north. After much contention, he was chosen provisional head of the proposed republic. The greatest disorder prevailed. Prince Jacques-Victor-Henry, heir to the throne, Prince Eugène, Christophe's natural son, and a number of others were brutally bayoneted in the prison yard on the night of October 18, but the lives of the Queen and the two Princesses were spared. The conspirators had won their first objective, the destruction of the kingdom, but they were soon to discover that it is easier to overthrow a government than to establish a new one.

While these events were in progress, President Boyer marched into the territory of the former king at the head of a large army and took possession of Saint-Marc. Although he had not instigated the insurrections, he seized the opportunity to reunite Haiti under one government. Romain, Marmelade, and the other leaders of the revolution tried to forestall him and sent a message indicating that they were setting up a republic to replace the fallen monarchy. They pointed out that they had come into possession of the letters and papers concerning the attempt of Sir Home Riggs Popham to establish cordial relations between Christophe's kingdom and the Republic. In these documents, they asserted, Boyer had manifested his desire to have his government recognized by that of Christophe, and had declared that he would not interfere in any manner with the regime in the north. Boyer, however, was not to be turned aside from his resolution and sent word that he demanded the absolute submission of all the chiefs. He thereupon continued his march toward Cap Henry with twenty thousand men, and the insurgents, capitulating to his demands, hastily proclaimed him President on October 21. On the twenty-eighth, Boyer arrived at Cap Henry and incorporated the former kingdom into the Republic. He appropriated Christophe's private as well as public treasury, abolished all titles and distinctions, altered the names of Cap Henry and the Citadel Henry to Cap Haïtien and La Ferrière, and after a military tour through the country returned to Port-au-Prince. The last vestiges of Christophe's monarchy had been obliterated.

Thus the magnificent plans of Henry Christophe came to an end. All work stopped at his death. The laborers left the fields untilled. The workers on the Citadel dropped their tools. An enormous cannon being hauled up the mountain to the fortress was abandoned halfway to the summit, where even today it can be seen amid the jungle. The schools were immediately closed, and the white teachers whom Clarkson and Wilberforce had so painstakingly selected were left with neither students nor salary. The soldiers broke discipline and soon became slovenly and careless. Swarms of idlers and vagrants crowded the roads. Abundance was replaced by destitution. The iron hand, the invincible will, and the insatiable ambition of the King were gone. The people had their freedom, the tyrant was dead; but for many a year black men and women spoke of him simply as *L'Homme;* and looking up at the mighty Citadel, or gazing on the Palace of Sans Souci, or remembering the former days of prosperity, were accustomed to refer to Christophe's death as *le temps de notre malheur,* "the time of our misfortune."

AFTERMATH

The death of Christophe and the overthrow of the kingdom were matters of bitter regret to Clarkson. Not only were the brilliant projects of the former king laid in ruins, but Clarkson and other friends of the Africans in England had lost in the wreck of Christophe's well-organized government their opportunity to prove to the world what a free and independent Negro state could accomplish. The letters Clarkson received from Haiti were most depressing. They give a graphic account of Christophe's illness, the insurrections, the death of the King, and the final destruction of the monarchy, and show how every beneficial aspect of the royal regime—the improvement of agriculture, the development of education, and the prosperity of the nation—rapidly disappeared. Especially significant are the attempts to evaluate the character of Christophe. Every writer bears testimony to his greatness. Both Wilson, the English teacher whom Clarkson had sent to Haiti, and Stewart, the King's physician, agreed that Christophe had become undisciplined and cruel and that the revolution was the inevitable result of his tyranny. Sanders, on the contrary, praised Christophe and maintained that his downfall was due wholly to the machinations of his enemies. All the correspondents concurred in their low opinion of Boyer's character and administration and painted a gloomy picture of conditions in Haiti. Sanders even went so far as to beg Clarkson "to come over and help us."

Almost at once Clarkson was bombarded with appeals for money from the funds Christophe had entrusted to him for his French mission. Boyer, though he had made off with the treasury of the dead king, absolutely refused to pay any of Christophe's obligations. Wilson, Stewart, Sanders, and even an English business house presented their claims, and Clarkson set about evaluating them with his usual thoroughness.

The sudden transformation of Christophe's kingdom from its high level of law and order to one of confusion and turbulence filled Clarkson with foreboding and alarm, and he was especially concerned over the unhappy plight of Madame Christophe and her two daughters, who were now at Port-au-Prince under the protection of President Boyer. He noted, too, with the greatest uneasiness, the ominous upsurge of French interest in Haiti as manifested by the French journals. His letter of inquiry to Dupuy remaining unanswered, he wrote directly to President Boyer on May 25, 1821, warning him of the duplicity of the French and indicating the solicitude of many people in England for Christophe's widow and children. His letter was obviously designed to open a correspondence similar to that conducted with Christophe. Boyer's response was really a rebuff and rather bluntly maintained that the Haitians could take care of themselves—"only we can guarantee our rights." Clarkson's concern over the fate of Madame Christophe, however, seems to have suggested to her the advisability of going to England. Boyer wrote that the Christophes wished to "spend some time in England for the sake of their health" and that he had given them permission to leave. "As you seem to take a great interest in their welfare, I have no doubt you will do what you can to be of service to them."

The arrival of Madame Christophe and her two daughters in England placed the abolitionists in a new position. Heretofore their efforts had been at a distance; now they were confronted with the care of these unfortunate women. "I saw the ex-queen of Hayti yesterday and her two daughters," wrote Zachary Macaulay to his wife on September 20, 1821:

She and they are in deep mourning, which, with their coal-black countenances, gives them a somewhat sombre aspect. The mother is, I should think, about fifty-five years of age, pleasing and modest. The daughters are, I should think, twenty-four and eighteen, pretty good-looking; but you need be under no apprehensions respecting Madame Christophe. She is not likely to come near us. But if she had, you might have rested perfectly easy on the score of morals. I have no doubt whatever that the young women are perfectly modest and virtuous. Neither mother nor daughters will be dependent on any one except for counsel and kindness in this land of strangers. They will be amply provided for from their own resources.

There was, as Clarkson himself remarked, "a sort of shrink at admitting them into high society," but he and his wife shared none of this prejudice and hospitably received them as house guests for nearly a year. "Their amiable dispositions, their gentle and correct manners, and their enlightened minds" soon won the affection of the Clarksons.

Nowhere does Clarkson's altruism show to better advantage than in his activities on behalf of the Christophes. If Wilberforce, in referring to their proposed journey to London, could say, "I should be cordially glad to render them any benefit, . . . but I have no time to spare, and she [Mrs. Wilberforce] has not at present spirits to undertake an office which would require a considerable share of them," Clarkson, for his part, was ready to assume every responsibility. His two letters to Zachary Macaulay, for example, indicate that there were many vexing problems attendant upon the domestication of the Christophes at Playford Hall. Wishing to free them from pecuniary worries, Clarkson not only insisted upon a curtailment of their expenses while they were his guests, but also supervised the investment of their funds, including the money realized by the sale of their jewels and the balance ($£5,700$) of the $£6,000$ which the King had sent to him. Christophe, indeed, could not have had a more loyal friend than Clarkson or one more willing to succor and advise his bereaved and unhappy family.

The last letter in this collection, dated September 13, 1824, was written by the three Christophes on the eve of their departure for Italy and forms a fitting conclusion to this Haitian story.

Christophe grows in stature in the correspondence which follows, but the contradictions in his character remain. He was often cruel and overbearing, yet in his letters he manifests a spirit of liberality and toleration and a disinterested love of his subjects. Was he, therefore, merely a crafty deceiver? Surely the practical benefits he bestowed upon his nation during his lifetime are witnesses in his favor. When he came to power in the midst of anarchy and disorder, he correctly estimated the people he was called upon to rule. The severest measures were necessary. Any sign of weakness threatened the success of his ambitions and his very life as well; but even as he failed in self-mastery and abused the power which destiny had placed in his hands, his restless and impatient spirit, rising above personal gratification, never ceased to envisage the future of the Haitian people. "If God blesses my handiwork, and grants me sufficient time," he had written, "I hope that the inhabitants of Haiti, overcoming the shameful prejudice which has too long weighed upon them, will soon astonish the world by their knowledge." He was cut off in the midst of his endeavors, his work unfinished. Yet he was, in the fullest sense of the term, a great man. "When we consider his whole history," wrote Zachary Macaulay, "raised from a slave to the command of armies and absolute power, and call to mind his military achievements, and the propriety and dignity with which he exercised the functions of government, we may rank him among the eminent men who have brightened the pages of history in different ages of the world."

THOMAS CLARKSON

from the original in the Municipal Museums, Hull, England

81

CITADEL HENRY
on the peak of La Ferrière

RUINS OF
THE PALACE
OF SANS SOUCI

(in center background)

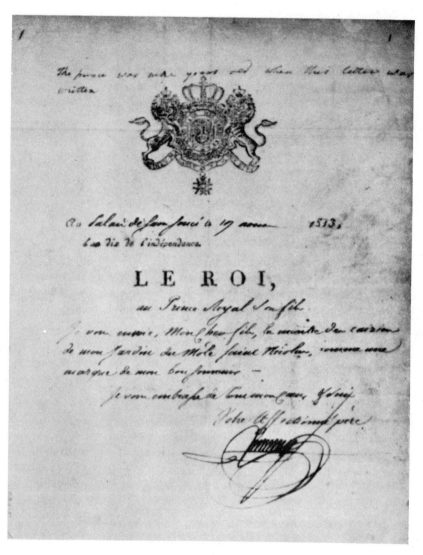

FACSIMILE OF LETTER 1

PART

2

LETTERS, 1813-1824

1

King Henry to his Son[1]

{ENGLISH TRANSLATION}

At the Palace of Sans Souci, this 19ᵗʰ of August, 1813,
in the 10ᵗʰ year of our Independence

THE KING,
to the Prince Royal, his son

I am sending you, my dear son, a sample of the grapes from my garden at
Môle Saint-Nicolas, as a mark of affectionate remembrance.

I embrace you with all my heart, and am

Your loving father,
HENRY

---

[1] This letter and the three following were salvaged after the Prince's murder and sent to
Mrs. Clarkson by William Wilson, one of the English teachers in Haiti. See Letter 51, p. 235,
and also Letter 54, p. 242. A marginal note, probably in Wilson's hand, reads, "The prince
was nine years old when this letter was written."

LETTER

2

King Henry to his Son
{ENGLISH TRANSLATION}

At the Palace of San Souci, this 17ᵗʰ of October, 1813,
in the 10ᵗʰ year of our Independence

THE KING,
to his dear Son, the Prince Royal

I received successively, my son, the four specimens of writing you addressed
to me; and, though I find nothing to criticize in your hand, which seems to
me rather good, I have reason to complain of your behavior and of your
character. Those in charge of your deportment and instruction are dissatisfied with you; do you imagine I can feel otherwise myself? I am informed that you have mistreated your servants. That is not commendable.
If you are anxious to merit my esteem and affection, that is not the way to
go about it, but rather by means of a more proper conduct, submissiveness
to the counsel and advice of those qualified to give them to you, and an
affability and kindliness which will make all cherish you. Though I have
delayed writing you until now, because of the press of affairs, and though
I have been unable to return to the capital, I shall not forget to speak to you
in person about this, the first time I see you, and I shall make you more
docile to the counsel and advice of those who have a right to offer them to
you, and more affable toward the persons who serve you.

HENRY

LETTER

3

King Henry to his Son

{ENGLISH TRANSLATION}

At the Palace of Sans Souci, this 12th of December, 1813,
in the 10th year of our Independence

THE KING,

to the Prince Royal, his son

While examining your latest specimen of writing, my dear son, I noted three erasures, and several other mistakes. Your intention in sending me the samples of your work was doubtless to offer me proof of your application, and to put me in a position to judge of your progress; consequently you should take care to send nothing unworthy of being seen by me. That is what you fail to do, since you allow me to note careless errors. Try, then, again.... [The remainder of this letter is missing.]

LETTER

4

King Henry to his Son

{ENGLISH TRANSLATION}

At the Palace of the Citadel Henry, June 15th, 1816,
in the 13th year of our Independence

THE KING,

to the Prince Royal, his son

My dear Son,

Since tomorrow is Sunday, I can permit you, by way of recreation, to take your horse and come to visit the work of the Citadel Henry. You will always have enough time to amuse yourself, and people would say that no celebration can take place without your wishing to be present, whereas your studies should receive all your attention. I do not find that you are devoting yourself to them with all the application they merit.

[No signature]

LETTER

5

King Henry to Thomas Clarkson
{ENGLISH TRANSLATION}

At the Palace of Sans Souci, this 5ᵗʰ of February, 1816,
in the 13ᵗʰ year of our Independence

THE KING,
to Mr. Thomas Clarkson,
Member of the African Institution, etc.

Dear Sir,

I received with great satisfaction Mr. Prince Sanders.[2] Your recommendation, and those of Messrs. Wilberforce and Stephen, insured him of being shown every possible consideration.

For a long while my intention, my dearest ambition, has been to secure for the nation which has confided to me its destiny the benefit of public instruction. Pétion's revolt, his betrayal of the Haitian people, and the civil dissension he created among us, arrested the impetus I wished to give to education, that first duty of sovereigns. I am completely devoted to this project. The edifices necessary for the institutions of public instruction in the cities and in the country are under construction. I am awaiting the professors and craftsmen I requested, who will take upon themselves the training of our youth. I intend to accord them every encouragement, protection, and tolerance in the exercise of their religions, along with whatever advantages may be just and reasonable. So if God blesses my handiwork, and grants me sufficient time, I hope that the inhabitants of Haiti, overcoming the shameful prejudice which has too long weighed upon them, will soon astonish the world by their knowledge. It is thus I should like to refute the calumny of our detractors, and justify the high opinion our friends, the philanthropists, have conceived of us. I would indeed be unworthy of the high rank to which Providence has called me, of the duties

---

[2] For an account of Prince Sanders (also spelled Saunders) see p. 45.

which are mine to perform, of the great hopes our friends place in me, if I did not strive to merit their approbation and fulfill their just expectations. Then, too, I have before my eyes the record of history, and the approval of posterity which I covet.

I rejoice, along with our kind friends, the philanthropists, at the action of the French Government in consenting finally to the abolition of the impious and abominable slave trade, and in abandoning the evil and impracticable idea of sending an expedition against Haiti. That Government should have taken such action long ago, instead of allowing itself to be led into disastrous measures by the claims and recriminations of those enemies of the human species, the ex-colonists, who declared in print that all our population above the age of six must be destroyed.[a] We hope, if the French Cabinet is ever again led to attempt inhuman measures against us, that our virtuous defenders will enlighten European public opinion and strive to prevent the execution of such a project. If our friends do not succeed in the praiseworthy design of halting this abomination, we count on them at least to inform and warn us of any enterprises which may be undertaken for our destruction, so that we may be upon our guard.

The British Nation has long since earned a right to the gratitude of all Haitians. What it has just done, when it used its influence to obtain of France the abolition of the infamous slave trade, gives us new reasons for admiration and thankfulness. We are grateful also for the share which Their Majesties, the Emperor of Russia, and the Sovereign of Germany, had in the abolition of the trade.

I felt it necessary to ask Mr. Prince Sanders to return to England, in order that he might bring back with him the teachers whom I requested Mr. Wilberforce to procure for me, and who are to instruct our youth according to the approved English educational system. I have entrusted Mr. Sanders with the delivery of the various letters which I am addressing to our friends, and with our public papers, because I have been informed that certain letters written to us, and some sent by us, along with our papers,

---

[a] Christophe kept himself well informed on the publications being issued in France: "The ex-colonists ... published thousands of pamphlets in which they unblushingly disclosed plans of destruction which make nature shudder.... These pamphlet-mongers propose to EXTERMINATE our generation *without distinction to* SEX *or* AGE!!—infants under the age of six years alone excepted, to be retained in bondage, because these little innocents could not at so early an age have received the first impressions of FREEDOM." Baron de Vastey, *op. cit.,* Appendix, p. lxxxix.

have been intercepted by French ex-colonists in London, Jamaica, and St. Thomas.[4]

Upon delivering to you my letter, Mr. Sanders has been asked to express to you, as well as to our friends, my warm and sincere thanks for all the efforts you have made, and the zeal you have shown for the triumph of the cause of the Africans and of their descendants. The gratitude which I feel toward you, and toward our good and virtuous defenders, will never be effaced from my heart, and I shall ever seize all occasions to give you proof of it.

HENRY

---

[4] Since the ejection of the French, the Haitians had lacked regular direct mail service to Europe. Letters were usually routed through the English West Indies, occasionally through the United States.

LETTER

6

Thomas Clarkson to King Henry

Playford Hall
Suffolk, England
May 4, 1816

[No salutation]

I had the honour of receiving your Majesty's letter, dated at the Palace of Sans Souci February 5ᵗʰ, which was brought to me by Mr. Prince Sanders, and it is my intention to return an answer to it by the same person, as well as to enter into some particulars which I think may be acceptable to your Majesty. Having however heard that my esteemed friend, Mr. Stephen Grellet,[5] who is a Minister of the Gospel belonging to the Religious Society of the people called Quakers, and who is now in North America, intends with other Ministers of the same Society to visit some of the English West Indian Islands, and also Hayti, for the purpose of preaching the Gospel for a season in those parts, I have thought it proper to send him this letter for your Majesty in order that he may not go into your Island without a suitable introduction. I am sensible how vigilant it becomes you to be with respect to strangers, some of whom may possibly visit Hayti for the purpose of plotting against its liberty and Independence.... [This] induces me to lay before you the character of Mr. Grellet and his friends, in order that they may come among you without suspicion, and that they may experience the protection which all those persons ought to find who feel it to be their duty, like the Apostles of old, to visit foreign climates and to hazard their lives for the sake of promoting the religion of Jesus Christ.... Mr. Stephen Grellet was born in France, but ... left his country during the Revolution, and went to the United States of America where he embraced the principles of the Religious Society of the Friends, or as they are more commonly called Quakers. After this he became a Minister of the Gospel in that Society, and in this capacity he visited England, Germany, and France. During his stay

---

[5] In the *Memoirs of the Life and Gospel Labours of Stephen Grellet,* 1860, a considerable account is given of Grellet's visit to Pétion, but no mention is made of an excursion into Christophe's kingdom.

in London for many months I had the happiness of knowing him. . . . It also happened that his Imperial Majesty, the Emperor of Russia, arrived in England. Mr. Grellet had the honour of an audience with that noble and august personage, and I know that he advocated before his Imperial Majesty in a very forcible manner the cause of all the injured children of Africa. As to Mr. Grellet's private character, I may compliment it in a few words by saying that he clearly affords in his own person a proof of modesty, humility, charity, and those other virtues which belong [to] the Christian character. . . .

I feel myself bound to say a few words in behalf of the Religious Society to which he belongs, for it is possible he may have companions with him, and it is right that your Majesty should know some of the civil and political principles of the Quakers.

In the first place, they consider it to be their duty to obey the civil magistrate, as the ruler under God for good, except in their religious customs and cases where their consciences would be wounded by it.

In the second place, they conceive it to be their duty never to go to war, or to take up arms even in their own defense. They had rather submit to the most cruel injuries, than shed the blood of any of their fellow creatures. Hence there is no rebellion, no insurrection, no plotting against governments wherever the Quakers are.

And thirdly, they have long ago conceived it to be their duty to consider all the children of Africa as their brethren, and to have no concern whatsoever either in buying, or in selling, or in holding them in bondage. In all America there is not one Quaker whose character has been stained by such infamous practices. The Abolition of the Slave Trade and of Slavery also has become a principle, and has been incorporated as such into their Religion. . . . They have been constant fellow labourers in England of Mr. Wilberforce and myself in this great and noble Cause from the first moment in which we ourselves embarked in it, and in North America they have been the original instruments of effecting whatever has been done in that Country in behalf of the injured Africans and their descendants. In fact, whenever you see a Quaker, you see a friend to the distressed, but more especially to those of the African race, and I cannot doubt, therefore, that every Quaker will experience your Majesty's kind protection and regard, but more particularly when he comes to you, not for the purposes of commerce, but as a promoter of the interests of Religion.

I shall only add to these remarks that the Quakers are in many respects a singular people. They are singular in their language, dress, and customs.

They have laid aside the usual ceremonies and formalities of the world in saluting or addressing themselves to others. Some years ago I wrote their history,[6] and if Mr. S. Grellet should receive this letter in time, he will probably present your Majesty with a copy of it.

I am your Majesty's [Friend]

[No signature]

---

[6] Clarkson refers to his *Portraiture of Quakerism, as Taken from a View of the Moral Education, Discipline, Peculiar Customs, Religious Principles, Political and Civil Economy and Character of the Society of Friends,* 3 vols. (London and New York, 1806).

LETTER

7

King Henry to Thomas Clarkson[7]

{ENGLISH TRANSLATION}

At the Palace of San Souci, this 18th of November, 1816, in the 13th year of our Independence

THE KING,

to Mr. Thomas Clarkson, etc.

Dear Sir and Friend,

I have read and meditated upon the contents of your letter of the 5th of August[8] with all the attention of which I am capable.

I am deeply appreciative of and touched by the great interest which you take in the cause of the Africans and their decendants, in the prosperity of Haiti, and in my personal reputation, and, therefore, I will reply to you with the frankness and sincerity which the relation in which we stand to each other requires. I hope that you will thus become acquainted with my character and motives, as I am with yours, and with those of my other estimable friends.

Entirely devoted to my project of establishing public instruction, of extending moral principles as widely as possible, and of concurring with the noble and generous views of our friends in England, I have welcomed with gratitude the masters and professors, whom they sent out to me. As soon as Messrs. Gulliver[9] and Sanders arrived here, I set them up in the capital, and

---

[7] "I lent the original to the Emperor of Russia at Aix-la-Chapelle, who was so much struck with it that he carried it to the Emperor of Austria and the King of Prussia for their perusal, and they pronounced it to be as good a letter as any of their own Cabinet-Ministers could have written on the occasion." [Note by Thomas Clarkson.] For the French original of this letter see Appendix, p. 276.

[8] Clarkson's letter of August 5 is missing from this collection.

[9] W. W. Harvey, during his stay in Haiti in 1820, made a visit to Gulliver's school at Cape Henry, and was very much impressed by the definite progress made by the students in reading, writing, arithmetic, English, and French. "The place appropriated to this purpose was a large building, situated in a retired and elevated part of the town, and was as properly arranged, and as perfectly furnished with all the necessary apparatus, as the best schools . . . in England. This school contained from one hundred and fifty to two hundred boys, from eight to sixteen years of age. . . . The master . . . had conducted it from its commencement; and his ability and attention appeared from the perfect order which prevailed throughout." W. W. Harvey, *op. cit.*, pp. 202–203.

procured them scholars whom they are to instruct according to the Lancasterian method. I am astonished at the effects of this new system, and at the precocious intelligence which it develops in the pupils. In fact, I consider the sending of these masters as the greatest favor my friends have done me.

Mr. Evans,[10] the teacher of drawing and painting, is established at Sans Souci, and his school is also functioning.

I am awaiting the other masters and professors my friends are to send me, and intend to station them in various cities of the kingdom and to staff the Royal College, so as to extend more widely the benefits of education.

I am too desirous of meriting the kindness and esteem which have been shown me, not to make every effort in my power to fulfill the expectations of our estimable friends.

Since the first Declaration of our Independence, the maxim of the government which preceded mine, as well as my own, has been not to interfere with the internal affairs of our neighbors. We have made this a fundamental article of our constitutions. We have always believed that we ought to confine ourselves solely to the defense of our own territory, to establishing the dominion of law in place of the licentiousness which is the natural consequence of all revolutions, to the rebirth and prosperity of agriculture and commerce; in short, that we should enjoy quietly within our frontiers the liberty and peace which we have bought with our blood. This truth is so evident that it has never even been suggested that we had tried in any way to disturb the peace of our nearest neighbors, the Spaniards, or to interfere with their Government, though their borders touch ours, and slavery is established among them. They are united to us by the ties of good neighborliness and commerce; when the French occupied their capital, I furnished them gratuitously with arms and ammunition upon their own request, to help them to drive the invaders out. My plan of action at that time agreed perfectly with that of the English Government, which furnished them with forces and supplies with the same end in view.[11]

---

[10] This was probably Richard Evans (1784–1871), who painted the portrait of Christophe reproduced as the frontispiece of this volume.

[11] When General Rochambeau evacuated Cap Français in November, 1803, the French general, Ferrand, held control of Spanish Santo Domingo, which had been ceded to France in 1795. The usurpation of the Spanish throne by Joseph Bonaparte in the spring of 1808 was a signal for an uprising in Spanish Santo Domingo, under the leadership of Juan Sánchez Ramírez, against Ferrand. At this time Christophe began sending arms and munitions to the Spanish rebels. His assistance and two expeditions sent out by the English from Jamaica enabled them to drive the French from the territory in 1809, and it reverted to Spanish control.

For a long time past my ships of war have been used only along the coast, and have never travelled any distance from our own shores. The Government of His Britannic Majesty cannot, I am certain, be ignorant of this fact; it surely cannot give credit to the false allegations of the planters. Perhaps, indeed, the knowledge of these facts is not sufficiently circulated throughout the British Nation, but the truth must one day be evident, for in the long run it is sure to triumph over imposture.

Why then should it be supposed that we intend to deviate from the principles which we have always professed? How can anyone do us the injury of suggesting that we, who have so much reason to be grateful to the Government and people of England for the interest which they have always taken in our welfare, should ever seek to upset the regime of the British colonies?[12] Is it because these same colonies have experienced troubles and internal commotions? But these have nothing and can have nothing in common with the cause which we defended for more than 27 years.

The cause of the Spaniards in South America is no less foreign to us. Nevertheless it is true, to our deep regret, that in the part of this island which is under the rule of General Pétion, the privateers of the Spanish patriots are permitted to take in provisions, arms, and ammunition, and to complete their number of men. There also they are allowed to sell their prizes. The Haitian ships of that part of the island even sail in company with those of the Independents.[13] This is probably what has given rise to the rumors which have circulated. But it would be unjust to confuse that part of the island, where disorder still reigns, with this Government, and to attribute to us actions which are contrary to our principles.

In common with every good Haitian, and with our estimable friends in England, I deplore the cruel necessity which forced me to take up arms to repel the invasion of General Pétion. My own life, as well as that of my comrades in arms, was at stake, and I had no other recourse; but what have

---

[12] See pp. 52–53.

[13] In 1815, Simón Bolívar and many of his fellow patriots, after two years of successful rebellion against Spanish authority, were driven from Venezuela. In December of the same year, Bolívar arrived at Les Cayes, in Pétion's part of Haiti, and was shortly followed by Commodore Aury, commanding ten Venezuelan men-of-war, and many refugee families. Pétion extended every aid to them. Toward a new expedition against the Spanish in Venezuela in the spring of 1816, he contributed 4,000 rifles, powder, cartridges, all kinds of provisions, even a printing press; and he authorized Haitians to join the rebels. Bolívar's expedition failed; he again took refuge in the Republic of Haiti, where he remained for six months. Fitting out a second force, Bolívar finally defeated the Spanish and proclaimed the independence of Venezuela, Colombia, Ecuador, Peru, and Bolivia.

I not done to minimize, as far as I could, the affliction of our civil war! Knowing from experience that our domestic quarrels would serve only to comfort our enemies, I remained on the defensive, and trusted that time would calm passions and cool heads. I repeatedly took the initiative and tried to bring General Pétion back to a proper sense of the duty which he owed to himself as well as to his country. Though my attempts to restore peace represented a sacrifice of pride, I felt that the good of my country and the happiness of my compatriots made such action necessary. Such was my conduct, and I can say with satisfaction that my advances towards a reconciliation were made with all the frankness and sincerity which are natural to my character. What was the result? Each time an absolute refusal on his part to unite with me for the defense of our endangered country, new insults, threats, and outrages in answer to the most just and honorable proposals which I could offer him.

General Pétion has embarked in a cause not his own, and his efforts to mislead the Haitians under his command will prove fruitless. They are no more disposed to resume the yoke of slavery than are the inhabitants of the Northern, Eastern, or Western parts of the kingdom. It is a consolation to me to see that the great majority of Haitians have reached an understanding, and that a common danger has tacitly united us all, from one end of the island to the other, for we all abhor the French and their oppressive Government.

General Pétion, by refusing to make common cause with me, by keeping up a correspondence with the enemies of the state, by accepting bribes from them, and by the asylum and protection which he gives the French ex-colonists, has excited just suspicions in the minds of even that part of our people which he has led astray. He is closely watched, and the ruin of his cause is not far distant. The reports I receive from his part of the island are highly satisfactory. The arrival of any sort of French forces would only hasten the complete reunion of all the Haitians.

I agree perfectly, dear sir, with all the arguments which you have brought before me. Every one, perhaps, of your just reflections and thoughts had occurred to me before. But what more can I do? My conscience is easy.

Despite the lies and calumnious reports continually circulated by General Pétion and his agents concerning my character and Government, I appeal to God and to mankind as witnesses to the justness of my intentions and actions. I leave it to my friends, my fellow citizens, my contemporaries, and to history, to decide between the General and myself.

It was indeed a great pleasure for me to hear of all that the magnanimous Emperor of Russia, the other chief potentates of Europe, and the illustrious General Wellington did to secure the abolition of the slave trade. I am aware how much you yourself labored to the same end, and I am very grateful to you for it.

I do not know of any better way of thanking you for your wise and good advice than to beg you to continue it, to impart to me those observations which your experience with the policy of the European cabinets may suggest to you, and to give me timely notice of any machinations which our enemies may devise against us. I shall always receive with pleasure any advice which has for its object the good of my country.

We shall never again be deceived by the French Government, for we know that so long as it is influenced by the ex-colonists, it can never entertain just notions concerning us; and even if it should in appearance agree to a few concessions, it would only be for the purpose of deceiving us more thoroughly. If France should demand the exclusive commerce of the island, what would this be but a breach of our independence? And what right or title has that nation to make such a demand?

Nor would France be more successful if she brought before the allied powers the principle of her right of possession. The example which she formerly gave by her conduct toward the United States of America would turn this argument against herself.

After having tried to massacre our entire population and failed in the attempt, how could France convince anyone by a declaration that she would rule in Haiti as over a free people?

Nothing short of absolute independence in both government and commerce will satisfy us. This we shall have, or cease to live.

The French Cabinet has just made a new attempt and again insulted the Haitian people by sending out as commissioners[14] three ex-colonists, all of them discredited and disgraced in Haitian eyes. You will see by the public papers which I am sending you the unbecoming and ridiculous manner in which these men attempted to open negotiations with us.

In order to put a stop to the indignities of the French, to end their last hope of deceiving and dividing us, or of achieving their criminal intentions by intrigue, I thought it my duty to publish the enclosed declaration.[15] In this document you will see the true facts of the situation of Haiti.

---

[14] See p. 60 for an account of these commissioners, of whom De Vastey identifies two.

[15] For a summary of this declaration see pp. 60–61; for the full text see Baron de Vastey, *op. cit.*, Appendix, pp. lxxxv–xcvi.

I beg of you to watch over the interests of the Africans, our brethren, and of the Haitians, their descendants, with your usual care, zeal, and humanity; you, who have been the champion of this noble Cause, cannot be indifferent to my solicitations.

Believe me, Sir, with the greatest consideration and the most cordial friendship,

HENRY

LETTER

8

King Henry to Thomas Clarkson

{ENGLISH TRANSLATION}

At the Palace of Sans Souci, this 18ᵗʰ of November, 1816,
in the 13ᵗʰ year of our Independence

THE KING,

to Mr. Thomas Clarkson

Dear Sir and Friend,

Your two letters of the 10ᵗʰ of June and the 16ᵗʰ of last August have reached me;[16] they refer to Mr. Grellet, minister of the Gospel belonging to the religious society of the Quakers, and to the political ideas which guide that estimable society, ideas which I fully understand.

If Mr. Grellet and his companions visit our country, I shall not fail to receive him with kindness, as you recommended, and to treat him with all the regard which is due him because of his character and the fact that he is your friend. I am delighted to hear that he is a champion of abolition and the unfortunate Africans and their descendants. These sentiments which distinguish the Quakers are certain to earn them my esteem and consideration.

I also received with pleasure the History of the Quakers which you sent to me by Mr. Prince Sanders, and thank you most heartily for it.

With the highest consideration and most cordial friendship,

HENRY

---

[16] Clarkson's letters of June 10 and August 16, to which this is a reply, are missing. This communication was written by Christophe on the same day as the preceding one. He was usually careful to treat different subjects in separate letters.

LETTER

9

King Henry to Thomas Clarkson

{ENGLISH TRANSLATION}

At the Palace of Sans Souci, April 26th, 1818,
in the 15th year of our Independence

H E N R Y ,
King of Haiti, etc.,

to Mr. Thomas Clarkson,
Member of the African Institution, etc.

Dear Sir and Friend,

I received your communications of the 18th of November, 1817, and the 4th of March of the present year.[17] Though I have had no secure way of replying, I flatter myself that you have no doubt as to the pleasure I feel each time I receive new proof of your zeal and your friendship for our cause.

It appears that the rumors concerning the cession of the Spanish part of Haiti to France are without foundation; at least, they have been so until now.[18]

A new Captain General has arrived in that part of the island; he is Don Sebastian Kindelan,[19] replacing Don Carlos de Urritin. The former sent one of his superior officers for the purpose of announcing to me his appointment and arrival, as well as his desire to maintain the same relationships of amity and good neighborliness which have heretofore existed between the Kingdom of Haiti and the Spanish colony. However, shortly afterward,

---

[17] There is an interval of nearly a year and a half between this letter and the preceding one. Clarkson's letters of November 18, 1817, and March 4, 1818, are missing.

[18] When the patriots of Spanish Santo Domingo succeeded in driving the French from that part of the island in 1809, they dispatched a commissioner to Spain to announce the restoration of the colony to Spanish authority. In 1814, the Treaty of Paris gave formal approval of Spain's claim to the Spanish part of the island. Samuel Hazard, *Santo Domingo, Past and Present;* ... (New York, 1873), pp. 156–159.

[19] Don Sebastián Kindelan y Oregon (1763–1826).

I was informed that this new Captain General was offering, especially to Frenchmen, tracts of land for settlement and many other encouragements to persuade them to immigrate to the Spanish part of the island. It would seem then, judging by this new system which she has adopted, that Spain is attempting to raise her colony from its present state of decay, and that she certainly has no intention of ceding it to France. On the other hand, she appears to wish to arouse in us the alarm which must inevitably be inspired by the residence near our frontiers of these trouble makers. The French colonists would assuredly use every means within their power not only to perpetuate slavery in the Spanish part of the island, but also to sow the germs of dissension and revolt in Haiti, and by their intrigues to rob us of the peace which we at present enjoy. We are profiting by our precious moment of tranquillity to devote ourselves to the tasks which are the object of all our desires: education and agriculture, which alone can make our people numerous and happy. What conduct should we observe under such trying circumstances? Shall we allow our most cruel enemies to establish themselves at our very gates under the specious excuse of Spanish protection? And if this Captain General should give asylum and overt protection to our enemies, could he complain if we in turn should harbor and aid the Spanish revolutionists? As yet we have taken no such step, but we reserve the right to do so if necessary.

Your proposal that I should write to the Emperor of Russia, as to an illustrious and magnanimous champion of the Cause of the oppressed Africans and their descendants, begging His Imperial Majesty to use his influence in the Congress so as to thwart the designs of the French against Haiti, appeals to me a great deal; but would not this request be premature? Should not the ground first be prepared? I believe, my friend, that you might rather sound out further the disposition of that power. Some time after receiving your letter, I read in the public papers that five Russian ships and three frigates of the same nationality had put in at an English port on their way to Cadiz; I understood then that you were mistaken in your conjectures when you did me the favor of writing that Russia had refused to give vessels to Spain.

I have read with attention your comments on the case of Davidson. Our enemies eagerly seized upon that affair, representing it under false colors and inventing aggravating circumstances which did not exist. You will see all the details of the matter in a report written by Baron Dupuy,[20] my

---

[20] For Dupuy's report, see Appendix, pp. 273–275.

secretary interpreter,[21] which I am sending to you; and you will be able to judge the hatred and malignity of our enemies in thus attributing to me something of which I was entirely ignorant. Neither Davidson nor any of his compatriots complained to me of the type of punishment [the use of thumbscrews] meted out to him. The only person who brought the matter to my attention at Sans Souci was Mr. Strafford, an English merchant, who came to ask for Davidson's release, a request which I immediately granted.[22]

Though this sort of punishment is not authorized by our laws, nevertheless, in accordance with your suggestions, I have given special orders that it shall never be repeated. I am grateful to you for the part you played in this affair. Those responsible for the scandal were not only serving the cause of our enemies, but also were attempting to draw pecuniary profit from the situation by pretending that their business had suffered. It did not take long, after they had presented their petitions, to show unmistakably what had been the real purpose of their intrigues: they were trying to make their creditors believe that a few days' imprisonment had been the cause of their bankruptcy.

We read with the greatest interest the treaty signed in Madrid, whereby the final abolition of the slave trade is fixed for the year 1820. It would be impossible to commend too highly the generous sacrifices made by England in order to obtain from Spain conditions so favorable to the cause of humanity; all will redound to the glory of the great and noble British Nation, which is constantly giving to Europe and the world new proofs of its unselfishness.[23] Who could speak of it without the heartiest admiration? The measures which England has taken to insure that the treaty will have the most fortunate possible effects have shown us with what unusual interest she regards its full observance. When we read this document, our affection for your incomparable nation redoubles, and we realize what

---

[21] For an account of Baron Dupuy and his position in Christophe's kingdom, see pp. 44–45.

[22] Concerning this affair Clarkson wrote as follows in his unpublished Autobiography: "Certain persons, coming from Hayti to London, brought word that the King . . . had thumbscrewed one Davidson, an Englishman, and kept him in torture several days. This news found its way into our papers and was there magnified. It was magnified again by certain planters, who carried it into the House of Commons, where it created a great sensation. . . . During this excitement, I wrote to the King, informing him . . . how much it had injured him in London; that the English people could not bear cruelty in any shape; that the news of it would travel over the whole Kingdom in four days; and that just when he was beginning to stand well with this country, . . . he would sink into disgrace. I told him that the thumbscrew was an *instrument of slavery,* which ought never to be seen in his dominions."

[23] Spain formally agreed to abolish the slave trade by 1820, in return for an indemnification of £400,000 paid by England. England herself abolished the slave trade in 1807.

efforts we in turn must make in order to fulfill your hope of being some day able to raise up Africa to the level of European civilization, in spite of all the machinations, calumnies, and insults of our detractors.

We have not yet seen the treaty made with Portugal, but we fear that that power will not be disposed to grant such generous conditions. She still depends heavily on the profits of the odious trade, which nevertheless will be fatal to her Brazilian colony in the long run.

The latest letters we have received from Europe mention the fact that the French are still discussing the question of a new expedition against Haiti. We are further informed that the allied powers are considering or perhaps are on the point of withdrawing their troops from French territory, and even of diminishing the debt which that nation had in the treaties promised to pay by installments.[24] The new Minister of War, Gouvion Saint-Cyr,[25] has gone so far as to present a project, which was discussed at a meeting of Louis XVIII's Cabinet, concerning the means to be used against Haiti. I am convinced that if an attempt is made to carry out this plan, you will not fail to warn me and to give me the benefit of your advice.

Meanwhile, I am profiting by the tranquillity we at present enjoy to put into effect several projects, conceived long ago, but the execution of which had been prevented by the difficult circumstances in which we found ourselves. I refer to the sale of all the national domain of the Kingdom, which has already taken place. I am trying, insofar as I can, to augment the number of property owners by granting equally to all Haitians, whatever may be their rank or station in life, the right to purchase land, plantations, and houses. I have given special consideration to the heads of families and to the most laborious and deserving tillers of the soil. This measure has already had the most fortunate effects on our agriculture and has fulfilled all my expectations.

Farming has been greatly extended both by the increase in the number of proprietors and by the steps I have taken against men of no known profession, the idle and vagabond, who had taken refuge in the cities and towns where they were leading a useless and dissolute existence. By send-

---

[24] Metternich succeeded in making the future of France the chief business of the Congress of Aix-la-Chapelle. In October, 1818, the Congress determined that the evacuation of foreign troops from French soil should be accomplished by the end of November of the same year; and the greater part of the French debt was, in fact, canceled. In return France consented to join the Quintuple Alliance.

[25] Laurent Gouvion Saint-Cyr (1764–1830), one of Napoleon's marshals, became Minister of War under Louis XVIII in 1815, and was maintained in that post, except for a brief interval, until the assassination of the Duc de Berry in February, 1820.

ing them back to the land, I put them in a position to lead a securer life and one more profitable to public morality.[26]

Inspectors have been appointed to visit each farm and see that the fields are cared for, and that they correspond in extent to the number of arms which cultivate them. The inspectors are instructed to make sure that foodstuffs and grains have been planted in sufficient quantity to permit laying up a reserve, so that we shall not find ourselves in the penury in which we were left last year, when the hurricanes and too abundant rains caused in all the western islands food shortages, though these were not so severe here as elsewhere.

I greatly regret that it is still impossible for me to put into practice, as extensively as I should have liked, my favorite plan, that of returning the soldiers of the army to agricultural pursuits. In order to do this, I should have to be able to assure my fellow citizens positively that the measure would in no way endanger their safety; I should also have to persuade the soldiers that there is no further need for them to remain under arms. Nothing in the world, my friend, would give me as much pleasure as to be in a position to carry out in a determined and general manner this great plan of improvement. It is true that I have made a beginning, but only peace and security will permit pushing it through to a satisfactory conclusion.

When I read your letters and those of our mutual friends, when I see that our ideas are in perfect harmony and understand that these ideas—concerning the necessity of devoting ourselves wholly to agriculture, morality, public instruction, and religion—are capable of great extension, I cannot but bewail and deplore this imperious necessity which prevents the execution of my projects in their entirety. I repeat that I must have the positive assurance that England will recognize our independence, or will take some equivalent step such as promising that the French will undertake no expedition to blockade our ports and harass our territory, and also that Spain will not be permitted to cede her part of this island to our enemies, thus leaving the latter established at our rear.[27]

---

[26] Cf. p. 46.

[27] The possibility of the cession of the Spanish part of the island to France was to remain a constant source of uneasiness to Christophe, and it was not until two years later that Clarkson was able to give any positive assurance that Spain would not thus dispose of her colony. Writing to Christophe in April, 1820, Clarkson reported: "A revolution has taken place in Spain, in consequence of which the Government . . . has become a limited monarchy. According to the new constitution the King cannot sell, alienate, or dispose of any part of his territorial dominions either at home or abroad without the consent of the Cortes. I hope, therefore, that your Majesty's mind will now be at ease with respect to the Spanish part of Hayti, for I can never suppose that the Cortes will consent to dispose of it to France."

I do not find, my friend, in the letters of our friends—I look in vain for—this positive assurance, so necessary, so indispensable, that I may disband the army and persuade the soldiers that they should devote themselves to agriculture. Nevertheless, in order to consecrate without inquietude all our energies to the regeneration of our country (though this task may seem a hard one to foreigners, and though certain delicate points are in fact difficult to accomplish, I indeed do not find it an impossible undertaking), the Haitians must have this assurance, this guarantee, this perfect security, which alone can tranquillize them and free them of their dread of being again molested by the unexpected attacks of an enemy whom they know only too well through bitter experience.

We should never be willing to lay ourselves open to the same charges with which the Haitian people reproached the late Governor Toussaint, accusations which he merited because of having allowed himself to be surprised by the French at the very moment when he was assuring his compatriots that the French would send out no expedition, was disarming his troops, and sending them back to the farms. That unfortunate chief was the victim of his own errors.[28]

I am confident, dear Sir and Friend, that you will always continue to aid me with your sage advice and your wide knowledge, and beg of you that you will not fail to write to me as often as possible. Please believe me when I say that your letters always give me the greatest pleasure; each communication I receive from you serves only to increase the esteem, confidence, and perfect amity which you have inspired in me. It is with these sentiments that I subscribe myself, your sincere friend,

HENRY

---

[28] Christophe's statement appears to be an exaggeration. Toussaint had long feared an invasion. He had 20,000 men well armed and a plan of defense. Perhaps he diversified his troops too much and, as Christophe says, he had sent too many men back to agricultural labors, but the fact is that it cost the French two-thirds of their army to gain only a temporary victory. After three months' fighting across jungle and mountain they were glad to accept into the French army the services of Christophe and other Negro generals, and did not dare to begin immediately to disarm the Negro soldiers. After Christophe had capitulated to the French, he realized the advantages of guerrilla warfare; indeed, he remarked to one of the French generals: "If instead of fighting we had fled before you, and alarmed the negroes of the country, you would never have succeeded over us." J. Brown, *op. cit.*, Vol. II, p. 122.

LETTER
10
Thomas Clarkson to King Henry[20]

[No salutation]   *London, August 26, 1818*

It was with double pleasure after so long a silence that I received your Majesty's letter of the 26th of April last, and I shall endeavour to answer the contents of it in as clear and as frank a manner as I can.

I have read with satisfaction the report of the Baron Dupuy in the case of Davidson. The facts, however, which it contains were known to me before, and they have been all used to your Majesty's advantage. The noise has now happily blown over, and tho' you return me your thanks for the part I took in that affair, Mr. Wetherby, who is now at Vienna, is much more deserving of them. He was indefatigable while he was in England, in advocating your Majesty's cause not only in the case of Davidson but also against other calumnies which found their way into the English newspapers from France.... I cannot express to you with what pleasure I received your Majesty's assurance that the cruel instruments of punishment mentioned in my former letter were no more to be used in Hayti. Such instruments have been expelled from all free and enlightened countries. They are tolerated only in ignorant and barbarous places, or in the land of slavery....

You seem to me to have misunderstood the circumstances of the Russian ships of war, which lay for some time in our ports on their way to Spain. The King of Spain was then in great want of ships to send troops and stores to South America. He employed agents to buy them where they could find them.... A few old ships half rotten were found in the royal dockyards of Russia, which the Emperor had no objection to sell. These were bought and conducted by Russian officers and sailors to Cadiz. It was a simple bargain of accommodation on both sides, but the Emperor of Russia seems to have taken no part in the war between Spain and her Colonies, for the officers and crews before mentioned, having delivered up the vessels to the purchasers at Cadiz, returned to their own country....

---

[20] "For want of a proper conveyance to Hayti," this communication, an answer to the preceding one, was dispatched along with Letter 12 on October 30, 1818, more than two months after it had been written. See p. 120.

There does not now appear to be any disposition in France to send an expedition against Hayti. Your Majesty seems to have been alarmed on this subject by the proposal of Gouvion Saint-Cyr as detailed in the French papers. I saw this account myself, but I believed it to be a fabrication. If I had supposed it to be true, you may be assured that I would have given you timely notice of it. You seem also to have been alarmed at the report that the allied armies were to be withdrawn from France and that her debt to Europe was to be diminished. I believe it to be true that these troops will leave France before the end of the present year, but ... that a considerable part of them will be stationed close upon her frontiers, at least for another year. ... I believe the debt has been diminished a little but not much. Security has been taken for the payment ... upon certain Rentes in France, and this ... will keep France poor for some little time to come. ...

My reasons for supposing that France will not fit out an expedition against Hayti are much the same as those contained in my former letters, and Mr. Wilberforce and all our other friends agree with me on this subject. 1. Such an expedition would be unpopular in France, because it would be thought impracticable. 2. France has at present no money to spare for a foreign armament. 3. She has not ships sufficient in number to support it. 4. It is the opinion of many that there will be another revolution in France after the allied armies are withdrawn, so that the present Government would not think it prudent or even safe to send their soldiers from home into foreign parts. And 5. ... what interest can France have in regaining Hayti, when she has abolished the Slave Trade?

To enable your Majesty to judge more clearly of this matter I shall give you the following short account of the progress made within the last 4 years in the great work of the Abolition of the Slave Trade.

In the year 1814, when the allied Sovereigns made their first Treaty with Louis the 18th, that King yielding to the advice of his ... Cabinet and to the cries of the ex-colonists, *reserved to himself* the power of *continuing the Slave Trade for five years.* The reservation seemed so horrible and unjust that the whole English Nation rose up to express their public abhorrence of it. 1,370 petitions which were signed by 1,350,000 individuals were presented to the English Parliament, ... praying that this wicked part of the Treaty with France might be done away. ... The consequence was that at the Congress at Vienna, ... France ... agreed to give up this article of the Treaty. ... This agreement, however, was not followed ... by any royal decree; ... accordingly, French merchants continued their depredations on the coast of Africa.... In this state of things the English Government thought it their duty again to apply to the Court of France.... [Their] representations had the desired effect, for in the autumn of the year 1817, a royal ordonnance appeared which proclaimed that no French subject should for the future supply the French colonies with slaves.... The French merchants evaded it. They continued the trade, but under a new destination; they now avoided the colonies of the mother country, but supplied foreigners with slaves. In this manner the trade was still continued.... The Duke of Wellington at Paris... laid... [the facts] before Louis the 18th in person and requested that the royal ordonnance... of 1817 might be so amended as to answer the end intended.... Another royal decree... followed in January 1818, which made it unlawful for any French subject to be concerned at all in this odious traffic. In the month of April following, both... Chambers... confirmed this decree. It was then ordained that both ship and cargo should be forfeited, if taken, and that the captains and officers should lose the right... of navigating any French vessel for the future. From this moment the Abolition of the Slave Trade may be considered as solid and substantial on the part of France.... The English Government... [then] set on foot... a project for an allied maritime force to cruise on the coast of Africa, and to protect it from future ravages on the North of the Line, that is, from the great River Senegal to the Kingdom of Angola.... It is, therefore, understood that 12 or 13 ships of war are to be kept crùising in these seas for this noble purpose. In April last the King of France sent the Goélette, Iris, from Rochefort to Senegal where she captured two French slave vessels. This Goélette was followed by the Brig, Argus, from L'Orient, and... by le Moucheron from the Port of Toulon. These vessels are to watch the coast of Africa from the Senegal to the Gambia. Three English ships of war are now watching the coast from the Gambia to Angola, but as this is a vast extent of coast, I am told that other foreign ships of war are to join the English, and that these are to be fixed on by Russia, Austria, Prussia, Holland, Sweden, Denmark, Spain, Portugal, and others in conjunction....

If these things are so, what has your Majesty to fear from France with respect to Hayti? While France conducted herself in such a manner as to make us doubt her sincerity as to the abolition of this wicked traffic, you had just reason for alarm. But she has now pledged herself to this great measure. The Law for the Abolition of the Slave Trade is now recorded as a Law of France.... Hayti could not be useful to France unless France could send slaves to make new plantations there or reduce the Haytians themselves to slavery. To send slaves there would be to break the Treaty with Europe and to make slaves of the Haytians would be impossible. To suppose on the other hand, that France would make war upon Hayti for the sole purpose of extermination would be absurd; for besides her own immense loss of men and money in such an attempt of what use would Hayti be to France without its inhabitants?

I come now to a very delicate point noticed in your Majesty's letter. I agree with you that if England would acknowledge the Independence of Hayti, you would enjoy tranquillity, and that you would be able to disband a part of your troops and realize your great project of agriculture. But I fear that such a conduct on the part of the English Government, though very desirable, is not practicable at *the present moment*. If England were publicly to acknowledge the Independence of Hayti, I am sure she would give offense to the French Cabinet, with which she is at present in habits of friendship. Such a measure would be considered as a direct and public insult upon the French Nation, and I think would endanger the throne of the King himself, whose continuance there contributes towards the repose of Europe. The French are a high-minded, vain, and conceited people. They fancy themselves to be the greatest Nation upon earth and are infinitely jealous of everything that appears to affect their honour or their supposed greatness. Their cry against Louis the 18th ... is that he was put upon the throne of France not by the choice of his subjects, but by the bayonets of the English, and that he is even at this moment ruled by the English Cabinet. Hence he is unpopular in France.... The English name is unpopular there also....

I leave you to judge ... whether it is not probable that the acknowledgement of the Independence of Hayti by the English Government would be attended with bad consequences. I think the French Nation would consider it to be such an insult, that they would urge the King either to hostilities against England or against Hayti, and who knows whether he would be able to resist the tide of popular opinion.

But suppose that it would be impracticable at the present moment to obtain from the English Government the acknowledgement of Hayti, I do not see why that circumstance should hinder your Majesty from disbanding a part of your troops and transferring their labours to agriculture. In England we have a regular army, ... but besides ... [this] we have another armed force in the time of peace, which we call the militia. This latter force amounts to about 50,000 men. Every county ... furnishes its quota ... according to its population. ... Every regiment is called upon to assemble ... for one month in the year, which is always before the harvest begins. During this time they receive pay, but no longer. It is surprising what experience they gain in military tactics in this short time. At the end of the month they return home. ... In this manner they serve one month in the year for five years, when the time of their service is completed. I must observe, however, that though they are only called upon to assemble for one month in the year in the time of peace, they are liable to be called upon at all times of public danger, and in the case of war they are continued in arms as long as the war continues. Something like this might be adopted by your Majesty for the present. You might disband one-third or one-half of your army. You might give the disbanded soldiers certain portions of land, partly as a reward for their services, and partly on condition that they should assemble for one month in the year to keep up their military knowledge. ... By such a plan your Majesty might increase the number of your cultivators and yet not diminish the number of the defenders of your country.[30]

I am sorry to hear of the conduct of Don Sebastian Kindelan and of the Spanish Court in inviting Frenchmen in particular to settle in your neighbourhood. ... I hope it was a mere act of colonization without any intention of vexing you, and I am inclined to this opinion because the Spanish Government has invited foreigners of all countries to settle in Cuba, where it is not likely that such settlers can injure you. But whatever be the motive, I entreat your Majesty to be tranquil and to act with prudence and dignity in the occasion. I can show you that you have no just occasion for alarm from that quarter, and I think I can submit to you a proposition which will render you secure without bringing upon you the necessity of any measures that may be offensive to the Court of Spain. ... I hope you will find upon a more mature consideration of the subject, either that you have no just cause for alarm, or that you have the remedy in your own hands. Your Majesty should never lose sight of this noble idea that the Slave Trade may now be considered to be abolished. This idea should accompany all your reasonings, either as they relate to the affairs of Hayti, or as they relate to your connection with other countries in your own neighbourhood. Things are entirely altered there by this new event. ... In the first place there can be no extension of slavery (which is one of the things you fear)

[30] Within a year Christophe adopted Clarkson's suggestion for the distribution of land to the soldiers and stated that he intended to create a militia as soon as security warranted. See Edict of the King, pp. 268–271, and Letter 21, pp. 150–151.

in the Spanish part of the Island, except by birth, for the French settlers who are invited there, cannot now procure any more slaves from Africa. The Abolition of the Slave Trade has been agreed upon by all Europe. No French ship can carry them there. No Spanish ship can carry them there, except she brings them from the South of the Line, and this only till May, 1820. No Portuguese ship can legally carry them there at all, for though Portugal is allowed to carry on the Slave Trade for some time to come she is only allowed to do it under restrictions. She cannot take any slaves from Africa on the North of the Line, and she can only carry them to her own South American possessions.[31] Secondly, the new French settlers (whose residence in your neighbourhood is the thing you dread) can never become formidable to you in point of numbers, even if they should accept the invitation of the Spanish Captain General; for, not being able to get slaves, they cannot open any new plantations; ... and if a few miserable French settlers, without money or without the means of a livelihood, should attempt to raise disturbances in your part of Hayti, you have ... the remedy in your own hands. The first thing ... would be to complain of their conduct to the new Captain General, and to demand of him that they should be sent off the Island, and if he should refuse to listen to your complaints, you would then be justified in the eyes of all Europe, in attempting to punish them yourself.

It appears to me ... to be perfectly clear that if you wish to prevent the settlement of the French or of others in the Spanish part of Hayti, your Majesty has nothing to do but to prevent them from importing ... slaves there.... You will now probably ask me how you can prevent the importation of slaves into the Spanish part of Hayti.... You may fit out a small ship of war to watch this part of the Island, and to act as a magistrate by taking up all offenders, that is, by enforcing the agreement of the different Sovereigns of Europe.... I do not know whether there has yet been any friendly communication between your Majesty and General Boyer, the successor of General Pétion.[32] If there has been such an intercourse, permit

---

[31] In 1815 Portuguese subjects were prohibited from prosecuting the slave trade north of the equator, and Portugal agreed to abolish the trade entirely in 1823, the date later being extended to 1830. England paid £300,000 as compensation to Portugal.

[32] Just before his death in March, 1818, Pétion chose, with the consent of the Senate, Jean-Pierre Boyer, one of his generals and a mulatto like himself, to be the new president of the Republic. Boyer, fearing that Christophe might seek to profit by the unsettled conditions attendant on Pétion's death, strengthened border defenses and set out on a tour of inspection of his military posts. Christophe had watched with great interest the change in the leadership of the Republic, hoping that perhaps he might be able to reunite all of Haiti under his authority.

me to say that I think that both of you ought to agree not only upon some plan of defense against foreign invasion, but also upon fitting out, each of you, a small ship of war to prevent the landing of slaves in the Spanish part of the Island.... You will probably ask me ... whether, if you should adopt my proposition, you would not be giving offence to some of the powers of Europe.... You would only be doing what they themselves have agreed to do. You would only be assisting them in confirming and enforcing their own law.... To elucidate this, suppose that a ship of war fitted out by your Majesty were to capture an English slave ship off the Spanish part of Hayti, what would be the consequence? Would you by so doing involve yourself in a quarrel with the English Government? What damages could any English merchant or captain whose ship you had taken, obtain against you by making a complaint at home? None at all.... And this rule will, I believe, hold good in all cases except in the case of the capture of a Spanish slave ship. The Spaniards are allowed to supply their own possessions, and of course the Spanish part of Hayti till May, 1820; but you might even capture a Spanish vessel if you could prove that she brought her slaves from any part of Africa North of the Line.

I have submitted this proposition to your Majesty's serious and deliberate consideration. You will, of course, not ... put it into execution, even if you approve of it, till we have communicated again with each other. It is possible there may be some new law on the subject at the approaching Congress of Sovereigns at Aix-la-Chapelle, which will take place in about 2 months. Besides many things ought to be done, before you enter upon such a measure. You ought ... to acquaint the new Spanish Captain General with your intention. You ought also ... to issue a proclamation to the allied Sovereigns of Europe, stating not only your intention, but your motives, and also your determination to give orders to the officers you may employ to keep as close as possible in their cruises to the coast of Hayti, and not to go near any of the European Islands in the neighbourhood. This proclamation should appear in the London papers, from which it would soon find its way throughout Europe. If I should find from your Majesty's next letter that you are inclined to adopt my proposition, I will consult Mr. Wilberforce and your other friends, and we will give you our best advice

---

He had long given aid to the bandit chief, Gomar,—even making him Count of Jérémie,—to encourage depredations against Pétion in the Grande Anse district of the South Province. At about the time this letter was written, Boyer organized a force to destroy Gomar, but Christophe created a diversion by threatening an attack on Port-au-Prince, and Boyer was forced to abandon temporarily his campaign against Gomar.

how far you ought to go and how far you could count upon the protection of the English Government in such a case.

I am very much pleased to find that Messrs. Gulliver and Daniel, who were the bearers of my last letters to you, are likely to be useful in your schools. I hope to be able to hear an equally good account of Mr. Simmons, of whom the Committee of the Foreign and British School Society speak very highly both as to character and talent.

My friend, Mr. Allen, is going next week to St. Petersburg.... I wish he may arrive in time to see... [the Emperor] before he leaves... for Aix-la-Chapelle. Should he be so fortunate, I am sure he will endeavour to inspire his Imperial Majesty with an esteem for your character and with a regard for the prosperity of Hayti.

I am with esteem and best wishes

Your Majesty's friend,
THOMAS CLARKSON

LETTER
11
The Count of Limonade to Thomas Clarkson
{ENGLISH TRANSLATION}

KINGDOM OF HAITI

At Cape Henry, September 14ᵗʰ, 1818,
in the 15ᵗʰ year of our Independence

THE SECRETARY OF STATE,
Minister of Foreign Affairs of Haiti,[33]

to Mr. Thomas Clarkson

Dear Sir and Friend,

You will doubtless learn with regret of an accident which occurred at the Citadel Henry on the 25ᵗʰ of last August. A bolt of lightning struck a magazine, setting off some powder and a store of cartridges. The explosion destroyed most of the apartments and set the structure afire. Thanks to the heroic action of His Majesty, who hastened forthwith to the spot, followed by the officers of his General Staff, his personal guard, the troops of the garrison, and the inhabitants of the near-by towns, it was possible to arrest the progress of the fire. Most of the apartments of the interior of the Citadel's enceinte, which were exposed to the open air, were consumed; but the bombproof powder rooms, all the casemated batteries, and the supply magazines were preserved, suffering absolutely no damage. In short, and God be thanked, the Citadel still remains capable of offering a stout resistance.

The most cruel blow and the one which most afflicts His Majesty is the irreparable loss of his brother-in-law, Prince Noël, Duke of Port-de-Paix and Governor of the Citadel, as well as the destruction of a number of the brave officers and soldiers of the garrison. We have 159 of these deaths to bemoan.

---

[33] For an account of Count Limonade and his position in Christophe's kingdom, see p. 44.

I am acquainting you with these sad details so that you may reassure our friends; our enemies will not fail to represent this misfortune as infinitely more disastrous than it really was.

There is in our correspondence a break caused by the serious illness I have had and from which I have not yet fully recovered, but you may rest assured that His Majesty's sentiments toward you are still the same, that he continues to appreciate you as you merit, and that he is counting on you, your zeal, your friendship, and your devotion to his cause, to keep him informed of all developments which may interest him. You doubtless received letters from His Majesty carried by Mr. Thompson.

I have the honor of saluting you with highest esteem,

DE LIMONADE

LETTER
12
Thomas Clarkson to King Henry

[No salutation]   *Oct. 30, 1818*

Mr. Thompson having offered to take charge of any packet which I might have for your Majesty, I entrust him with this letter, and also with another which I had written to you in August last and which has lain there ever since for want of a proper conveyance to Hayti....

Understanding some time ago that several of the European Sovereigns would meet at Aix-la-Chapelle in the month of September to adjust the affairs of Europe and its dependencies, I determined to go thither in person to avail myself of my personal knowledge of the Emperor of Russia, and of the Duke of Wellington and Lord Castlereagh, the English Ambassadors there,... in order that I might procure, if possible, from the Congress ... some resolution which should give the finishing blow to the Slave Trade.

Your Majesty knows already that the Spaniards have bound themselves by Treaty to give up the Slave Trade entirely and forever after *May, 1820,* and that after this period no European nation can be legally engaged in it but the *Portuguese,* whose time for continuing it will expire *in 1823.* I wished, therefore, to persuade the Emperor of Russia and our own Ambassadors to try to obtain from Congress two resolutions: 1st, that the Portuguese should be obliged to give up the Slave Trade at the same time as the Spaniards, that is, after May 1820; and 2ndly, that if any persons of any nation should be found carrying on this bloody traffic after May 1820, they should be taken and punished as pirates....[34] I had a long and interesting interview with the Emperor of Russia. His Imperial Majesty told me in the most unequivocal manner that he approved of both my measures ... [and] that he would support ... [them] in Congress to the utmost of his power.

While I was at Aix-la-Chapelle I was not unmindful of your Majesty.... I was very earnest with the Duke of Wellington to inform me whether the French still entertained any design of invading Haiti. He said he believed

---

[34] The Congress of Aix-la-Chapelle did not pass either of these resolutions.

that they had given up that intention; for having given up the Slave Trade, they had now no motive for an invasion. It would be but of little advantage to them to possess Hayti unless they could stock it with slaves.... He assured me that the great families in France who had formerly an interest in Hayti, [and] who had been constantly urging the King and his Ministers to invade it under the hope of regaining their estates there, were now quiet. Finding to their disappointment that the Law for the Abolition of the Slave Trade had been passed ... they had now given up their estates as lost forever, and therefore they ... no longer took a part against Hayti.... He was informed, however, that the French Government intended to try to make a commercial treaty with General Boyer, the successor of Pétion, as the only thing they ever expected to gain from Hayti.... [This] throws light upon a paragraph which I read about a fortnight ago in a French paper, ... "that *General Boyer* had *made a proposal* to the French Government to pay an *annual tribute* to France, and to give *her all his commerce* provided France would acknowledge *him* and the *Independence of the territory* he possessed." Now, I do not believe the account as it stands in the French newspaper, ... for to pay an annual tribute is irreconcilable with Independence, but I do believe ... that the French will try, or that they have already tried, to gain the trade of General Boyer's part of Hayti, and that they would be very willing to acknowledge his Independence in return. I hope, however, that General Boyer will have sense enough to reject such a proposition. It would do him no good. It would bring you into trouble. It might ultimately be calamitous to both.

I return now to the Emperor of Russia.... I ... should have thought my journey to Aix-la-Chapelle very incomplete unless I had endeavoured to interest him in your Majesty's welfare also; and to do this with the more effect, I took the liberty ... of shewing him *confidentially* one of your letters to me,[35] which I had taken with me from England for that purpose. This letter produced upon his Imperial Majesty the effect I had anticipated. He expressed his obligations to me for having shewn it him; for he confessed it had given him new ideas both with respect to Hayti and to your Government. He had been taught by the French and German newspapers (and he had no other source of information) that Hayti was inhabited by a people little better than savages. He now saw them in a very different light. The letter which I had shewn him was a letter of genius and talent. It contained wise, virtuous, and liberal sentiments. It would have done honour to the

[35] The letter referred to is Letter 7 of this collection.

most civilized Cabinets of Europe. To see, said his Imperial Majesty, a person rising up in the midst of slavery and founding a free Empire was of itself a surprising thing, but to see him, in the midst of ignorance and darkness, founding it on the pillars of education under Christian auspices was more surprising and truly delightful. He hoped he should see the spectacle of a new Empire rivaling the whites in all that was great and good.

I replied that I was sure you would do great things for Hayti, but that you were crippled in your exertions by the fear of a French invasion.

The Emperor said it was undoubtedly true when the French expected a renewal of the Slave Trade for five years that they had in contemplation a diabolical attempt against Hayti, but since the five years had been given up, he had heard nothing of an expedition against that country; and he thought he should have heard something of it, if it had been seriously intended. He hoped and believed that nothing of this sort was in contemplation. . . .

I then told the Emperor what your Majesty had been doing. You had had it in contemplation to found a University. You had sent for professors of the languages, for ministers of the Gospel, and schoolmasters from England, and at this moment you had made such good use of the latter that the means of education were becoming general through your part of the Kingdom of Hayti. I then told the Emperor that you had many thousand men in arms, the greater part of which you wished to disband that you might put them upon farms, and thus make them useful in promoting agriculture and population, but that you dared not realize this, your favourtie idea, while you were in fear of an attack from the French Nation. . . . I earnestly entreated him, if ever an expedition should be seriously intended by the French against Hayti, to use his high influence . . . with the King of France to prevent it.

The Emperor said that he had just received a letter from Mr. Wilberforce on the same subject. He would not lose sight of it. Your good efforts . . . must not be allowed to be undone . . . He would speak to Lord Castlereagh and see what could be done in the affair. . . .

In my letter of August last I suggested to your Majesty that you might prevent the introduction of a population (that might be injurious to you) into the Spanish part of the Island, by cruising about and seizing all Portuguese slave ships *immediately,* and all Spanish slave ships after May, 1820, should such ships be found on the shores of your Island for such a purpose. This I suggested to you rather *to think* upon, than to act upon:

and indeed it would be wise to suspend all provisions of this sort, till we hear what Congress have done. . . .

I am happy also to inform you that there is a growing spirit of rational liberty among the French people, which cannot but be favourable to you. The greatest enemies you had in France were the Ultra Royalists; . . . but it is remarkable that in the late elections . . . not one of these has been returned to the Lower Chamber, but instead of them, several friends to liberty, and also friends to you and to the Independence of Hayti. Among these is my much esteemed friend, General Lafayette. Should the French Minister ever have it in contemplation to invade Hayti, this estimable man, with many others, will lift up their voices in the Senate against him. The greater number there are of liberal men in the Lower Chamber of the Senate in France, the more secure will your Majesty be from French invasion.

I cannot close this letter without recommending to your Majesty to consider whether an union with General Boyer is practicable. You best know what success your Proclamation[86] has had among the Haytians on his part of the Island. If they are not likely to come over to you, surely concord is better than variance. It is impossible to foresee human events. It is possible, however, that your union might be very useful against any attack from the Spanish side of the Island, and certainly it would be very useful against an attack on the part of the French. What I most fear is that if you should keep General Boyer in a state of fear or alarm respecting your own intentions, you will oblige him to have recourse to France for protection, though probably much against his will. In this case he will offer France his trade, but he will call upon her in return not only to acknowledge, but to *guarantee* his Independence; and if France should guarantee his Independence and your Majesty should afterwards see occasion to quarrel with him, he will call in the French to his assistance, and you will then see French armies finding a safe and easy passage through his territories into yours.

I remain with my best wishes

Your Majesty's friend,

THOMAS CLARKSON

---

[86] For details of this proclamation, see Letter 15, p. 130.

L E T T E R

13

Thomas Clarkson to King Henry

[No salutation]

[February 20, 1819]

...Having just received a letter from a friend of mine in the United States of America, I am desirous of making you acquainted with its contents.

It appears from that letter that there is a great number of *free* people of colour settled in different parts of the United States. I believe their number may amount to about 200,000. They live chiefly by their industry, and many of them have acquired property. There has been a general wish among the citizens of the United States that they should be sent to Africa, the land of their ancestors, to live there as an independent people, either under the protection of the American Government, or under a guarantee of the different Powers of Europe, that they shall not be molested there. But of late this opinion has been changed, and there seems to be now a desire that they should be sent to Hayti, provided they should wish to immigrate there, and provided that your Majesty and General Boyer would have no objection to receive them and to take them under your protection. Many meetings have been held by the friends of the Abolition in the United States, and are still to be held there, to take into consideration this important subject. I have thought it proper, therefore, to advise your Majesty of these circumstances, that in case any application should be made to you for this purpose, you may be put upon your guard.

There can be no doubt that such an immigration, if it consisted of persons of character, would very much add to your population, and of course to the security of your Dominions, but there is another point of view, in which it might be far more advantageous. If the American Government were to apply to you on this subject, you might stipulate to receive them, *provided the American Government would purchase the Spanish part of the Island* and cede it to you, but upon no other terms. I am told that the Spanish Ambassador to the United States is of opinion that his own Government would dispose of this part of the Island for this purpose. Spain would probably sell it to America, though she would not sell it to your Majesty.[37] Should such an event take place, it would take away one great cause of uneasiness from you. You would then have no fear of France, either by a direct invasion of Hayti, or by the settlement of Frenchmen on the Spanish part of the Island. I do not know whether this project of taking the free people of colour to Hayti will ever come to anything, but yet I thought it proper to apprise you of it.[38]

I felt myself obliged to your Majesty for desiring the Count de Limonade to inform me of the death of Prince Noël, because I always take an interest in what may concern you....

I am with great respect and regard, your Majesty's friend,

THOMAS CLARKSON

Since writing the above, I have had some conversation with Mr. Wilberforce, who is of opinion that you should not refuse to receive the free people of colour from the United States, provided the Government of the United States would buy the Spanish part of the Island for that purpose. I am very glad to find that Prince Sanders has been impressing the citizens of North America with a most favourable idea of your Majesty's character, both at Boston, New York, Philadelphia, and other parts, which has caused them to turn their attention towards you.[39]

---

[37] Nothing came of the plan for the purchase of the Spanish part of the island and its cession to Christophe. Even if the United States had been willing to agree to such a proposal (which seems most unlikely), a revolution in Spain in January, 1820, put an end to such a possibility.

[38] Although the death of Christophe brought to an end the project to settle free people of color from the United States in Haiti, nevertheless, as the subsequent letters show, Christophe did everything in his power to make possible the immigration of the American Negroes. Just before his death he prepared a formal agreement providing, among other things, a ship and a sum of $25,000 towards incidental expenses. Only his signature was wanting to set the plan in motion. See Letter 48, p. 226.

[39] In 1818, Prince Sanders published an American edition of *Haytian Papers*, "to excite a more lively concern for the promotion of the best interests, the improvement, the definite independence, and happiness of the Haytian People."

LETTER

14

King Henry to Thomas Clarkson

{ENGLISH TRANSLATION}

At the Palace of Sans Souci, March 20ᵗʰ, 1819,
in the 16ᵗʰ year of our Independence

THE KING,
to Mr. Thomas Clarkson,
Member of the African Institution

Worthy and respected Friend,

My confidence in your friendship and great knowledge leads me to send you a copy of a letter written by the French general, De Vincent,[40] to Count Limonade, my Minister and Secretary of State. There is also a copy of the reply which was made to De Vincent.[41]

When you read these two missives, I shall be greatly obliged if you will express yourself very frankly and tell me what you think of the matter.[42]

You will see that the French Government is looking for the means of sounding us out; but, before I undertake any negotiations, I am anxious

---

[40] General de Vincent, an ex-colonist, had played a prominent role in Haitian affairs during the period of Toussaint L'Ouverture's rise to power, as an emissary of the Directory of France and later of Napoleon. Enjoying the confidence of Toussaint, he remonstrated with the Negro over the flagrant provisions of the Constitution of 1801, but his efforts to effect any modification were unavailing. Ordered by Toussaint to present the constitution to Napoleon, Vincent did so and tried in vain to dissuade Napoleon from attacking Haiti in 1802. Since he was respected by both the French and the Haitians, he was in an excellent position to act as an intermediary between the French Government and Christophe. The latter once said to him, "You are the only Frenchman who loves the inhabitants of Saint-Domingue; all the others deceive them and work for their ruin." Thomas Madiou, *Histoire d'Haïti*, 3 vols. (Port-au-Prince, 1923), Vol. II, p. 96.

[41] Christophe did not send this reply to France because in the meantime his minister received a "more aggressive" letter from De Vincent. See Letter 18, p. 138.

[42] These letters are not among Clarkson's papers, but the import of De Vincent's communication is clear from the correspondence which follows. By early 1819 France, having given up all idea of reconquering Haiti by force of arms, determined to try diplomatic means. De Vincent's first letter, written in early 1819 at the instigation of the French Government, was an attempt, as Clarkson wrote, "to try privately how far your Majesty would be disposed to make any treaty" with France. See Letter 25, p. 159.

to have your advice and to profit by your wisdom. I shall be deeply grateful if you will write to me in your usual plain-spoken way, telling me what course I should follow in case the French Government proposes the signing of a treaty with us. You have long known my thoughts concerning the conditions under which Haiti would be willing to deal with France. My ideas were made public in my Declaration of November 20, 1816.[43] That is why I told you in a confidential letter that my dearest wish was to have England recognize the independence of Haiti before we listened to any proposal put forward by the French Government.

Since you, my friend, are fully acquainted with the politics of all those capitals which are interested in Haiti and know what is happening just now throughout Europe, your advice will be of unusual value to me under these circumstances. I shall await your answer with considerable impatience.

With sentiments of esteem, friendship, and deep regard,

HENRY

---

[43] See p. 60.

LETTER

15

King Henry to Thomas Clarkson

{ENGLISH TRANSLATION}

At the Palace of Sans Souci, March 20ᵗʰ, 1819,
in the 16ᵗʰ year of our Independence

THE KING,

to Mr. Thomas Clarkson

My Worthy and respected Friend,

I received with great satisfaction from the hand of Mr. Thompson your letters of the 28ᵗʰ of August and the 20ᵗʰ of November of the past year.[44] I have read them with lively interest, and I know not how to express to you all the gratitude I feel for the outstanding services which you never cease to render the cause of the Africans and the Haitians, their descendants.

In your communication of the 28ᵗʰ, you discussed the Spanish part of Haiti. Since I last wrote, nothing new has happened there, and you may be sure, my friend, that if anything worthy of my attention should occur, I shall be guided by your wise advice, and that under all circumstances I shall conduct myself with dignity and prudence.

Though it is only with the greatest grief that I can bear to see Spanish vessels engaged in the slave trade within sight of our coasts,[45] it is not my intention to fit out ships of war against them, because I should never wish to give our enemies any excuse for molesting us. You are aware that they watch our each and every action, and that nothing would make them happier than to find some way of discrediting us in the eyes of the world.

Your opinion and that of our mutual friends in England is that France is not at present in a position to undertake any expedition against Haiti.

---

[44] The two letters referred to are very probably Letters 10 and 12 of this collection, though the dates do not agree.

[45] Since Spain was permitted to carry on the slave trade until 1820, she continued to import Negroes into Spanish Santo Domingo.

The reasons you give me seem plausible; since the slave trade has been abolished, France would have nothing to gain by the conquest of this island; and, moreover, the expedition might well be unpopular in France.

You come then to a very delicate matter upon which I had until recently based my dearest hopes. If England had recognized the independence of Haiti, our tranquillity thus assured, I should have been able to carry out my great plan for general improvement and the development of agriculture. It is a plan which I cannot abandon, but I learn with distress that, for the reasons which you explain, England could *not just now* recognize publicly the independence of Haiti without antagonizing France.

Though what you have said brings me a certain degree of security, still it is all based on supposition. I can conceive of nothing which would re-assure me completely, except the support of England, and you demonstrate to me that she can do nothing openly in our favor. With respect to France, too, nothing is positive; the ultra-conservatives may at any moment triumph over the constitutional party, and should that happen, the ex-colonists would certainly again stir up the resentment of the French Government against Haiti. We therefore have at present no real guarantee in which we can have confidence. Nevertheless, you advise me, my worthy friend, to disband a portion of my troops in order to increase the number of those engaged in agriculture, and to organize a militia according to the English model. This measure has an unusual appeal for me. Even before the reception of your letter, I had already sent a certain number of soldiers—older men and the physically unfit—into agriculture; but I cannot yet risk dis-missing a large part of my army, without being able to give positive assur-ance to the nation that it will not be troubled by the French. Even so, I propose to bring up this great and salutary measure for discussion in my Council.

Public instruction is making steady progress. The Royal Chamber is zealously fulfilling its functions:[46] regulations for the organization and control of the national schools and academies have been drawn up,[47] and now we are considering the means of establishing new schools and making education available to all Haitians. In the publications which I am sending to you, you will learn of the present situation of the institutions of learning.[48]

[46] For the ordonnance establishing the Royal Chamber of Public Instruction, see Part III, Document 1, pp. 257–260.

[47] For this ordonnance, see Part III, Document 2, pp. 261–267.

[48] Since Clarkson forwarded the printed report on the national schools to the Emperor of Russia, it is missing from this collection. See Letter 19, p. 140. However, five national schools

Mr. Simmons, the young man whom you recommended to me, has been made master of the school in Gonaïves.

You ask me, my friend, if any communication exists between myself and General Boyer. The situation is this: upon receiving word of Pétion's death, I made overtures to Boyer in an attempt to bring about a reconciliation. I pointed out to him that justice, reason, and the best interests of the Haitian people all demanded *our union and the formation of a single government.* My efforts were unavailing, because ambition and the baser passions speak more loudly in corrupt breasts than the desire for the well-being of the nation. At least, I have the consolation of having done once more all that was in my power to reunite our country. You must have seen, in the proclamation dated from Saint-Marc,[40] the offers which I made to Boyer; but I must tell you, my friend, that in Port-au-Prince there exists a group of trouble makers from all parts of the world who always make every effort to mislead public opinion. These men take the greatest pains to intercept any writings which might inform the people concerning their own best interests.

We have heard that the French were trying to come to terms with Boyer, and there can be no doubt that they are still trying to carry on intrigues with him as they did with Pétion. I myself believe, as you do, that Boyer might well lead astray the unfortunate Haitians of that part of the island. He is the pupil and emulator of Pétion, and is following in the latter's footsteps. If you add to that fact the presence of the great number of Frenchmen of both colors who have taken refuge in Port-au-Prince, you may be able to judge the influence of the French party, and to understand how constantly I must be on my guard against what could happen there. I beg of you that, for your part, you will pass on to me any information which reaches your ear. I promise you that I shall take no step which might frighten Boyer and induce him to throw himself into the arms of the French. If he does anything of the sort, it will be of his own accord, since he is well informed of my intentions toward him.

---

taught after the British system were now in operation. The dates of their founding and the instructors are as follows:

October	1816	at Cape Henry	under T. B. Gulliver
April	1817	at Port-de-Paix	under T. Papillon
May	1817	at Sans Souci	under J. Emmanuel
May	1817	at Gonaïves	under W. Simmons
November	1817	at Saint-Marc	under T. Duchèsne

Cf. Baron de Vastey, *op. cit.,* Appendix, p. cxvi.

[40] For Christophe's proclamation and letter, as well as the indignant refusal of the Republic, see Vergniaud Leconte, *op. cit.,* pp. 409–412 and 453–454; and Baron de Vastey, *op. cit.,* Appendix, pp. cvi–cxi.

How can I express to you, my friend, the satisfaction I felt upon reading in the public papers that you had gone to the Congress of Aix-la-Chapelle. I was immediately sure that it was only your indefatigable zeal in the defense of our cause which called you to that meeting of the Sovereigns of Europe. It was with the greatest emotion and the most lively interest that I read of the gracious way in which the noble and magnanimous Emperor of Russia had received you; my pleasure was extreme to note his conduct, reflecting an attitude which honors both that illustrious Sovereign and you, my worthy friend. The conversations you had with Emperor Alexander, the letter of mine which you showed him and which His Imperial Majesty communicated to Their Majesties, the Emperor of Austria and the King of Prussia, all were extremely flattering to me and made me understand the intensity of your concern for all that concerns Haiti. The information you received from Lord Wellington and Lord Castlereagh confirmed my already high opinion of these noble gentlemen. We surely have cause for great hope when we see the cause of the unfortunate Africans defended and furthered by the most illustrious men of Europe.

In accordance with the suggestion made in your last letter and with what I have read of the generous character of Emperor Alexander, I have decided to write a letter to His Majesty, Emperor of all the Russias.[50] I am sending you this dispatch unsealed; please read it, my friend, and if you judge that it may be sent on to him, I beg of you to forward it to its destination.

I cannot end this letter without expressing again to you, my true and worthy friend, all the thankfulness I feel, not only for what you have done for the general cause, but for the aid you have given us in particular. The frankness, wisdom, and sound advice that I find in your letters are most precious to us. Please continue your support, and our gratitude shall be limitless.

HENRY

---

[50] See the next letter in this collection.

LETTER
16
King Henry to the Emperor Alexander
{ENGLISH TRANSLATION}[51]

To his Imperial Majesty of all the Russias

Sire,   [March 20, 1819]

Fame has spread to the most distant countries the report of the noble and generous feelings with which your Imperial and Royal Majesty is inspired towards all nations. This universal benevolence has excited my admiration, which has been increased by the accounts I have received from my worthy friend, Mr. Clarkson, of the humane and beneficent disposition of your Imperial and Royal Majesty towards the unfortunate Africans and their descendants, the Haytians; my gratitude and respect for your virtues have inspired me with the desire of addressing this letter to your Imperial and Royal Majesty as a tribute which I feel justly due.

I have always believed that a Sovereign so enlightened, just, and humane, who in the midst of his conquests and victories gave the strongest proofs of justice and moderation, must take a lively interest in the situation of the Haytians, that unfortunate people who have risen from the midst of ignorance and barbarous slavery to the rank of a free and independent nation, after having experienced the greatest misery and misfortune, and I am happy to see my hopes realized.

Your Imperial and Royal Majesty must be undoubtedly aware of the events which have taken place in this country during the last thirty years; it may, however, be well to revive in your memory the steps which have led the Haytians to liberty, and from liberty to independence.

I shall not fatigue your Imperial and Royal Majesty with the afflicting details of the deplorable situation in which this nation was plunged before the period of its freedom. How it groaned under the yoke of the most frightful slavery is well known to the world; the recital of its long misfortunes and the picture of the horrible tortures that it experienced under

---

[51] This is Clarkson's translation of Christophe's letter to Emperor Alexander, the original of which was forwarded to the Emperor.

the colonial government for more than a hundred and fifty years would only wound your magnanimous and generous soul. I therefore hasten to the period in which general liberty was proclaimed by the agents of the French Government in 1793 and afterwards sanctioned by a legislative act of France herself [and] maintained for twelve years by mutual and uninterrupted intercourse, communication, and correspondence between the two countries.

During these twelve years of liberty which the people enjoyed with the French Government, the virtuous general, Toussaint L'Ouverture, then Governor of the Island, established laws, morality, and religion; under his paternal administration, commerce, agriculture, and industry flourished, and the European planters were not only protected but respected in their habitations. The people had given unequivocal proofs to the Metropolis of their attachment and devotedness, making it triumph over its numerous enemies, after having braved misery, famine, and privations of every kind. Full of confidence in the French Government, the Haytians were far from anticipating that after they had shed their blood in her service France would reward their constant attachment and fidelity by depriving them of liberty twelve years after she had granted it [to] them.

At the time the peace of Amiens was negotiated, we imagined ourselves in the utmost security and were so far from apprehending the misfortune which threatened us, that the Governor, Toussaint L'Ouverture, had sent almost all his troops to agriculture, flattering himself that he should enjoy in the midst of his family and fellow citizens the fruit of his glorious labours, when a formidable army suddenly overspread the country, sent with the criminal intention of destroying a peaceable and defenseless population, or to plunge it again into the horrors of slavery.

Your Imperial and Royal Majesty would scarcely credit this excess of injustice and perfidy, had you not yourself sorrowfully experienced it. But the French were not satisfied with coming upon us as armed men; in order to secure the success of their expedition they took shameful and perfidious means to deceive the people. The proclamation of the French Government declared *you are all equal and free before God and the Republic*—whilst its intentions and formal orders were for the establishment of slavery or our entire destruction; the people, deceived by these fallacious promises and also long habituated to consider themselves as Frenchmen, gave themselves up without resistance; but scarcely had they extended their dominion by cunning and persuasion, scarcely was Governor Toussaint dismissed from command, when they seized him by the blackest treason in the retreat where he was confined, took him away with his family and a great number of his fellow soldiers, and transported them to France, where the unfortunate chief with these unhappy victims worthy of a better fate ended their days in dungeons and galleys. From this moment slavery was proclaimed, a signal for proscription and massacre was given, gibbets were raised in all parts, funeral piles, bloodhounds, and the most horrible punishments were used to exterminate us. Your Imperial and Royal Majesty cannot form a just idea of the atrocities and horrors that have been committed. None but those who have witnessed the scene can believe them. The barbarities exercised by the French upon the Haytians have surpassed all the crimes of destruction in the new world.

After fighting many battles and at the expense of rivers of blood, we have driven these oppressors from our borders notwithstanding all their efforts; and to secure ourselves from the repetition of such unheard of barbarities and crimes, such injustice and perfidy, the people of Hayti in a general assembly proclaimed their Independence the 1st of January, 1804! During sixteen years that the nation has enjoyed independence, it has advanced rapidly towards civilization and is continually improving its social situation.

As soon as the reins of government were consigned to me, it became my first care to give my fellow citizens a code of laws suited to their wants and to their morals. I then felt the necessity and advantage of public instruction in order that the virtues incalculated by religion and morality might be practiced in their families, and in order that they might appreciate the benefits of liberty. For this purpose I requested my English friends to send me schoolmasters, professors, and artists in order to diffuse the arts and sciences. In viewing their progress I already gather the fruits of my labour. By the encouragement that I give to marriage and protection to good morals, I have the satisfaction of seeing a sensible amelioration every day in our situation. Ignoble vices, depraved morals, the bitter fruits of slavery and ignorance, disappear or scarcely dare to show themselves.

Agriculture has received all possible encouragement by the multiplicity of farms; commerce and industry prosper, labour is honoured as the source of all blessings.

I trust that the motives which inspire me will influence your Imperial and Royal Majesty to excuse this apology for my labours. Too long has the African race been unjustly calumniated. Too long has it been represented as deprived of intellectual faculties, as scarcely susceptible of civilization or government by regular and established laws: these false assertions spring from the avarice and injustice of men who have had the impiety to degrade the finest work of the Creator, as if mankind had not one common origin. These persons attribute to difference of colour that which is only the result of civilization and knowledge. The religious principles and superior intelligence of your Imperial and Royal Majesty enable you to feel better than I can express these eternal truths, and when in the Council of the Sovereigns of Europe you condescended to speak in favour of the oppressed Africans, you proved to the world that your noble heart was penetrated with the sublime truth of morality and religion. In the effusion of my gratitude and the admiration with which the virtues of your Imperial and Royal Majesty have inspired me, I thought that I could not do better than address myself to the most illustrious protector of the African cause, that I might open my heart to him, tell him the situation of the people who have confided their destiny and dearest interests to me, and disclose to him my projects for their happiness.

In the bloody contest which your Imperial and Royal Majesty has had to support against the unjust aggression of France, we have not ceased to offer our prayers for the success of your arms, and we cherished the hope that when a general pacification took place in Europe, the people of Hayti would have partaken with the other nations in the blessings of peace, instead of which for sixteen years we have been obliged to be continually on the watch until our independence should be acknowledged by France.

When the Government of France was changed, we hoped that the Cabinet of his Majesty Louis XVIII would have been directed by principles of moderation, justice, and humanity, and that he would have acknowledged the independence of the people of Hayti, but it was a vain hope! He *openly showed* his disposition to make use of the same system of duplicity and perfidy that the preceding Cabinet had employed; Europe knows that without the latter events which have taken place we should have had to sustain a war of extermination with France!

I shall not suffer myself to enlarge further on the subject. I fear that I have already trespassed on the precious time of your Imperial and Royal Majesty. I believe I have sufficiently informed you of our situation to authorize the hope that you will grant your powerful and generous protection and benevolence to the cause of the unfortunate, oppressed Africans, and of the good and interesting people of Hayti. It is in their name that I have the honour of addressing myself to your Imperial and Royal Majesty and that I beg you to accept the testimony of our great respect and gratitude and of the admiration which we feel for your virtues.

HENRY

LETTER
17
Baron de Vastey[52] to Thomas Clarkson
{ENGLISH TRANSLATION}

Dear Sir,   *At Cape Henry, March 24th, 1819*

Mr. Birt has been so kind as to offer to deliver my correspondence, so I am taking advantage of the opportunity to write you this letter. Since the ship is to sail for England tomorrow morning and my health is not at all good just now, lack of time and of strength will prevent my expressing myself as fully as I should wish to have done with a person like yourself, my dear Sir, who has always shown himself to be the sincere friend of humanity and the zealous champion of the unfortunate Africans and the Haitians, their descendants.

I have never for a moment forgotten the wise advice you gave me in your last letter, and I can hardly find words to express my gratitude. I beg of you, Sir, to continue enlightening me with your counsel. You can never write at too great length about anything related to our national interests; nor will you ever be able to realize what an eminent service you render us when you explain the underlying principles of government and guide us along the paths of wise and good policy.

"Sound counsel," says the proverb, "is worth a thousand men." Each time I reread your letter I again appreciate the truth of the axiom.

I have the honor of presenting you with a copy of my "Political Reflexions,"[53] as a small token of my respect and admiration for you. The book is drawn from my observation of the internal and external situation of Haiti. You will understand my motives and will appreciate my fears and hopes. I beg your indulgence toward the errors which the work must contain in large numbers; you will surely pardon me in the light of my good will and inexperience.

---

[52] See p. 44 for an account of Baron de Vastey.
[53] De Vastey refers to his *Réflexions politiques sur quelques ouvrages et journaux français concernant Hayti* (Sans Souci, 1817).

It is certainly unnecessary for me to urge upon you the importance of your concern for the cause of Haiti and of the aid which I am requesting so insistently, for you know even better than I do what serious consequences *a grave political blunder* can have. Since I may, any day now, find myself forced to make a decision, your wise suggestions will be infinitely precious to me.

I have the honor of sending you along with this letter a report on the national schools which are already functioning. We intend to establish a school in each parish. You will also receive the King's proclamations regarding public instruction.

With renewed assurances of my profound respect and veneration, I have the honor of remaining, Sir,

Your most humble and obedient servant,

BARON DE VASTEY

LETTER

18

King Henry to Thomas Clarkson

{*ENGLISH TRANSLATION*}

*At the Palace of Sans Souci, this 8ᵗʰ of June, 1819,
in the 16ᵗʰ year of our Independence*

THE KING,

*to Mr. Thomas Clarkson,
Member of the African Institution*

Worthy and respected Friend,

With one of my letters of the 20ᵗʰ of last March I sent you a copy of a letter from the French general, De Vincent, addressed to Count Limonade, my Minister and Secretary of State. I also sent the reply which had been made to De Vincent. Scarcely had my missive to you been dispatched, when my Minister received another communication from the same general, much more aggressive than the first one. For that reason I judged it best not to send to General de Vincent the answer which had first been prepared.

I am now sending to you, along with the present letter, a copy of General de Vincent's second communication, as well as the reply which I had drawn up and which will be dispatched very shortly.[54]

---

[54] De Vincent's "much more aggressive" letter, which was dated February 17, 1819, and Limonade's reply have not come to light, but it is easy to surmise their contents. Following his first communication, which was designed to discover how far Christophe was amenable to any overtures from France, De Vincent now obviously offered him "a constitutional regime," but his letter certainly revealed France's intention not to relinquish the sovereignty of Haiti.

"I am sorry to find," Clarkson says in referring to this letter, "that General de Vincent should have shown himself ... far more friendly to the interests of France than to the interests of Hayti. If Hayti is not to be allowed to be independent, what is she to be? She must either be an independent kingdom or a vassal of France. I know of no medium between the two situations."

Clarkson went on to say: "It is, therefore, with peculiar pleasure that I have read the copy of the answer of the Count de Limonade on this subject. Your Majesty has replied, through him, in a frank and open manner. You have been firm and courageous. You have maintained your dignity and asserted your independence." Limonade's letter undoubtedly reaffirmed the stand taken by Christophe in his declaration of November 20, 1816, in which he declared that he would not negotiate with France "on any other footing than that of power with power," and that the preliminary basis of any negotiation must be the unqualified recognition of the independence of the whole of Haiti. This letter, expressing Christophe's inflexible attitude, was the only communication actually sent to De Vincent. See pp. 60–61 and 159.

I am again asking you, my friend, as I did in my letter of March 20th, to express yourself very frankly and tell me what you think of the matter. I need your advice and the wisdom of your experience, and shall await them with the anxiety which the seriousness of the subject justifies.

Allow me to renew, my friend, my best wishes for your good health and the assurance of my esteem, friendship, and veneration.

HENRY

LETTER

19

Thomas Clarkson to King Henry[55]

June 28, 1819

[No salutation]

I received your Majesty's letter of the 20th of March, which was conveyed to me by Mr. Birt.

I read with interest and satisfaction the letter which you enclosed to me for the Emperor of Russia. Nothing could have been more proper. I sent it without delay to Count Lieven, his Imperial Majesty's Ambassador in London, and also your printed list of the National Schools in Hayti. I wrote also a letter to the Emperor.... Since that time I have received an answer from Count Lieven, in which he promises that he will forward my packet in the very first dispatches which go to Russia.

I have the pleasure of informing you that our great cause, the Abolition of the Slave Trade, is in a progressive state. The Spanish Slave Trade will now soon be at an end. That of Portugal will then only remain. In November last the Sovereigns who were assembled at Aix-la-Chapelle did not think it right to adopt at once the severe measure of making this Trade piracy, but they determined to call the attention of the King of Portugal towards it, and accordingly they wrote to him an affectionate letter, signed by their own hands, conjuring him to give up, as the rest of Europe had done, this execrable Trade. In March last a new event occurred in our favour. The Government of the United States had long ago decreed the Abolition of the Slave Trade, and they punished such of their citizens as they found violating the Law at home, but they never followed up the decree, as the English have done, by arming cruisers, with a view of punishing those who violated it abroad. This error they have now repaired; for in March last they passed an Act, by which they voted 100,000 dollars for equipping vessels of war to capture their own slave vessels, wherever they

---

[55] This letter was confided to the care of Mr. C. Davis, who was about to depart for Haiti. However, the boat went down at sea and both Davis and his wife perished. Clarkson sent a duplicate of this letter by Mr. Birt, who was likewise shipwrecked just before his arrival in Haiti. This time the crew survived, and the letter was delivered late in November, 1819. See p. 164.

could find them on the high seas. Their vessels are to go to the Coast of Africa and other parts of the world for this purpose.

On the 20th of February last I wrote to your Majesty concerning a plan, which was then in agitation, of sending the free people of colour who live scattered about in different parts of the United States of America, to Hayti.... That unhappy distinction between black and white, which originated in the execrable Slave Trade, follows them wherever they go except among the more liberal and religious, so that though they are citizens of the United States, they are looked upon in a degraded light. They are also subject to be stolen, ... dragged away privately, ... and sold into slavery in the southern states of America, though the law would punish the aggressors if they were found out. Their situation being such, a number of worthy persons in the United States, friends to the Abolition of the Slave Trade, formed themselves into Societies, some years ago, for their protection. These Societies have been accustomed ... to send deputies every three years to hold one common meeting ... at Philadelphia. Here they report everything that has come to their knowledge relative to these poor people, and here also they resolve upon such new measures as they think most likely to improve their condition. The last of these Triennial Conventions took place at Philadelphia in December last (1818).... It seemed to be the opinion of the deputies ... that the most satisfactory and permanent way of providing for the free people of colour would be to send them to Hayti, provided they were willing to go there and provided your Majesty or General Boyer would be willing to receive them and to grant them lands and citizenship. It was resolved accordingly that the President, Mr. Richard Peters, Jr., "should open a correspondence with influential and philanthropic individuals in Europe on the present state of Hayti to promote such arrangements as will render that Island a safe asylum for such free people of colour as may choose to immigrate there."

In consequence of this resolution, Mr. R. Peters has opened a correspondence in England on this subject.... I wrote him a letter ... [and] advised ... [him] not to think of obtaining information relative to Hayti from England, but to assemble the Convention ... and to recommend to it to send one or two persons on whom it could rely direct from Philadelphia to Hayti, to communicate in person with your Majesty there. I assured him that you would receive these deputies and converse with them with your usual frankness: that you yourself would give them all the information they desired and much more than they could get in England, and that you would treat them with all due respect and attention, not only on my account, but because you had a regard for all those who were the friends of Africa and their descendants. I told him also that, in order to remove all difficulties, I would inclose him a letter of introduction to your Majesty.... This letter I wrote accordingly....

The whole matter ... resolves itself into two questions. The first is whether the immigration of the people of colour to Hayti is to be on a large and unlimited scale, that is, whether they are all willing to go there, either now or at a future time,... so that Hayti may be considered as the constant asylum for all such free people of colour as may be inclined to immigrate there from the United States. In this case your Majesty would have a right to stipulate that the American Government should buy the Spanish part of the Island, and cede the whole of it to you, or a part of it, according to the proportion of population you should be willing to receive; and I have no doubt that the American Government would be willing to treat with the Spanish Government for this purpose. This stipulation, if acceded to, would be of great advantage to your Majesty, because you would then be relieved from all fear either from France directly, or from France buying the Spanish part of Hayti and colonizing it with Frenchmen.

The second question is whether the immigration before spoken of will be only upon a small and limited scale.... In this case I think that the American Government ... would not consent to purchase the Spanish part of Hayti.... It is, therefore, for your Majesty to consider how far you would be willing to take ... [a limited] number ... without the compensation of the Spanish part of the Island.

It must be obvious, however, at the first sight that such an addition to your population would strengthen your own Government both at home and in the eyes of foreigners, and of France in particular. You would also be able to realize more rapidly your project of introducing the English language into Hayti because all the free people of colour speak that language. Many of them also would be very valuable to you because they are skilled in different trades; and if only two-thirds of them were to be put upon farms, cultivation would be going on to a considerable extent, while you would not be obliged to disband your present military.

There is one consideration particularly worthy of your Majesty's most serious attention.... If you yourself should be unwilling to receive the free people of colour without the stipulation in question, it is probable that General Boyer would be glad to take them upon any terms, and that he would thus be making a very formidable addition to his population, which you would not like to see in your own neighbourhood.

I come now to a very important part of your Majesty's last letter, and I only wish that I had the ability to answer it either to your satisfaction or to my own. I told you, ... upon the authority of the Duke of Wellington, that the French Government had given up all idea of making a conquest of Hayti, but that an attempt was to be made to obtain its trade by means of some treaty to be proposed. General Vincent's letter, a copy of which you sent me, seems in some degree to confirm this statement, but I am more convinced of the truth of it by what passed a few days ago in the Chamber of Deputies in France. On Monday, June the 7th, a discussion took place there relative to the sums of money to be voted for keeping up the French Marine and Colonies. Among those who spoke was Monsieur Laisné de Villevêque,[56] who in the course of his speech alluded to Hayti. He gave it as his opinion "that if a constitutional regime were offered to the Blacks there (I use his own words) the Government might succeed in restoring to France the Colony of St. Domingo, formerly so flourishing." The Minister of Marine and Colonies immediately rose up.... "He deprecated any allusion of this nature on account of the delicate situation of the relation of France with Hayti." I judge from this very short conversation either that the French Ministers had at that moment some proposal in view which they intended to make to your Majesty and General Boyer relative to your commerce, or that they had already sent off to you, or to both of you, some proposal to that effect, which was then on its way to Hayti. But whether my conjecture be right, or whether it be wrong, I am persuaded that though the French Government has wisely abandoned the idea of using force against Hayti, it will never give up the idea of having some right to the advantages of its commerce; and as money is to be voted every year in the French Chamber of Deputies for the expense of the Marine and Colonies, I feel certain that whenever this vote is proposed, some Deputy, like Monsieur Laisné de Villevêque will rise up with some resolution or other unfavourable to the Independence of Hayti. It is, therefore, evident to me that sooner or later some proposal must be made to your Majesty by the French Ministry on this subject; and I think it would be proper for your own peace of mind to set the matter at rest by speedy determination on your part either to refuse or to agree to a treaty with the French Government. I confess my own inability to advise you for the best in this affair. I will, how-

---

[56] Gabriel-Jacques Laisné de Villevêque (1767–1851), who was elected to the Chamber of Deputies in 1817, as a Liberal candidate.

ever, throw out a few ideas for your consideration, after which your Majesty will adopt your own course.

I shall begin by taking it for granted that your Majesty proposes to adhere to the grand fundamental proposition laid down in your Declaration of the 20th of November, 1816: that you will make no treaty with France but upon the acknowledgement of the Independence of Hayti; that this treaty shall be conducted on both sides after the manner and usage of two independent nations; and that this treaty shall not be considered as valid until it be guaranteed by the English Government.

I may now observe, that there can be but two kinds of treaty between your Majesty and the Government of France. You must either admit France to a *participation* of your commerce with other nations, or you must admit her to a *monopoly* of your commerce, and thus exclude all other nations from it. Let us suppose for a moment that you offer her the first kind of treaty.... I think that the French Government ought to be satisfied with [such] a treaty.... It would be unreasonable in France to expect that you should abandon an intercourse with those nations with whom you have been long on friendly terms and whom you have had reason to esteem. Let it be remembered, also, that at this moment no French vessel is allowed even to enter your ports and no Frenchman ever to land upon your soil. The permission, therefore, of these to come and trade with you must be a great change in favour of France.... Now I am sure that England, if called upon, would very readily guarantee such a treaty as this, for France having once acknowledged the Independence of Hayti (which she must do before she could obtain the treaty), England would feel no indelicacy nor fear of offending an ally by seconding it; and besides, England would have an interest in the guarantee, as your Majesty would have reserved for her a part of your commerce. You would be placed then in very happy circumstances if all these objects could be realized. You would then have a treaty on an equitable basis. You would have given to France a part of what she considered to have been forever lost. You would not have offended any of your former friends. You would have secured the acknowledgement of your Independence, and you would have obtained a powerful guarantee at the same time....

Now ... suppose that France, not satisfied with a participation of the commerce of Hayti, would insist upon a monopoly of it, and that you would agree to the demand. In what situation would your Majesty then stand? In the first place you would have turned your back upon your old connections.... Should a war arise between England and France, many of the vessels which supply you with articles of trade would be captured, and you would not be able to replace their cargoes from other parts. Perhaps your very ports would be blockaded. You would have gained, indeed, the acknowledgement of your Independence, as it relates to your Government; but you would have lost your Independence, as it relates to your commerce. But how could even the Independence of your Government be secured to you without a guarantee? and with what hope could you ask England to guarantee it, if you should have excluded her from the advantages of your commerce?

Your Majesty will see by the foregoing statements that there would be a very material difference between the effects of the two treaties. At the same time, I candidly acknowledge that if the salvation of Hayti, that is, the preservation of her Independence as it now exists, *could be really secured, and could only be really secured, by granting to France a monopoly of your commerce, I would advise your Majesty to grant it:* for what is England or any other country to you compared with your own Independence and the liberty and happiness of your people?

The great difficulty which I see in a treaty which should give to France a monopoly of your favours would be in finding a guarantee for it on the part of England; and yet I think there are circumstances which might induce England, even though you excluded her from your commerce, to become a party to such a treaty. You are well acquainted with the internal situation of our West Indian Islands. They are peopled by men who have been robbed of their liberties and who by the laws of nature have a right to regain them, if they can. Our Islands, therefore, are full of combustible materials, and you have only to apply a candle to them to set them on fire. Any King of Hayti, if he had the resources of a powerful population, could command their destruction at any time. Our Government knows this. Our West India merchants and planters know it also; and hence the latter have a jealousy and fear of your Majesty's rising greatness. I am of opinion, therefore, that though you should exclude England from your commerce, her Government might be induced to guarantee a treaty of monopoly with France, provided you would bind yourself in the same treaty not to molest any of our West Indian Islands as now established....

If your Majesty should make a treaty with France, *but particularly an exclusive one,* I think you ought to stipulate: 1. that no French troops should ever be allowed to land on any part of the Island of Hayti; 2. that no French ship of war should be allowed to enter its ports, except it should bring dispatches to your Majesty or be forced there by want of provisions or stress of weather; and 3. that you should be allowed to be neuter in case of war. I think the name of Hayti should be used in the treaty (and not that of St. Domingo) because the former name acknowledges and identifies the Island in its new situation and under its new kind of Government. I am of opinion also that your Majesty would do well to make it a fundamental law of the realm (and this immediately) that no Europeans should purchase land or reside in the interior ... of the Island. It is sufficient if you allow them to make purchases and to reside at Cape Henry or other maritime places for the purpose of carrying on their trade; but if you have no such fundamental law it is possible that the French, when once admitted into your maritime towns, ... might, under the pretence of examining, purchasing, and cultivating land for plantations, creep out of the towns and spread themselves by degrees in your villages, for the real purpose of overthrowing the Government. Now the term *Europeans* would include the French, though it would not have the hateful appearance of being levelled against them in particular; and if this were made a fundamental law of Hayti before you entered into a treaty with France, the French Government would be obliged to respect it as a law of the realm, existing when she acknowledged your independence.[57]

I would advise your Majesty, when you have made up your mind on this subject, to draw up the outlines of such a treaty as you would be willing to make with France, and to send these outlines in a Letter to Mr. Wilberforce, and to desire Mr. Wilberforce and Mr. Stephen conjointly to show them to our Government and to inquire how far it would be willing to guarantee such a treaty. I am sure they would do their utmost to procure for you a favourable answer, and your Majesty would then know on what you had to depend, and you might act accordingly.

I am very much pleased to find that Prince Sanders has been representing your Majesty's Government in a very amiable light to the citizens of Boston, New York, Philadelphia, and other places, the consequence of which I hope will be that they will be disposed to offer you a very considerable part of the population of the free people of colour, should they be sent to Hayti.

[No signature]

---

[57] Almost as soon as Christophe received Clarkson's suggestion, he acted upon it. Writing to Clarkson he said, "I thoroughly approve the steps to be taken relative to the property which the ex-colonists might attempt to acquire, should a treaty be signed with France.... My two Councils will shortly be called ... and ... the situation will be clarified by a special law." See Letter 27, p. 165.

L E T T E R

20

The Count of Limonade to Thomas Clarkson

{ENGLISH TRANSLATION}

KINGDOM OF HAITI

At the Palace of Sans Souci, July 25ᵗʰ, 1819,
in the 16ᵗʰ year of our Independence

COUNT LIMONADE,
Secretary of State, Minister of Foreign Affairs,
Member of the Royal Chamber of Public Instruction of
Haiti, Honorary Member of the English and Foreign
School Society of London, etc.,

to Mr. Thomas Clarkson,
Member of the African Institution

Dear Sir,

I have been kept from the pleasure of writing you by a long and painful illness which made it impossible for me to work and to serve my beloved Sovereign. Now that I am well again, God be thanked, the fact that my first letters are written to you and the friends of the Cause makes it an even greater satisfaction to resume my ordinary occupations.

I congratulate you heartily, first for your zeal in going to the Congress of Aix-la-Chapelle so that you might serve the Cause you have so long championed with the warmth and energy of the virtuous, and secondly for your speech before the illustrious Sovereigns assembled there and your conversations with the Emperor of Russia. The estimable character of that admirable Sovereign and his good will toward Haiti merit our gratitude and veneration. But you, how can we ever repay you for all you have done for us and our African brothers and for all that you still intend to do for us?

We well know then, Sir, that in the quiet of your heart you will enjoy a sense of self-satisfaction, our blessings and those of our posterity, and the certainty of heavenly reward.

His Majesty writes to you, opens his heart to you, and has as much confidence in you as in himself.

Please believe, Sir, that my wishes for your health equal my respect and affection for you.

COUNT LIMONADE

LETTER

21

King Henry to Thomas Clarkson

{ENGLISH TRANSLATION}

At the Palace of the Citadel Henry, July 29th, 1819,
in the 16th year of our Independence

THE KING,
to Mr. Thomas Clarkson,
Member of the African Institution

My worthy Friend,

When this letter reaches you, you doubtless will have already received my preceding communications which were entrusted to Messieurs Birt and Waldkierch. I understand that Mr. Birt has arrived safely and has already delivered the first of these two communications; along with this letter I am sending you a duplicate of the second.

Since I last wrote, I have received several indirect messages from agents of the French Government, urging me to come to an understanding with France. I have not seen fit to answer, on a subject of such importance, without having first benefited by your wise advice. Your suggestions are therefore being awaited so that I may make a decision; for, allow me to repeat, if I could be certain that Great Britain would recognize the independence of my country, I should pay no attention to these overtures which are being made.

I read attentively your remarks concerning the emigration of colored people from the United States of America, and appreciate fully what you say about the advantages and disadvantages which might result. Approaches have been made to me from the United States by several persons, in particular by the President of the Emancipation Society of New York. I have replied only to the latter, and am sending you a copy, so that you may know my views on this subject.[58]

---

[58] Christophe's letter to the Emancipation Society is missing from this collection.

I have heard nothing from Mr. Prince Sanders since he left Haiti by stealth, and feel that I owe you this word of warning in case he should try to take advantage of you, using my name. We dealt with him most generously during his stay among us.

Since I last wrote, we have been visited by Admiral Home Popham[59] of the Jamaica Station, who was received in a manner befitting his rank. I gave him a personal audience. While he was here, he was encouraged to visit our institutions, our hospitals, and the interior of the island; no doubt he has informed his Government of conditions as he saw them in Haiti.

Shortly after the departure of Sir Home, Commodore George Collier, commander of the African Coastal Station, spent some time here on his way back to England. He gave us very gratifying information concerning the progress toward civilization which our African brothers in Sierra Leone[60] are making, to my own great satisfaction. Through him we learned then that our friends are forging ahead, and we continue to hope that all their efforts will be crowned with success.

Acting in accordance with your wise suggestions for the improvement of my country's agriculture, and reassured by the fact that certain highly placed individuals have informed you that the French will not undertake any hostile action against Haiti, I have judged it advisable to take advantage of the favorable moment and put into effect a project which has long been very dear to me: that of giving all members of the armed forces concessions of land from the public domain. You will see in the public papers which I am sending you[61] that when making this distribution I did not

---

[59] See p. 53.

[60] Sierra Leone, a British colony on the west coast of Africa, owes its birth to a group of British philanthropists who wished to alleviate the lot of the victims of the slave trade. The first settlement of 1787 had an unfortunate beginning, although a strip of land providing the best harbor on the west coast of Africa was purchased. In 1791, the Sierra Leone Company was incorporated. Its purposes were to provide a haven for liberated Negroes, to colonize a small part of the coast of Africa, to discourage slave trading among the neighboring tribes, and to promote Christianity. In 1792, about eleven hundred Negroes, who had been settled in Nova Scotia following the American Revolution, were taken to Sierra Leone by Clarkson's brother. The colony was transferred to the British Crown in 1807. The slave trade having been abolished by England in the same year, thenceforth slaves captured by the Royal Navy from English vessels illegally engaged in the slave trade were taken to Sierra Leone, thus greatly augmenting the population. Writing to Christophe in 1819, Clarkson says, "We have now there nearly 10,000 Africans who have been captured from the slave ships by British Frigates." See p. 161.

[61] Christophe refers to his edict of July 14, 1819, a carefully thought out document. It provided for concessions of land from the public domain to soldiers of all ranks. Later he intended to add regulations governing the period of military service and the time the soldiers were to devote to the cultivation of their land. See pp. 268–271. It will be seen that Christophe readily accepted Clarkson's plans for the establishment of a militia.

depart from the plan which you proposed to me. I shall begin little by little to familiarize the troops with the transition from the soldier's life to that of the farmer by giving them leave, a group at a time, to go and cultivate their land for brief periods; then, when I can do so with complete security, I shall go even further and carry out in its entirety your plan of maintaining only a militia. You see, my friend, how much value I attach to your kind advice, as well as to that of our common friends Wilberforce and Stephen. Please believe me when I tell you that I have always agreed heart and soul with you. However, my position is really difficult, since I simply must guarantee the safety of my fellow citizens and relieve their fears concerning the future. I shall not fail to keep you informed as to the results of this experiment.

It is with regret that I announce to you that the Reverend Mr. Morton,[62] professor of the French and English languages, disregarding his promises and alleging the most frivolous of excuses, has requested permission to leave for the United States, though he has been given absolutely no reason for complaint. Because it has always been against my principles to make anyone remain who wished to leave, I have granted his request and have had him replaced by Mr. Daniel, master of the National School of Sans Souci. A well prepared monitor is taking Mr. Daniel's place.

The National School directed by Mr. Gulliver is doing very well; likewise that of Mr. Simmons at Gonaïves. In general, our students are progressing satisfactorily.

Mr. Moore,[63] the mathematics professor, has arrived among us, and he will shortly proceed to choose a group of students to be trained in his profession.

The interior of the island is completely tranquil.

Word did reach me that General Boyer had sent troops against the Count of Jérémie in the mountains of Jérémie; I know no more about it than that

---

[62] Mr. Morton had been instrumental in founding the Royal College at Cape Henry. Harvey says in this connection: "A considerable number of the Haytian youth were now instructed in Latin, English and French composition, history, geography, and mathematics.... The ... professor, on whom at first devolved the entire charge of the college, devoted himself to the task ... with the utmost zeal and diligence.... Being a clergyman of the Anglican Church, he added to his usual engagements, that of occasionally instructing them in the doctrine and precepts of the Christian religion." *Op. cit.*, p. 212.

[63] "Nor was the mathematical professor," declares Harvey, "less indefatigable in his endeavours to promote the improvement of those committed to his charge. He was a gentleman of considerable scientific attainments, highly respected by Christophe and the Board of Instruction.... He occasionally delivered lectures on mechanics and chemistry; and being provided with the apparatus necessary for the purpose, he illustrated their principles by suitable experiments." *Ibid.*, pp. 212–213.

the troops have been on the move since last February.⁶⁴ As for myself, I assure you that I have no intention of committing any hostile act against Boyer. You may, therefore, boldly deny the rumors which may be circulated to the effect that I am plotting an attack against his part of the island.

I shall continue to rely on you, my friend, to keep me informed about all developments which I should know of.

Please believe that my concern for your health and happiness is as great as my esteem for you.

HENRY

---

⁶⁴ In the summer of 1819, Boyer succeeded in annihilating Gomar (Count of Jérémie) and his bandits without any interference from Christophe. Since Christophe had long supported Gomar, his neutrality is another indication of his willingness to follow Clarkson's advice. See pp. 115–116 and note; also p. 123.

LETTER

22

The Count of Limonade to Thomas Clarkson

{ENGLISH TRANSLATION}

At the Palace of Sans Souci, September 3ʳᵈ, 1819,
in the 16ᵗʰ year of our Independence

to Mr. Thomas Clarkson

Dear Sir,

The King, my august and beloved Sovereign, had the pleasure of writing to you the 29ᵗʰ of last July; I also had the honor of writing you on that same date.[65] Today I am taking this occasion to send you a work just published by Baron Vastey.[66] In it you will find authentic details concerning the history of our country, and a study of the character of the King. You will find successfully refuted, I believe, the calumnies referring to his person which the enemies of the African race have delighted in spreading. In short, I believe that you will discover new reasons for esteeming him ever more highly. You will see in His Majesty a man frank, upright, patriotic, loving his fellow men and his country, incapable of ever betraying his people.

I have the honor of signing myself, with all possible consideration,

Your faithful servitor,

COUNT LIMONADE

---

[65] Limonade probably refers to his letter of July 25, 1819. See Letter 20.

[66] *Essai sur les causes de la révolution et des guerres civiles d'Hayti, faisant suite aux réflexions politiques sur quelques ouvrages et journaux français concernant Hayti* (Sans Souci, 1819); later published in English as *An Essay on the Causes of the Revolution and Civil Wars of Hayti, Being a Sequel to the Political Remarks* . . . , translated from the French by W. H. M. B. (Exeter, 1823).

LETTER

23

Thomas Clarkson to King Henry

[No salutation]   *September 7, 1819*

I had the honour of writing to your Majesty in June last by Mr. C. Davis in answer to your letter relative to a treaty with France, and I now send you a duplicate of that letter by Mr. Birt, to whom I feel much obliged for his politeness in giving me timely notice of his intention to return to Hayti....

Since that time, Monsieur Laisné de Villevêque has again introduced the Island of Hayti to the notice of the Chamber of Representatives... of France. He read a report there, which was so far approved of that it was ordered to be printed and to be recommended to the attention of the King's Ministers. He advised France to use a liberal policy towards the chiefs of Hayti. He had no objection to acknowledge their Independence, but he expected that they, on their part, should pay a sum of money to France, as an indemnification to the ex-colonists for the loss of property which they had experienced in consequence of the revolution, and also, that they should allow to France the advantage of their commerce. As the report of Monsieur Laisné seemed to be generally, if not universally approved of, I should suppose, that the Ministers of Louis the 18th would offer to your Majesty and to General Boyer a treaty upon this basis. The report now mentioned was read in the Chambre Basse at the latter end of the month of July. I need scarcely observe that the sentiments of Monsieur Laisné,... having appeared in the public journals, have become known throughout all France.

Your Majesty will find, on reading over my last letter to you, that I did not anticipate Mons. Laisné's idea of an indemnification to the ex-colonists.... This new idea... has greatly altered the face of things since I last wrote to you: for if you should consent to pay to France an indemnification, you ought to consider such a payment as the price paid for the acknowledgement of your Independence;... and if this be so, you will have a right to demand of France not only a free trade, but you will have a right also to insist upon her finding a guarantee....It is the business of France if she receives the money, and not yours, to find a proper security for it; and in this case, it might be advisable to tell her that you yourself would give the preference to Great Britain.

Should such a treaty ... as that proposed by Mons. Laisné be offered you, it becomes an important question with your Majesty whether you ought to accept it....It is my sincere advice to you to accept such an indemnification in exchange for the acknowledgement of your Independence,[67] and to demand of France in return a guarantee, and a free trade in which she may participate like other nations. I take it for granted, however, that the indemnification will be reasonable and moderate, and such as you can pay without any great sacrifice, either at once or by installments in a course of years. My reasons for giving you this advice are the following.

1. It is a fact that a great number of the ex-colonists are reduced to beggary and that they depend upon pensions from the French Government for their support.[68] These men are constantly troubling...it for money and urging it to acts of hostility against Hayti for the recovery of what they have lost. This is one reason why the French Government hesitates to acknowledge your Independence, for if it were to make this acknowledgement, then (the ex-colonists losing all hope of recovering their property in Hayti) it would have the burthen of supporting them and their families forever. By agreeing, therefore, to an indemnification...you would thus remove a constant source of discord between you and the French Government....

2. You would not only get your Independence acknowledged by France, but secured also, and let me observe that no nation, after this, would hesitate to acknowledge you as an independent State.

3. You will never probably have an opportunity of making peace on such fair and honourable terms as under the reign of Louis the 18th....England would be more likely to become a guarantor at *his* particular request, than she would hereafter at the request of his successors.

4. France, by means of the frugal and wise administration of Louis the 18th (who is an amiable man himself, though he may have rash counsellors) is increasing her finances and her power in a manner far exceeding

---

[67] Although Christophe readily accepted most of Clarkson's recommendations, it is significant that he was adamant on this important point and refused to consider indemnification in any form whatsoever.

[68] These pensions amounted to the sum of 1,000,000 francs annually. See pp. 202–203 of this collection.

the calculations of politicians, so that in a few years she will become ... by far the most powerful nation in Europe, and I could wish that your Majesty should make a treaty with her, before she assumes so powerful an attitude.

I have communicated my views on this subject both to Mr. Wilberforce and Mr. Stephen, and I am happy to announce to your Majesty that they concur in them most cordially. If I should collect any farther intelligence from France, I will omit no opportunity of sending it to you. You may rely upon my constant vigilance for the good of Hayti and upon my best efforts to promote it. I have the honour to be with great respect and esteem,

Your Majesty's friend,

THOMAS CLARKSON

L E T T E R

24

King Henry to Thomas Clarkson
{ENGLISH TRANSLATION}

At the Palace of Sans Souci, September 10th, 1819,
in the 16th year of our Independence

T H E   K I N G ,
to Mr. Thomas Clarkson,
Member of the African Institution

My esteemed Friend,

The ill health of our dear mutual friend, Wilberforce, his multiple occupations, and the trouble I have already caused him in the matter of choosing schoolmasters and professors for us, all make me fear to importune him by asking for further services.

I am therefore turning my eyes toward you, as the friend best placed to understand our needs in the field of education. I therefore beg of you to do us the favor of securing two professors of belles-lettres, in the French and English languages, men who are well prepared and to be recommended for their ideas, their behavior, and their character. I want to place them in the Royal College of Haiti.

We need these two professors especially, since the departure of Mr. Morton has brought to a stop the education of the young people who had been confided to his care. Mr. Morton asked for and obtained permission to leave because of illness.

It will indeed be a great favor, my friend, if you will find these two professors for me just as soon as possible. To that end I authorize you to sign an agreement with them for seven years, under the terms of which each of them will be paid a yearly salary of three thousand gourdes,[69] to begin the day of their arrival in Haiti. Their own traveling expenses, as well as those of their families and any children they may care to bring with them, will

---

[69] £675, according to Clarkson's estimate.

be paid by the government; also their return passage to England will be provided for upon the expiration of their contracts.

Out of the three thousand gourdes which will be paid to them regularly each month in cash, at the rate of 250 gourdes per month, they must provide food and lodging for themselves and their families, since this government does not attempt to provide food and housing for the schoolmasters and professors in its employ.

They will be honorably treated, and will enjoy in Haiti all the consideration which their profession merits. These then, my friend, are the conditions you may incorporate in the agreement you may eventually sign with the two professors.

I shall have full confidence in your choice, for I know you will pick out only such men as we can use.

Allow me to renew the expression of my highest esteem and warmest friendship.

HENRY

L E T T E R
25
Thomas Clarkson to King Henry

September 22, 1819

[No salutation]

As Mr. Birt informed me some days ago that he was about to return to Hayti, I sent him the duplicate of a letter which I wrote to your Majesty in June last relative to your expected treaty with France, and also another letter dated September 7, on the same subject, both which letters he has promised to deliver [to] you. Yesterday I was agreeably surprised by receiving a letter from your Majesty, dated June 8, enclosing the second part of the correspondence between the Count de Limonade and the French general, de Vincent; and as I understand that Mr. Birt will not leave London till the day after tomorrow, I hasten to communicate to your Majesty my sentiments upon it....

When I read the first letter of General de Vincent to the Count de Limonade, I suspected that the former was employed by the French Government to try privately how far your Majesty would be disposed to make any treaty with it. His second letter of February the 17th confirms the opinion which I had then formed. There can be no doubt that the French Government has made him the organ of communication in this affair. But I am sorry to find that General de Vincent should have shown himself, notwithstanding his professions, far more friendly to the interests of France than to the interests of Hayti. If Hayti is not to be allowed to be independent, what is she to be? She must either be an independent kingdom or a vassal of France. I know of no medium between the two situations. It is, therefore, with peculiar pleasure that I have read the copy of the answer of the Count de Limonade on this subject. Your Majesty has replied, through him, in a frank and open manner. You have been firm and courageous. You have maintained your dignity and asserted your independence.

I ... hope that the French Government has already changed its views upon this subject. It was in February when Gen. de Vincent's second letter was written; but it was not till the end of July ... that Mons. Laisné de Villevêque made his report to the lower chamber, in which he recommended to the King's Ministers an enlightened policy towards the two chiefs of Hayti. I am of opinion that this report will produce a new overture to your Majesty on the part of the French Government, and I hope it will be more frank and more liberal than the former. As to Louis the 18th, I believe him to be an amiable and a just man, and a man whose word may be taken, but I have not the same opinion of his Ministers.

I hope that your Majesty will soon make up your mind as to the different articles of the treaty that you would be willing to agree to with France. ... I shall be glad to hear the result of your deliberations and shall wait with impatience for it. When I know what kind of treaty your Majesty has resolved upon, I think it possible that opportunities may occur when I may be able to promote your wishes concerning it.

It was reported some time ago in the public papers that General Boyer had sent an agent to Paris to make a treaty with the French Government, but I find from the *Constitutionnel* (French paper) that no such agent has yet arrived.

I am with great esteem and regard

Your Majesty's friend,

THOMAS CLARKSON

L E T T E R

26

Thomas Clarkson to King Henry

September 28, 1819

[No salutation]

I write in great haste to your Majesty, for it was only last night that I received your letter of the 29th of July, and if I do not answer it by this day's post to London, I shall lose the opportunity of answering it by Mr. Birt. . . .

The Colony at Sierra Leone, concerning which Sir Geo. Collier has given your Majesty information, has repaid us for all our labours. We have now there nearly 10,000 Africans who have been captured from the slave ships by British Frigates, all of whom are living in a state of freedom and of civilized society. . . . All these poor people have been rescued from the jaws of slavery, and they are now living as monuments of God's mercy. . . .

I have many things to recommend to your Majesty for the improvement of Hayti, but at present these would be premature, for I think that we ought at this moment to bend all our thoughts to two things, namely, to the accomplishment of a treaty with France, through which only your Independence can at present be firmly established, and to the increase of your population by just and rational means. When your Majesty shall have gained these two points, you will find no difficulty in performing what remains to be done for the good of Hayti.

With respect to a treaty with France, I have conveyed to you my sentiments fully in the letters which will be given you by Mr. Birt. I have nothing to add to them. I wish, however, to know from your Majesty . . . the kind of treaty you would be willing to agree to with the French Government, and also, whether you would permit me, as a private individual, to use my own discretion in selecting proper opportunities of making your sentiments known on this subject to persons in authority in France. I may have delicate opportunities of doing this, which you cannot have in Hayti.

With respect to the increase of your population by emigrations from the United States, I admire the letter of the Count de Limonade to the President of the Society at New York, a copy of which you sent me. . . . I have reason to think that the people of colour, who have been manumitted there, are in general persons of sober and industrious habits. It must, however, be in the very nature of things that there will be some idle and dissolute persons among them. Your Majesty ought to have the power of selection and not to take any but such as are of approved life and character.

There is one article which I wish the Count de Limonade had mentioned in his letter to the President of the Society at New York and which I should be unhappy unless it were adopted. If it had been inserted, it would have had a considerable effect both on that Society and on the free people of colour themselves. . . . I wish his Excellency had said that your Majesty would permit the manumitted people, if they should come to Hayti, to exercise freely their own religion and to hear their own preachers, if they preferred it, and that you would not allow any of their meetings of worship to be disturbed on any pretence whatever. If your Majesty should have occasion to write again to New York I could wish you to state [this policy]. . . .

Among the persons of colour who might be induced to leave the United States for Hayti there are many who have acquired property from 50 to 2 or 3000 dollars! Such persons would be very useful to your Majesty. They would form that middle class in society which is the connecting medium between the rich and the poor and which is the great cause of prosperity in Europe, but which cannot at present have been raised up in your Majesty's Dominions. If your Majesty, then, were able to select from the free people of colour some who had property and the rest of industrious, sober, and religious character, you would confer an essential benefit on your country. You would of course give to each family a few acres of land. . . .

The only difficulty I anticipate is this, namely, you would not be able to give to these emigrants of colour such privileges as they have been accustomed to see or to enjoy without infringing upon the general laws of your Dominions. In the United States, being free men, they were accustomed to go where they pleased in search of their livelihood without any questions being asked them or without any hindrance by the Government. No passports are ever necessary there. This I apprehend is not the case in Hayti in its present state. Again, they would not have the advantage, if accused, of being tried by a jury of their fellow citizens. This noble custom cannot at present exist in Hayti, because your Majesty's subjects are not yet sufficiently enlightened by education to compose so distinguished a tribunal.

Again, they have had the privilege, being free men, of meeting in public to discuss their grievances and to make their observations freely upon the conduct of their Government. This would not be allowed in the present infant state of Hayti: your Majesty would consider such a privilege as dangerous at the present time.

In the different letters which I have written to my friends in the United States ... I have uniformly endeavoured to make the following stipulation in your Majesty's favour, viz., that the American Government should buy the Spanish part of your Island and cede it to you as an indemnification or recompense for receiving the free people of colour into your Dominions and under your own protection; but ... as your Majesty never mentioned any such stipulation in the Count de Limonade's letter to the President of the Society at New York, I take it for granted that you are willing to receive these free people of colour without it. ...

I am glad to find that you are willing to aid the emigrations of the free people of colour ... by pecuniary assistance. This was perhaps not looked for by the Society of New York, but it will have the effect of making this and other societies turn their mind rather towards you than towards General Boyer. ...

THOMAS CLARKSON

LETTER
27
King Henry to Thomas Clarkson
{ENGLISH TRANSLATION}

At the Palace of Sans Souci, November 20ᵗʰ, 1819,
in the 16ᵗʰ year of our Independence

T H E   K I N G ,
to Mr. Thomas Clarkson,
Member of the African Institution

My esteemed and worthy Friend,

Mr. Birt delivered to me upon his arrival a duplicate of your letter of the 28ᵗʰ of June, as well as your letters of the 7ᵗʰ and the 22ⁿᵈ of last September.

I am sorry to have to inform you that the brig Ann, in which he made the journey, went on a reef the night of the 9ᵗʰ of this month at Point Caracolle, the entrance of the bay of Cape Henry. Fortunately, the crew was saved, as was the debris of the cargo, but the ship itself was totally lost. Mr. Birt, because of this misfortune, finds himself forced to leave again for England by way of the United States, and I know of no better way to see that my dispatches reach you than to confide them to his hands. The trustworthiness and zeal he has always shown in obliging me give me confidence that he will acquit himself faithfully once more.

I am also sorry to announce to you that, according to the American papers, Mr. Davis and his wife, who you tell me were bearers of your original dispatches, were lost along with all their goods when the ship on which they were coming to this island from New York was destroyed. I now know why I had been deprived of the pleasure of hearing from you for so long a time.

I have read your letters with the greatest interest and attention.

I am delighted that you transmitted to the Russian Ambassador the letter I wrote to his Sovereign, and that you also wrote directly to the Emperor, sending him the report on the situation of our schools. In that action I saw a new proof of your zeal and devotion to our cause.

What you tell me concerning the steps taken by several different nations to put an end to the infamous slave trade can only make me rejoice; I am indeed anxious to see the moment arrive when Spain must abandon this abominable traffic entirely, for we are informed from Havana that the trade is still carried on very extensively and in the most abominable manner.

In your decision to write to Mr. Richard Peters, President of the Triennial Convention of Philadelphia, I recognize your usual wisdom and philanthropic views. You were right, my friend, when you assured him that I would welcome the envoys of the Convention, not only because of your recommendation, but also because they are friends of the Cause. Have no doubt that they will be received with distinction, and that I shall make every effort to satisfy them by explaining to them the measures I shall adopt to facilitate the immigration of the unfortunate descendants of the Africans and to help them to become established in their new home.

It is true that matters of religion were not discussed in my Minister's letter; that was not felt to be necessary, since everyone knows that all religions are tolerated and protected in Haiti.[70] Nevertheless, I profit by your judicious observations.

I received, almost at the same time your letters arrived, a communication from Mr. Evan Lewis of Wilmington, dated the 10th of September. He too writes to me of this matter and expresses a wish to come to Haiti. I answered that he would be favorably received. This worthy Quaker was so kind as to send me your book on the Abolition of the Slave Trade, which I esteem very highly.

I appreciated what you said to me about the Spanish part of this island, and am in complete agreement. The project would be an important one, and I hope you will keep it in mind.

I thoroughly approve the steps to be taken relative to the property which the ex-colonists might attempt to acquire, should a treaty be signed with France. You may be sure that my two Councils will shortly be called together to consider this important point, and that the situation will be clarified by a special law.

Please do not forget to procure for me at your earliest convenience the

---

[70] The Haitian Constitution of 1807, written in accordance with Christophe's wishes, declares: "The catholic, apostolic, and Roman religion is the only one acknowledged by the government. The exercise of other religions is tolerated, but not publicly." Sir James Basket, *op. cit.*, p. 241. The fact that Christophe was ready to welcome Stephen Grellet the Quaker, and the Methodists, Harvey and Jones, and permitted the Reverend Mr. Morton, an Anglican, to teach in the Royal College, indicates that he practiced religious tolerance.

works of Pamphile Lacroix and Guillermain de Montpinay,[71] and any other recent publications which concern Haiti.

I did give orders to Baron Dupuy, my Secretary Interpreter, to give preference to our common friend Allen in the matter of the medicines which he had to import. I am glad he carried out my wishes in this respect.

I see by your letter that our friend is on a trip to Russia; there is no nobler or greater cause than the one which makes him undertake this journey. It will surely achieve the most fortunate results. When he returns, please offer him my compliments.

Farewell, my friend, with the assurances of my esteem and friendship,

HENRY

---

[71] The works mentioned are: Baron Pamphile de la Croix, *Mémoires pour servir à l'histoire de la révolution de Saint-Domingue* (Paris, 1819), 2 vols.; and Gilbert Guillermin de Montpinay, *Colonie de Saint-Domingue, ou appel à la sollicitude du roi et de la France* (Paris, 1819).

LETTER
28
King Henry to Thomas Clarkson
{ENGLISH TRANSLATION}

At the Palace of Sans Souci, November 20ᵗʰ, 1819,
in the 16ᵗʰ year of our Independence

THE KING,
to Mr. Thomas Clarkson,
Member of the African Institution

You will see, my friend, in the letters which accompany this one, that I have given full and confidential answers to all the important questions you raised in your own recent communications. I have answered from several different points of view.

Since the negotiations which I am authorizing you to undertake will necessitate traveling and incurring various expenses, permit me, my friend, to present you with the attached letter of credit drawn on Reid, Irving and Company of London; you will thus have at your disposal the sum of six thousand pounds sterling. I cannot allow you to spend any personal funds on my behalf. If you should need any further sums in order to complete your mission, please let me know so that I can see they are provided.

I remain your faithful friend,

HENRY

LETTER

29

King Henry to Thomas Clarkson

{ENGLISH TRANSLATION}

At the Palace of Sans Souci, November 20ᵗʰ, 1819,
in the 16ᵗʰ year of our Independence

T H E   K I N G ,
to his friend, Mr. Thomas Clarkson

My Friend,

Following the suggestions made in your letters of the 28ᵗʰ of June, the 7ᵗʰ and the 22ⁿᵈ of last September, we have determined to ask you to make an overture toward opening negotiations for the signing of a treaty between Haiti and France.

Fully convinced of your zeal and your friendship for our person, of your complete devotion to the cause of Haiti, which is that of justice and humanity, I have decided that there is no one in whom I could better place my confidence than in yourself, my worthy friend. I know of no one else who has more constantly and ardently dedicated himself to this sublime cause than you, who have devoted time, life, and fortune to its defense.

In order to enable you to undertake this important mission, I have ordered our Minister of State and of Foreign Affairs to send you such credentials and instructions as will permit you to begin negotiations in whatever way you think preferable.

There is no need for us to indicate to a friend as informed and wise as yourself the essentials upon which we must insist in the projected treaty. You know as well as we do the points on which we can never yield, because you are fully aware of the best interests of Haiti.

We ask then of you, my worthy friend, and of the others who are champions of the Cause, from the vantage point you occupy to tell us the first steps we should take and how we can best serve the general interest of the

Haitian people. We are counting heavily that your great political experience, your particular affection for us, will make it possible for you to show us the way with your advice and to suggest the steps which would most benefit Haiti; we trust that you will be aided by our friends, Messieurs Wilberforce and Stephen, and by others who like yourself are guided by principles of humanity and whom you judge capable of being of assistance. Rest assured that we shall be ready to do and accept anything which is just, reasonable, and compatible with the welfare of Haiti and our own honor.

From what I have just said, you will see, my friend, how well disposed we are to come to terms.

The most important items from our point of view are *that Haiti be recognized as a free, sovereign, and independent nation; that her commerce be free; and that the demands of the ex-colonists be abandoned.* We desire that all the rest be settled according to the terms and stipulations which will be most advantageous to both countries.

One of the points which may cause some difficulty in your negotiations is the friction which exists now between the northwest and the southwest of Haiti; it is therefore essential that we should explain the situation to you fully and frankly. We have always believed that this friction could not prevent us from negotiating in order to further the common interests of all Haitians. Naturally, the basis of an eventual treaty would be the Act of Independence to which both parts of the country have already subscribed. At any rate, we know that in dealing with this important question you will present our own point of view in as favorable and advantageous a light as possible, and that you will seize any chance which may present itself to bring about an arrangement of things which would serve the true interests of the Haitian people.

Convinced as we are, my friend, that you will do nothing which will not redound to the profit and honor of my country, it is not our intention to limit your freedom of action in such a way as to prevent your serving our best interests in whatever manner your heart and your exact knowledge of the situation may indicate. We leave it to you then, my friend, once you are on the spot, to calculate the strong and the weak points of our position, and to act according to the circumstances in which you find yourself placed and within the spirit of your instructions.

There is another matter which concerns us seriously and which I feel that I must speak to you about: we had always cherished the hope of seeing the independence of Haiti recognized by England prior to French recognition. That is why, as we now make overtures to France, we are happy that they are to be made through you rather than anyone else. Never doubt for a moment that we would have been satisfied with an English *guarantee* instead of a treaty.

We beg of you, my friend, to do everything within your power to keep us informed of your progress as you carry out the details of the negotiations. In the interval, we may again be approached by the French. Since our correspondence will undoubtedly become more and more active and we shall need to communicate with each other often and through a reliable intermediary, it will be easier for you to send us your dispatches in care of Reid, Irving and Company of London, which firm has been requested to send out a ship to Cape Henry every three months, news of each sailing to be given to you in advance. In case you are in such a hurry to send your letters that you feel it would be unwise to wait, I authorize you to charter a light ship for the express purpose of carrying your dispatches whenever you feel that to be necessary.

I am your sincere and faithful friend,

HENRY

LETTER
30
The Duke of Limonade to Thomas Clarkson
{ENGLISH TRANSLATION}

KINGDOM OF HAITI

At the Palace of Sans Souci, November 20th, 1819,
in the 16th year of our Independence

THE DUKE OF LIMONADE,
Secretary of State, Minister of Foreign Affairs,
Member of the Royal Chamber of Public Instruction of
Haiti, Honorary Member of the English and Foreign
School Society of London, etc.,

to Mr. Thomas Clarkson,
Member of the African Institution

Sir,

I have the honor to send you the credentials and instructions which His Majesty has requested me to convey to you, so that you may be in a position to make an overture and open negotiations with France.

I have the honor of being, with highest consideration,

Sir,

Your humble and obedient servant,

THE DUKE OF LIMONADE

LETTER

31

The Duke of Limonade to Thomas Clarkson

{ENGLISH TRANSLATION}

KINGDOM OF HAITI

At the Palace of Sans Souci, November 20ᵗʰ, 1819,
in the 16ᵗʰ year of our Independence

THE DUKE OF LIMONADE,

Lieutenant General of the King's Armies,
Commander of the Royal and Military Order of Saint
Henry, Major of the Light Horse of the Prince Royal,
Secretary of State, Minister of Foreign Affairs, etc.

Be it Known,

That the King, my august sovereign and master, desirous of reëstablishing peace between Haiti and France on suitable and honorable terms,

Has chosen his worthy and honorable friend, Mr. Thomas Clarkson, member of the African Institution of London, to aid him and use his good offices with a view toward ascertaining the disposition of the French Cabinet toward Haiti. Consequently, the aforesaid Mr. Thomas Clarkson is fully authorized by the present letters to make an overture to this effect, through whatever channels he may deem advisable, and to make known to us the conditions under which the French Government would be prepared to negotiate a treaty with Haiti. In faith of which, we have signed these letters and affixed to them our official seal.

THE DUKE OF LIMONADE

LETTER
32
The Duke of Limonade to Thomas Clarkson
{ENGLISH TRANSLATION}

KINGDOM OF HAITI

At the Palace of Sans Souci, November 20ᵗʰ, 1819,
in the 16ᵗʰ year of our Independence

THE DUKE OF LIMONADE,
Lieutenant General of the King's Armies,
Commander of the Royal and Military Order of Saint
Henry, Major of the Light Horse of the Prince Royal,
Secretary of State, Minister of Foreign Affairs, etc.

Instructions for
Mr. Thomas Clarkson

Mr. Thomas Clarkson is authorized to point out to the French Government that in the midst of a war of thirty years' duration the Haitian people, after shedding rivers of its finest blood, set itself up sixteen full years ago as a sovereign state, free and independent. Exercising its natural rights, the nation proclaimed its Independence before all men by its solemn Declaration of the 1ˢᵗ of January, 1804.

Since that great and glorious day the Haitian nation has created for itself a stable and regular government, national institutions, and a system of laws. A new and enlightened generation is replacing the former population; the ideas, morals, customs, and even the habits of the people have undergone a total change. In a word, nothing any longer exists of the former regime!

A constitutional and hereditary monarchy has been established, as have an order of nobility and a military order. An army and an agricultural system have been set up. The plantations, lands, houses, and other property which the ex-colonists owned in the cities and country have been given away, divided, or sold. Everything has changed. The colonial regime has been overthrown, destroyed from top to bottom. The last vestiges of that odious system have disappeared from the soil of Haiti.

For sixteen years the subjects of all maritime and trading nations (France alone excepted) have carried on a commerce with Haiti. These activities and mutual interchanges are in fact equivalent to a tacit, if not a formal, recognition of our independence.

Nothing then remains for the Haitian government but to see solemnized by treaties an independence which has already been implicitly recognized by the nations, been consecrated by the passage of time and by the institutions and privileges the people possess by right of conquest in a bloody and cruel war. The events which led up to our independence are best not recalled here, but they are known to the entire world, reinforce the cause of the Haitian people, and are more than sufficient justification for the separation of Haiti from the former mother country.

We have always felt that France, faced with such powerful arguments and moved by sentiments of justice and humanity, must unhesitatingly recognize by a solemn treaty an independence which she herself made inevitable and which can in no possible way be destroyed, as is clearly evident to every reasonable observer. It was then with great astonishment, grief, and regret, that we have seen her insist on maintaining her claims against Haiti, claims which are now meaningless and without foundation. France's former rights as the mother country of Haiti ceased to exist sixteen years ago by the very fact of our conquest of the Island and the Act of Independence by which the nation declared itself a free and sovereign state.

Under existing circumstances, any political or commercial relations between the people and governments of the two countries have been and are impossible, and will continue so until their respective rights have been stipulated and recognized in a formal treaty. This situation has brought about a painful state between the two nations, one might say a state of permanent hostility, equally disadvantageous to the commerce and prosperity of both.

His Haitian Majesty, impelled by sentiments of humanity and justice, wishes to discover the bases upon which a solid and durable peace may be built, and thus bring an end to an unfortunate state of affairs in a way mutually beneficial to France and Haiti.

In the overture which His Haitian Majesty has decided to make through his esteemed and worthy friend, Mr. Thomas Clarkson, it is his wish to give unmistakable proof of his deference toward His Christian Majesty, the King of France and Navarre, and to demonstrate his ardent desire to restore peace and commercial relations between the two countries.

In the negotiations to be undertaken, His Majesty is leaving to the discretion of Mr. Thomas Clarkson the choice of the means and avenue of approach. In case Mr. Clarkson's efforts are successful, and it proves possible to proceed to drawing up a draft of the treaty, the negotiator should demand as indispensable conditions:

1st. That His Christian Majesty, King of France and Navarre, recognize Haiti (that is, the territory of that part of Saint-Domingue which formerly belonged to France, along with the dependent islands, La Tortue, Gonave, the Cayemites, Isle à Vache, and Beata)[72] as a free, sovereign, and independent state; that he deal with Haiti as such; and that on his own behalf and in the name of his heirs and successors he renounce all claims to political, property, and teritorial rights over Haiti or any part thereof.

Once this *sine quâ non* condition has been agreed upon, the negotiator may offer in return:

2nd. That France will share in the commerce of Haiti as a most favored nation.

3rd. That, in case of a European war, Haiti will observe the strictest neutrality toward the belligerent powers.

4th. That steps will be taken to arrange between France and Haiti a commercial treaty safeguarding the interests of both countries.

A treaty embracing these conditions would be not only just and equitable, but equally honorable and advantageous to the contracting parties.

In no real sense would it represent a sacrifice for France to recognize the independence of Haiti; any sacrifice involved was made sixteen years ago, and was necessitated by the force of circumstances. By performing now an act of justice and humanity, France would secure the evident advantage of sharing in our commerce on a most favored nation footing.

In considering the terms of the proposed treaty, we have disregarded the following matters as inadmissible: (1) any indemnification of the ex-colonists; (2) any claim for exclusive rights to our commerce; (3) the existing difficulties between the northern and southern parts of Haiti. Nevertheless, since these different questions may be brought up, we submit our answers, so that the negotiator may be in a position to discuss them authoritatively.

[72] Ile de la Tortue lies directly north of Port-de-Paix off the northern coast. La Gonave, largest of the Haitian islands, is northwest of Port-au-Prince. The Cayemites, or Caïmites, include several islets, just off the coast between Jérémie and Anse à Veau. The Ile à Vache lies off the south coast, as does La Béate; however, the latter, now usually known by its Spanish name, La Beata, is today owned by the Dominican Republic.

The negotiator will point out that the ex-colonists were banished by the laws of Haiti; that, as outlaws, their former property was confiscated; that their goods were given away, divided, and sold. The present legal owners not only shed their blood to earn a right to this property, but have invested enormous sums of money in making it again productive, since most of it was burned or destroyed during the several wars which were waged on the Island.

What rights, what arguments can the ex-colonists then allege to justify their claim for an indemnity?

Is it possible that they wish to be recompensed for the loss of our persons?

Is it conceivable that Haitians who have escaped torture and massacre at the hands of these men, Haitians who have conquered their own country by the force of their arms and at the cost of their blood, that these same free Haitians should now purchase their property and persons once again with money paid to their former oppressors?

It is not possible; it is not for one moment to be considered. Free men could never accept such a condition without covering themselves with infamy!

The ex-colonists are our natural and implacable enemies; they tortured us while it was in their power to do so, and they never cease to seek an opportunity to renew their torture. It would, therefore, be altogether unjust and unreasonable to ask the Haitian Government to come to the aid of such men. In the face of such powerful reasons, we feel confident that the question of an indemnity to the ex-colonists will be disposed of.

With regard to the second matter, exclusive rights to our commerce, the negotiator will observe: (1) that any free, sovereign, and independent state must be master of its own commerce; (2) that it would be unjust to exclude now from all trade those nations which have maintained commercial relations with us for the last sixteen years; and (3) that an exclusive commerce with France would be contrary to our laws and best interests. It would then be impossible for us to grant any nation exclusive rights to our trade; justice, fairness, and good faith require that the Government of His Haitian Majesty should treat all countries favorably and on an equal footing as we expect them to treat us.

We feel that France should be satisfied to share in our commerce as a most favored nation. There is no doubt that, sharing thus, she would stand to profit enormously. The special protection which we accord agriculture and the resulting increase in our productivity, as well as the immense con-

sumption of European manufactured goods by our rapidly growing population, cannot but render commercial relations between the two nations
more and more lucrative.

Regarding the third question, the difficulties existing between the northern and southern parts of Haiti, the negotiator should point out: (1) that
the momentary division of the country is a family matter which is of no
concern to a foreign government; (2) our Declaration of Independence of
the 1ˢᵗ of January, 1804, declares one and indivisible both the territory and
the cause of the Haitian people; (3) that there is, therefore, nothing to
prevent His Haitian Majesty's signing a treaty in the name of all Haitians,
provided that he takes as his point of departure the Declaration by which
both parties are solemnly bound.

In wishing to negotiate for the whole of Haiti, His Majesty has no intention of trying to extend his Government over the southern part of the
country,[73] but rather feels that he is bound by his honor and patriotism to
further the highest interests of the entire nation. Consequently, any attempt,
proposition, or demand which would require him to depart from this point
of view would be regarded as inadmissible, for the simple reason that the
cause and the territory of the Haitian people are one and indivisible.

Though His Haitian Majesty is disposed to find a way of overcoming any
difficulties which may present themselves, there are certainly cardinal
points, such as those just enumerated, which he can neither surrender nor
compromise. For further guidance, His Majesty refers his honored friend,
Mr. Clarkson, to the principles expressed in his Declaration of the 20ᵗʰ of
November, 1816.[74] His Majesty cannot depart one iota from those principles.

Mr. Clarkson now knows the intentions of the Haitian Government and
the conditions under which it would sign a treaty; when he has learned
those of the French Government, if there is substantial agreement between
the two parties, he will draw up a draft which he will forward to me, so
that I may in turn submit it to my government as the basis for a definitive
agreement.

THE DUKE OF LIMONADE

---

[73] In view of Christophe's long-cherished desire to unite all Haiti under his authority, this
statement of policy is extraordinary. Clarkson's pointed insistence that Christophe avoid any
conflict with Boyer had been fully accepted.

[74] See pp. 60–61.

LETTER

33

Baron de Vastey to Thomas Clarkson

{*ENGLISH TRANSLATION*}

At Sans Souci, November 29ᵗʰ, 1819

Dear Sir and respected Friend,

Mr. Birt delivered to me your letters of the 28ᵗʰ of June and the 28ᵗʰ of September.[75] I was quite flattered by your expression of interest in my health, which is now, by the way, completely restored. May your own be as excellent as we should wish it.

I regret to inform you that Mr. C. Davis, who was the bearer of one of your letters to me, perished at sea along with his unfortunate wife. This has been a terrible year for shipwrecks. Mr. Birt almost suffered the fate of Mr. Davis within sight of our coasts. His boat went aground on Caracolle Reef, a spot which was rendered well known by the wreck of one of Christopher Columbus' caravels at the time of the discovery of the New World.[76] Fortunately, Mr. Birt escaped, but his ship was lost and only a part of its cargo was saved.

Mr. Birt had the honor of being presented to the King at Sans Souci. Your recommendation sufficed to insure him of a favorable reception. Because of his misfortune, he found it necessary to hasten his return to England by way of the United States of America. We confided to his care certain dispatches, which he promised to deliver to you personally.

I shall not go into detail about the content of our letters; when you read them you will be fully informed. In fact, you will have further proof of His Majesty's sincere friendship toward you and his great confidence in your zeal and personal devotion.

I am profiting by the occasion to send you a new work entitled *Essay on the Causes of the Revolution and the Civil Wars in Hayti.* Exasperated at seeing in the journals of the South and in those of France, their faithful

---

[75] These two letters to De Vastey are missing from this collection.
[76] The *Santa Maria* was sunk here on December 24, 1492.

echoes, the calumnies which the enemies of Haiti and the King endlessly repeat concerning his government and his person, I decided to tell the truth in the matter. That led me into the writing of a whole volume on the origin and cause of our civil dissensions. I was able to devote only two months to the composition of this work and furthermore I was ill most of the time, so you will undoubtedly find it full of imperfections. Though I did not have at my disposal enough time to do it properly, I nevertheless flatter myself that, with all its flaws, this book will cast a great deal of light on our wars. Each time you need to make up your mind about the nature and the origin of these struggles of ours, it may be of great service to you, for you will find in it an explanation of how it happens that the country is divided under two governments. You will doubtless come to realize that ambition and ignorance have caused us untold grief. You will find brought out through an analysis of the original documents how the rights of the King to govern are perfectly established and what a pity it is for the country that a Prince so worthy and capable of governing it, should have met with an unjust and ambitious rival to dispute with him the reins of government. So, whenever you need information about these two governments, you may wish to have recourse to this book and to certain other works which I am sending you. They will be useful to you in the course of your negotiations each time you wish to find arguments and review the facts.

I feel also that I should tell you a little about various persons who are in correspondence with Haiti; you will probably meet them and it may be useful to know them. You certainly know better than I do who are the greatest enemies of Haiti in France, but in order that you may be fore-warned against certain individuals I should acquaint you with certain facts. I am sorry to say that among our friends were a few individuals who have allowed themselves to be prejudiced against us by the perfidious suggestions of our enemies.

I am sending you a copy of a document, the original of which is in the handwriting of Abbé Grégoire;[77] in it you will see how this man, praiseworthy as he is in many ways, has allowed himself to fall into grievous injustices toward us. I am convinced that when his religious nature has made him see the light and he is truly informed of the existing situation, he will feel only regret that he has borne false and premature judgment against us. We have not lost our sentiments of gratitude toward this venerable man of good and we shall never forget that he has always been an ardent defender

---

[77] The Abbé Henri Grégoire (1750–1831) was one of the most famous French humanitarians. He wrote several works pleading for more just treatment of the blacks in Saint-Domingue.

of our cause. We believe that once he realizes that he has been led into error, he will render us the justice we merit.

It might not be inappropriate for me to give you a few details with regard to certain colonists, though you know them well. You have at hand the letters of Monsieur de Vincent. I have nothing to add, except that he is an ex-colonist of this country. Monsieur de Pradt,[78] the celebrated writer, is doubtless known to you. He wrote a note to my friend, Baron Dupuy, which contains ideas similar to those of Monsieur de Vincent, even though in general his political writings are full of liberal and progressive principles. There are a large number of others, such as Esmangart,[79] Count Laborde,[80] and the Duke de Lervis. You know them well, and I mention them only because they are the ringleaders. A complete list would be endless.

Your idea of establishing an African Institution in Paris is sublime. His Majesty is deeply interested in the realization of the project. The Institution would serve as a rallying point for the friends of the Cause, and would contribute not a little, as you observe, to keeping the Government within due bounds.

I have also read attentively what you wrote me with regard to the introduction of free people of color to Haiti and the acquisition of the Spanish part of the Island. These are such important projects that all the friends of this country should join with us in desiring their realization. I feel that the first point would be easy to achieve, since it might be done even without the active coöperation of the United States Government. The matter might be arranged privately, between individuals. However, the same is not true in the case of the acquisition of the Spanish part of the Island; if we are to achieve that, then it is necessary that our independence be recognized, so that we may carry on direct negotiations and conclude treaties with the Government of the United States. It would seem to me then, my worthy and respected friend, that we must first work for the *recognition of our independence*. Once we have that, the rest will come easily. All our projects looking to the advancement and the welfare of our fellow citizens can then come true. You have within your hands the instruments for making pos-

---

[78] Dominique Dufour de Pradt (1759–1837), author of *Trois âges des colonies*, 1802, *Des Colonies et de la révolution actuelle de l'Amérique*, 1817, and *Pièces relatives à St.-Domingue et à l'Amérique*, 1818.

[79] Charles Esmangart (? –1837) was an ex-colonist, and had been one of the commissioners sent out by the French Government to secure Haitian submission in 1816. In 1802 appeared his *Des Colonies françaises et en particulier de Saint-Domingue*, and in 1833, *La Vérité sur les affaires d'Haïti*.

[80] De Vastey apparently refers to Joseph-Alexandre, Comte de Laborde (1773–1842).

sible this first precious step forward. Everything depends on your zeal in your task, that zeal which has never heretofore flagged for a single instant and which will surely not fail at a moment so decisive as the present. You will have rendered humanity the greatest service a mortal can render here below, for there is no doubt whatsoever that the cause of Haiti is bound up in many ways with that of all mankind. May you then succeed; our hopes and prayers will accompany your steps as you make the effort which will be the crowning achievement of your immortal labors.

Each day the internal situation of our country seems to improve, and we are enjoying the most complete tranquillity. Public instruction is making great strides: we have established five new schools, and next year more will be founded.[81] His Majesty has lavished great care and attention on improving the morals of the masses and stimulating all the sources of public prosperity.

Allow me now to speak to you briefly of a few personal matters. It is well occasionally to lay business aside and concern oneself with things domestic.

My warm interest in all that has to do with you led me to inquire of Mr. Birt concerning your family, and it was with genuine pleasure that I learned from him many precious details. I beg of you to be the interpreter of my respectful admiration for Mrs. Clarkson, and to present my compliments to your son who, Mr. Birt informs me, is now studying law. May your son follow in his father's footsteps and, like you, dedicate himself always to the defense of frail and suffering humanity.

It was with deep regret that I learned from your letter that your health has been seriously affected by your ardous labors in behalf of the abolition of the slave trade. But Heaven is just, and will surely prolong your life until you have seen your work crowned with the fullest degree of success. Your desire to come and spend the rest of your days in Haiti flatters us immensely. It proves unmistakably your high opinion of us. We indeed hope that some day we may have the joy of seeing you, and we do not feel that our hope is necessarily an idle one.

Before closing, I must also tell you a little about my own family; a heart such as yours will not be indifferent to a friendly interchange of confidences.

I was born at Ennery, a parish in the interior of the country, in 1781, which means that I am now thirty-nine years old or almost so. At the age of

---

[81] In December, 1819, a national school was founded at Fort Royal; and in January, 1820, five additional schools were established at Limbé, Borgne, Saint-Louis, Jean Rabel, and Plaisance. Cf. Baron de Vastey, *op. cit.*, Appendix, p. cxvi.

fifteen I entered the service of my country under the command of General Toussaint of glorious memory; later I served under Emperor Dessalines and the present King, my august sovereign. I have been married for twelve years. I have two daughters, Malvina and Aricie, and am enjoying all the happiness possible in the bosom of my family....

I am, Sir, with the most sincere friendship and the feeling of the greatest veneration,

Your very humble and obedient servant,

DE VASTEY

L E T T E R

34

Duncan Stewart[82] to Thomas Clarkson

Cape Henry, Haiti, Dec. 4, 1819

Dear Sir

I hope you will excuse the liberty I take in addressing you. The welfare of the people of Haiti I have much at heart, and will always feel the greatest gratification in communicating to their friends in Europe any information that may be useful in enabling them to form a just estimate of the state of the country and how they may best advise the King and prosecute the Haitian cause.

I know that many of those who wish to befriend this country have formed from inaccurate and contradictory information very erroneous notions of the state of Haiti and that they suppose these people much lower in the scale of civilization and intelligence than they actually [are]. I speak of this side of the Island.

Perhaps there never was a man, who from the energy and acuteness of his mind and from an intimate knowledge [of] the character of the people he governs, [was] so well calculated to rule a kingdom as the present King of Haiti. He found the Haitians at the death of Dessalines in the most complete state of anarchy, and the soldiery abandoned to every species of licentiousness. His intelligent mind soon discovered that he had but one course to follow, and at the sacrifice of his natural disposition he was forced to employ severities for which he has been unjustly reprobated by those who were ignorant of their necessity. The good effect of his policy was soon evident. Great enemies became daily less frequent and are now unknown in the Kingdom of Haiti. In proportion as his people can bear it, their liberties are gradually increased. And altho' many of the disadvantages of a perfect military government still necessarily remain, the power of the chiefs over their inferiors is diminishing daily.

---

[82] Duncan Stewart, a Scotsman, was Christophe's personal physician and one of his most intimate friends and advisers. Stewart was in charge of a "school of medicine, ... which ... held out the fairest promises of success." *Ibid.*, p. cxv.

The Hospitals of the Kingdom I have wholly under my care, and the King has given me complete power to order what I think necessary for the dieting, clothing, and accommodation of the sick in his Hospitals. I can safely say there is not an hospital in England where the sick are better supplied with all conveniences and necessaries than the Hospitals of Haiti. At my recommendation the King has likewise much increased the rations of his troops and they are all well clothed. Every soldier receives per day 22 oz. of bread or a sufficient equivalent of some nutritious vegetable; besides they have ½ lb. of fresh beef made into soup; and by a late decree each soldier has a certain quantity of land given him, on which he is permitted to spend 4 months every year and where his family have a comfortable home. With these advantages the soldier does not require any pay in money.

The agriculturists are allowed one-fourth of the produce of the land, besides the privilege of the use of some land to raise fowls, hogs, and vegetables for their families and for the market. Their fourth of the produce is regularly calculated when it comes into market by officers appointed for that purpose and most punctually paid. The King himself is most particular in paying those on his own estates, and always attends in person on those occasions to see it done and to receive any complaints or petitions which his agriculturists may have to prefer. There is a King's lieutenant stationed over each district, whose duty it is to receive and transmit to the King any complaints which the agriculturists may have to make, and the proprietor if he cannot satisfy the King as to his conduct is sent to prison until the agriculturists' demand is paid. If any proprietor uses his labour ill, on complaint being made and found to be just, the labourer is sent to one of the King's estates, where all the labourers are well used and are as comfortable and happy as any peasantry I ever saw in any part of Europe.

His Majesty's present Ministers, at least those on whom the great weight of the Government rests, are mulattoes and are very intelligent well-educated men. The King's confidence in them is every day increasing, and consequently, he is relieved of much of the detail of business to which at one time he gave minute attention. This is particularly the case with the Baron de Dupuy, a man who might be thought clever in any country and certainly the most labourious and useful man in the Kingdom. What they chiefly are in want of in Haiti is true religion with its many beneficial effects on life and manners, and the education of the female sex, which would lead to their obtaining that rank in society to which they are entitled, and without which civilization can advance but very slowly. I am sorry to say that females are used very ill in Haiti, being often forced to submit to the hardest labour and the greatest iniquities, at the capricious will of their rulers.[83]

If you think I can be of any use giving you information on any point, I shall be most happy to do it. Excuse this hasty scrawl.

I have the honour to be, dear Sir,

Your most obedient and respectful Servant,

DUNCAN STEWART

---

[83] Clarkson seems to have been much impressed with Stewart's remarks concerning the state of Haitian females, for not long afterward he wrote to Christophe: "[Mr. Wilberforce and I] were both of opinion that nothing could contribute so much to the real civilization of your Majesty's part of the Island ... as the elevation of the female character. This might be done gradually by not suffering the females to undergo the most labourious and slavish employments, but those only ... most suitable to their sex. We were convinced also that this great work might be much advanced by giving the girls the same education which your Majesty is giving the boys. In Europe, but more particularly in England, the women are as well educated as the men, and education is extended to both sexes even in the lowest stations of life. To education should be added the force of good example. I have often thought of recommending to your Majesty, if you should want any more white people from England (whether as clergymen, schoolmasters, agriculturists, mechanics, or of any other description), to receive none but married men with wives and families. If these were to set an example ... of chaste, sober, moral, and earnest living, it is incalculable what good might be done to the Haytian female. ... I have no doubt that many English females of virtuous character might be prevailed upon in the case of such a society to go to Hayti as school mistresses, who are unwilling to go at present. ..."

Thomas Clarkson to King Henry

January 24, 1820

[No salutation]

I received your Majesty's letter of September the 10th, and now write to inform you that, after having made a proper inquiry, I have found out two young men, Mr. William Wilson and Mr. George Clarke, whom I consider to be fully qualified for the literary situation which you design them to fill in Hayti. The former has been a teacher of youth in the private family of a Gentleman, and the latter in an English school of reputation, so that they have already had considerable experience in their profession. I have seen them and conversed with them several times at my own house, and have been pleased both with their address and conversation. I ... believe, from the testimony which I have had concerning them, that they are young men of correct behaviour and of moral character.

Mr. William Wilson is acquainted ... with the elements of ... universal grammar. Though he has not been in France, he appears to me to speak French with more than usual elegance. He is acquainted with the Latin language also. Besides this, he reads the Italian, and he speaks and reads the Spanish, so that he may probably be useful to your Majesty, if you should have any message to the Spanish part of the Island. He is acquainted with the English classical writers both in poetry and prose, and also with ancient and modern history. His knowledge and conversation will make him interesting and ... useful to the Baron de Vastey, ... particularly when the Baron is engaged in his literary labours.

Mr. George Clarke acquired his knowledge of the French by residing for some months in Paris, and afterwards many months in Dieppe. Here he taught the English language to French scholars grammatically. On his return to England, he was employed in a school near London in teaching the French and Latin languages grammatically, which school he left to engage himself in your Majesty's service. He has a competent knowledge, like the former, both of ancient and modern history, and has acquired that diversity of reading and knowledge which is usually comprehended under the name of the "belles-lettres."

I have no doubt that the abilities both of Mr. Wilson and of Mr. Clarke are such as will enable them to fill the offices you propose with satisfaction to your Majesty.... I have also reason to believe that I have not been deceived as to their moral character.... I have engaged both of them for seven years, if their health permit, upon the terms mentioned by your Majesty. It is their desire to continue during the whole of this period in Hayti, and I am persuaded that no common illness will induce them to leave it.... They thank your Majesty for your kind consideration towards them in proposing to pay their salaries in equal divisions every month, and as they leave England too suddenly to be prepared as they could wish for their new situation, your first payment of it at the end of the first month from the day of their arrival will be particularly acceptable to them....

I congratulate your Majesty upon the plan you have adopted of disbanding a part of your military for the purpose of agriculture, and of placing them in such situations that they may be easily called together in case of invasion. I presume you will encourage honourable marriage among them. As the cultivation of the earth will now become an important object with you, I think it would be proper that your subjects should be taught the use of the plough and of other improved agricultural instruments; and on this account I was glad to learn from Mr. Wilberforce that he had sent out to you several ploughs, and, what is very desirable, two ploughmen.... If you should have occasion for an additional number of ploughmen, I think I could find out one or two, either single men or married men with families, who might suit you, if they would consent to go. At the same time, I confess I cannot see how common ploughmen, who can only speak English, can instruct the Haytians, who can only speak French. It seems to me, if you intend to extend your agriculture on a large scale, that you ought to have some middle man between the two, some very superior farmer, who should be able to speak French and English, and who should go about from farm to farm and explain to the Haytian farmer what the English ploughman wishes to communicate to him, and also instruct him ... in the most judicious application of husbandry to the soil, and in various other departments connected with that science.

I have heard nothing lately from France.... It happens that I have a friend, the Baron de Turckheim, who is ... the President of the electoral college of Alsace and the representative for that Province. He is a very worthy man and a great friend to the Abolition of the Slave Trade. He is, besides, well known to the Cabinet Ministers of Louis the 18th. I purpose writing to him ... to ask him to use his good offices with Mons. de Cazes,

the Prime Minister, in order that . . . the Baron and myself may be allowed
to mediate between the French and Haytian Governments, at least so far
as to try to open a road by which the two Governments may meet each
other in a frank and open manner. . . ."[84]

I remain,

THOMAS CLARKSON

[84] Clarkson wrote not only to Baron de Turckheim on March 11, 1820, but also to Lafayette.
The letter to Lafayette has not come to light, but Clarkson included a copy of his letter to
Turckheim in his unpublished Autobiography.

Clarkson begins by reminding Turckheim of the ill repute in which Christophe is held in
France; "but we who live in England," Clarkson continues, "having better opportunities of
knowing his character, . . . have good reason to esteem his talents and his virtues and to be
assured that he will be ranked by posterity . . . among the benefactors of mankind." Indicating
the tremendous task of civilizing a barbarous people, and reviewing the achievements already
made by Christophe, Clarkson points out that there is one great obstacle handicapping advancement—"the apprehension that France may wish some time or other to recover Hayti by
force of arms." This necessitates the maintenance of a large standing army, the greater part of
which would be disbanded and employed in agriculture if this apprehension were removed.
"I do not mean to imply . . . that he is afraid of the French armies," Clarkson hastens to add;
"he is well assured that France can never conquer Hayti."

On the other hand, Clarkson assures Turckheim that a reconcilement would be as advantageous to France as to Haiti. The French Government must pay annual pensions to the ex-
colonists; "but besides the burthen of all these pensions, France loses a considerable portion
of trade which she might carry on if she were upon friendly terms with the Haytian Government."

But how could a reconciliation be brought about? "No Frenchman could be employed for
this purpose. . . . The French name is odious in Hayti." Clarkson goes on to recall "the misery
which France inflicted upon this unhappy Island under the reign of Buonaparte," and the
intrigues of 1814 and 1816 conducted by French agents even under Louis XVIII. "All the
measures taken by France with respect to Hayti since the year 1814," he declares, "have been
calculated only to give the inhabitants of that Island an unfavourable impression of the French
character; . . . [and have] occasioned the two rival chiefs, who had no friendship for each
other, to come to an understanding, that if ever an invasion was attempted, they would unite
in one common defence."

How, then, Clarkson asks, are the two countries to be "brought into habits of commercial
friendship with each other"? Since such "an event is not likely to be accomplished through the
medium of any Frenchman," he continues, "in this difficult state of things, I think it my duty
to offer my services to the French Government through the medium of you to endeavour to
bring the parties together"; and he authorizes Turckheim to sound out the French ministers on
the subject of a treaty.

Clarkson concludes his letter as follows: "I am in frequent correspondence with King
Henry. . . . I sent him my ideas of what I considered to be a fair and equitable treaty between
the two countries, and I begged him to take it into his most serious consideration. As a pledge
of my sincerity and frankness . . . I have no objection whatever to send to you, and through
you to the French Ministers, the conditions which I proposed to him . . . if they . . . are desirous
of receiving them, and if they will frankly make their observations upon them to you. . . . I shall
then be able to judge how far the two Governments are likely to meet; and if I should think
such an event likely, I will then offer every assistance in my power to promote such a desirable
object. Permit me to observe that I have no interest in offering my mediation, nor any motive
but humanity and good will as it relates both to France and Hayti. . . . God grant that I may not
have written in vain."

This letter laid the basis for later conferences in Paris with Turckheim, who supplied Clarkson with the information sent to Christophe in the long letter of July 10, 1820. (Letter 41, pp.
200–207.)

LETTER

36

King Henry to Thomas Clarkson

{ENGLISH TRANSLATION}

At the Palace of Cape Henry, March 17ᵗʰ, 1820,
in the 17ᵗʰ year of our Independence

THE KING,

to Mr. Thomas Clarkson,
Member of the African Institution

My Friend,

The letter you wrote me last year on the 10ᵗʰ of November[85] was delivered upon the arrival of the two Methodists, Mr. Elliot Jones and Mr. Woodis Harvey.[86] I am sorry, however, to inform you that the former, Mr. Jones, was already ill when he landed, and therefore decided to go and pass the summer in the United States of America in order to recuperate. Mr. Harvey has remained with us. I ordered that he be accorded all necessary facilities and protection for the accomplishment of his mission, and I am told that he is living on terms of intimacy with the British professors.

Your account of the virtues of the Society to which these Methodists belong was alone sufficient to give me the fullest confidence in their principles.

I appreciated, my friend, the three points you made in your letter regarding the prosperity and happiness of a nation, and I shall profit by your welcome advice.

When this communication reaches you, Mr. Birt will surely have arrived, and you will have learned about the important dispatches which I sent you. I am impatiently awaiting your answer.

I am, with the highest esteem and consideration,
                              Your sincere friend,

HENRY

---

[85] Clarkson apparently did not keep a copy of this letter.
[86] William Woodis Harvey (1798–1864) published in 1827 his *Sketches of Hayti; from the Expulsion of the French, to the Death of Christophe*. The work is chiefly valuable for its first-hand accounts of Haiti in 1820 and for its analysis of Christophe's system of government.

LETTER

37

The Duke of Limonade to Thomas Clarkson

{ENGLISH TRANSLATION}

*At the Palace of Cape Henry, April 14ᵗʰ, 1820,
in the 17ᵗʰ year of our Independence*

THE DUKE OF LIMONADE,
*Secretary of State, Minister of Foreign Affairs,
Member of the Royal Chamber of Public Instruction of
Haiti, Honorary Member of the English and Foreign
School Society of London, etc.,*

*to Mr. Thomas Clarkson,
Member of the African Institution of London, etc.*

Dear Sir,

Upon the arrival of the two professors you sent out to us, I received your letter of the 24ᵗʰ of last January,[87] in which you acknowledge receipt of my preceding communication of the 23ʳᵈ of September of last year,[88] the work of Baron de Vastey, and the newspapers which I sent you.

In the future I shall follow your suggestion and be careful to give instructions that dispatches addressed to you should not be sent by post, but delivered to Mr. William Allen, Plough Court, Lombard Street, London.

The favorable opinion of General de Vincent which you express in one paragraph of your letter is in perfect agreement with our own impression of him: he is an honorable man, a man of integrity, truthful, and a person who, knowing our country very well, can speak of it with authority.

His Majesty was very fond of De Vincent when the latter resided in Haiti, and De Vincent bore the King and royal family a great deal of affection. In fact, he still seems to entertain the same sentiments toward His Majesty. When you are in Paris, you will probably find it possible to see De Vincent and to learn in some detail how he feels about Haiti, he and others who

---

[87] Clarkson's letter to the Duke is missing.
[88] Limonade refers to his letter of September 3, 1819. See p. 153.

seem to be working in our interest. You can well imagine, Sir, how eager we who live so far away are to know better the men with whom we may have to deal.

We are delighted at His Majesty's good fortune in having a friend like you, who has dedicated himself completely to the great cause of humanity and to the welfare of Haiti. You may be sure, my dear Sir, that we are indeed grateful for the new proof of devotion you give us when you declare that you will use all your wisdom, energy, and strength to further the interests of our country. We believe implicitly that you will do everything within your power.

I remain your faithful servant,

DE LIMONADE

LETTER

38

King Henry to Thomas Clarkson

{ENGLISH TRANSLATION}

At Cape Henry, April 14ᵗʰ· 1820,
in the 17ᵗʰ year of our Independence

THE KING,

to Mr. Thomas Clarkson,
Member of the African Institution of London, etc.

My Friend,

Mr. Wilson and Mr. Clarke, who come to me sent by you, have arrived safely in Haiti and have delivered the letters they brought with them. They were presented to me and I had a long conversation with them.

Allow me to thank you, both for the zeal and promptness with which you acted in finding them and for your care in choosing them. I have kept the agreement you made with them in my behalf, and they have received, not one month's, as you had promised them, but three months' salary in advance and a suitable lodging at government expense. After reading what you wrote about the talents and capacities of these young men, with my usual confidence in you I did not hesitate to install Mr. Wilson as the tutor of my son, the Prince Royal.[89]

Mr. Clarke I established as professor in the Royal Academy,[90] in the post formerly occupied by Mr. Daniel. Since the health of the latter has been bad for some time, he is profiting by the arrival of Mr. Clarke to take a leave of absence, and will leave for England bearing my letters to you. I have only

---

[89] In response to a request from Wilson for advice concerning the education of the Prince, Clarkson wrote a long and detailed letter of suggestions. See Introduction, p. 67 and note.

[90] The Royal Academy apparently progressed most satisfactorily under Clarke, who soon had sixty pupils. On November 4, 1820, four weeks after Christophe's death, he remarked in a letter to Clarkson: "In a few years, I should have conducted two or three young men so far in classical and general knowledge as to have left them without hesitation as my successors. Mr. Moore would have done the same in mathematics and chemistry; and Dr. Stewart's medical class was rapidly advancing." See Letter 43, p. 212.

praise for his quiet and seemly behavior since he has been in Haiti. I am glad to give him all due credit and to express my regret that he is leaving us just when the Royal Chamber of Public Instruction had decided to use him in the Western Province as supervisor of the schools which have been established there and to charge him with setting up new schools.

Mr. Gulliver, the oldest of our schoolmasters in point of service, is also leaving for reasons of health, having suffered various illnesses and frequent relapses. We trust that he will return, as he promises to do as soon as he has recovered. We have been very much pleased with his work and the period of his engagement is not yet over.

I agree perfectly with your feeling that it would be well to introduce Haitian agriculturists to the use of the plough. Our friend Wilberforce has already sent me two ploughmen who have been set to work near the capital cultivating potatoes and cereal grains. Inevitably, since they know not a word of French, they have been having some difficulty in instructing the young men who were sent to learn from them. I believe then that we shall bring in only these two, until we begin to see the results of the experiment.[91]

Please believe, my friend, that my wishes for your welfare are in proportion to my esteem and affection for you.

HENRY

---

[91] Harvey reports more fully concerning this experiment. On their arrival, the two ploughmen "were directed first to make a trial of the implement, and in case it should succeed, afterwards to instruct the natives in the manner of using it. But they were not in the first instance equally successful. The grounds allotted to one of them, having been prepared before his arrival, were cultivated with a great saving of manual labour, and produced a most abundant crop. The estate which the other was directed to cultivate, required the assistance of a great number of labourers, in order to clear it from weeds, bushes and cane-roots, before he could introduce his plough; and its soil proving less fertile than that of others, little appeared to be gained in point of labour, and nothing in produce. Their subsequent attempts, however, were attended with equal success; and Christophe, highly gratified ... proceeded to make arrangements for introducing the plough into general use." *Op. cit.*, pp. 249–251.

LETTER

39

King Henry to Thomas Clarkson[92]

{ENGLISH TRANSLATION}

At the Palace of Cape Henry, April 14ᵗʰ, 1820,
in the 17ᵗʰ year of our Independence

THE KING,

to Mr. Thomas Clarkson,
Member of the African Institution of London, etc.

My Friend,

The English brig Aimé, under the command of Captain Harvey, reached port on the 21ˢᵗ of March, and I received the letters of the 6ᵗʰ and 9ᵗʰ of last February[93] which you sent in the captain's care.

It was with real satisfaction that I learned that the dispatches I had entrusted to Mr. Birt were delivered by him into your hands. I have read with pleasure what you say about the steps you are going to take to discuss the mission with our friends before setting out to accomplish the task which my esteem and trust have led me to confide to you.

You seize my thought very well when you state that it is unjust that I should find myself forced to remain in doubt concerning the intentions of the French Government toward Haiti and that you feel I should go directly to the source of authority rather than depend on the indirect overtures which are still being made to me. Whether your trip is successful or not, it will be worth while, because I shall learn what to expect from France. I shall await confidently, then, the first communications which you say you will send me in April, and which I shall hope to receive toward the end of next June.

I am happy that you understood my intentions as to the destination of the funds I sent you; I leave them entirely in your hands.

---

[92] This was apparently Christophe's last letter to Clarkson. Within six months Christophe died a violent death at his own hands.

[93] These letters are missing from this collection.

Since we wrote the afore-mentioned dispatches, we have received letters from General de Vincent and Monsieur de Pradt; I am including a copy of them for your information.[94] You will also find in an unsealed envelope the answer my Minister wrote to General de Vincent.[95] I beg of you to read the latter and, if you judge it will not hinder the success of your mission, to seal it and have it delivered to the addressee; if you prefer not to forward it, please return it to me with a statement of your reasons, so that I may understand and profit by your observations.[96]

It is well for you to know that during the period of your mission no letter dealing with relations between France and Haiti will be answered or dispatched unless it has first passed through your hands. I should not wish anyone to offer as an excuse for delaying or weakening the reply which must be made to you the plea that a letter has been written to Haiti and that an answer is being awaited. You will be in a fine position to detect any ruses or attempts at evading the important question, the answer to which it is vital for you to learn.

We shall be looking forward to your first communications. May I reiterate to you the assurance of my consideration and esteem?

Your friend,

HENRY

---

[94] These communications are missing from this collection. In his previous letters to Christophe, however, Clarkson had traced the change in French public opinion to a more liberal attitude towards Haiti since De Vincent's "aggressive" letter of February 17, 1819. By the end of July, 1819, France was willing, he believed, to relinquish her claim to the sovereignty of Haiti under two conditions: that "the chiefs of Hayti ... should pay a sum of money to France as an indemnification to the ex-colonists for the loss of property ... in consequence of the revolution," and that Haiti allow France the advantage of her commerce. Clarkson felt that this "enlightened policy" would "produce a new overture ... on the part of the French Government," and the letters of De Vincent and De Pradt probably embraced the afore-mentioned terms. See pp. 143, 154–155, and 159–160.

[95] Christophe, too, had arrived at his own terms. The indispensable condition of any treaty was that the King of France first recognize Haiti as a free, sovereign, and independent state. Once this conditon was agreed upon, Christophe would offer in return that France share in Haitian commerce and that Haiti would observe neutrality in case of a European war. Christophe declared as inadmissible any indemnification of the ex-colonists or any claim to exclusive rights to Haitian commerce. Limonade's reply to De Vincent, therefore, probably included these terms. See p. 175.

[96] Clarkson left for France about the first of May, 1820, and if he received Christophe's letter and enclosures during his residence there, it seems safe to assume that he did not deliver Limonade's letter to De Vincent.

LETTER

40

Thomas Clarkson to King Henry

April 28, 1820

[No salutation]

I had the honour of informing your Majesty by Messrs. Wilson and Clarke that I intended to proceed to London, as soon as circumstances would permit, in order to consult Mr. Wilberforce, Mr. Stephen, and others on the subject of your last letter to me, and then to proceed to Paris (if it should be thought advisable) to endeavour to execute your commission there. Since that time I have been to London . . . and I now write to your Majesty to lay before you the substance of the conferences which took place. . . .

1. With respect to the Diplomatic Paper by which your Majesty author-ized me to act as your Envoy at Paris,[97] . . . we were unanimously of opinion that the French Cabinet would not receive it. By receiving it the . . . Cabinet would be acknowledging the Independence of Hayti at the very outset. . . . We were persuaded that they would not do this, unless it could be previously known that I had the power of making propositions to France which she would think equivalent to the surrender of the sovereignty of Hayti. It appeared, therefore, that to offer this Diplomatic Paper to the French Gov-ernment without the previous statement of some preliminaries advanta-geous to France would be to insure its immediate rejection by that Government. . . .

2. We were of opinion that the sudden proposal of a treaty by your Majesty to the French Cabinet would be rather injurious than favourable to your own interests, for hitherto you have stood upon high and independ-ent ground. You rejected the two commissions which were sent to you by the King of France in the years 1814 and 1816.[98] If, therefore, you were to apply, suddenly and without some arrangements previously made, to the French Government for a Treaty of Peace and Commerce, we fear the

---

[97] For the credentials and instructions sent to Clarkson see Letters 31 and 32, pp. 172–177.
[98] See pp. 57–61.

French Government would consider this application of yours as a ... sign
of your consciousness of your own weakness. ... This sudden change from
an austere inflexibility to a voluntary yielding on your part, so as even to
send an Envoy to that very Court whose messengers you have twice refused
to receive, would make you be considered by the French Government as an
humble suppliant for peace, a situation of which they would directly take
advantage, either by means of some well-concerted plan of intrigue, or by
an open invasion or blockade of your Dominions.

3. We were unanimously of opinion that the present was not the time for
your Majesty to send an Envoy to Paris. Since the assassination of the Duc
de Berry,[99] ... French affairs have assumed a new aspect. Though this
tragical event had no connection with political party, but was perpetrated
solely by Louvel, a desperate madman, yet the King of France has been
prevailed upon to act as if a conspiracy had been formed to overturn his
Government. He has accordingly changed his Ministry, and these have unhappily succeeded in making alterations in the laws of France,[100] which,
being contrary to the spirit of the Charter and ... therefore offensive to the
French Nation, have produced an irritation which may ultimately end in
revolutionary consequences. In short, the disturbed state ... renders the
present time a very unfit one for your Majesty to propose a treaty....
Another circumstance ... forbids such a proposition at the present moment.
The *new* Administration consists principally of *Ultra Royalists*, ... who are
enemies to your Majesty and to the liberty of the Africans. The Duc de
Richelieu is probably the only man in this Administration who is a friend to
the African race.

4. With respect to the grand preliminary article of the treaty, by which
the entire Independence of Hayti would be made a *sine quâ non* with
France, we ... feel as if we were called upon to decide a case which would
terminate *either in liberty or slavery;* ... and we wish on that account that
your Majesty should determine this awful question for yourself. At the
same time, we feel it our duty to declare to you that we think that no treaty
with France would be safe for your Majesty and the Haytian people, unless
your Independence ... be acknowledged by the French Government in its
fullest latitude and in terms so clear and explicit as not to be evaded.... If
France has not kept her Treaty with the Sovereigns at Vienna for the

---

[99] On February 13, 1820, the Duc de Berry, nephew of Louis XVIII, was assassinated by the
Bonapartist Louis-Pierre Louvel.
[100] Clarkson refers to the *lois d'exception*, which suspended freedom of the press and individual political liberty and transformed the electoral system.

Abolition of the Slave Trade, ... what prospect is there that she will keep her treaty with you, if she found it to be her interest to evade it? and if such a treaty were liable to evasion? ... Besides, we consider all French Governments as so loose or relaxed in moral principle that all human caution is necessary for those who have any dealings with them. ...

5. On the subject of indemnification, which your Majesty has forbidden me even to name to the French Ministers, we agree with you that, as far as justice is concerned, it is not due to the ex-colonists. ... But though we agree with you fully upon this point, we are unanimously of opinion that France will never give up the sovereignty of Hayti without some greater sacrifice on your Majesty's part than that which you propose. All that you offer to France in return for your Independence is a free trade and neutrality in time of war. ... We are very sorry, therefore, to be obliged to say that unless you can offer something more to France than these two conditions, all hope of a treaty then is at an end. ...

If your Majesty, therefore, should resolve to offer no other propositions than the two mentioned, we are unanimously of opinion that it would be more to your advantage to continue as you are ... than to offer a treaty, the very offer of which might be construed into weakness by the French Government, and in which you would have no chance of succeeding; and we are the more induced to this opinion, because, though we believe that France will one day or other be among the most powerful nations of Europe, and therefore in a situation to disturb your peace, yet we think that she is far from being in a situation to invade you at present, while you yourself will be growing more formidable with time.

These then are our sentiments on the different points contained in your Majesty's instructions to me; ... and though we believe the treaty in question to be quite hopeless, unless your Majesty will consent to enlarge your conditions, yet we think that something useful might be attempted ... on your Majesty's account. ... It strikes us as desirable that some person should go to Paris, not as a public agent but in his own individual capacity, and spend a few weeks there for the purpose of getting accurate information on the particular disposition and state of France as they relate to Hayti. ... I have taken upon me this important office, and I purpose, therefore, to leave England in the course of three days. Your Majesty may be assured that I will neglect nothing which may be of importance to you, ... and I hope to be able to procure such a fund of political knowledge as may enable you to see your way more clearly with respect to France, not only for the present but for the future. I expect to be absent from home many weeks. I shall go as a private individual, but shall take my Diplomatic Papers with me in case of an unexpected turn....[101]

[No signature]

---

[101] This letter was the last one from Clarkson to arrive before Christophe's death. Since Christophe had eagerly awaited news of Clarkson's French mission and since his letters, as well as those of Vastey and Limonade, are pathetically hopeful of a favorable outcome, the negative nature of Clarkson's letter, the advice "to continue as you are," must have left him heartsick and discouraged. The unfavorable news, however, did not deter him from pursuing his policies for the improvement of Haiti, and almost his last official act, performed, indeed, on the very eve of his death, was to provide financial assistance for the transportation of the free people of color from the United States, in order to increase his population.

For his part, too, Clarkson must have regretted sending such unsatisfactory tidings. He had strenuously urged Christophe to observe only the best interests of Haiti in making a treaty with France, even if it proved necessary to offer her exclusive commerce or to pay an indemnification, but Christophe had emphatically refused to compromise on either point.

LETTER

41

Thomas Clarkson to King Henry

July 10, 1820

My Friend

I had the honour of writing to your Majesty by Mr. Birt on the 28th of April last...on your proposed treaty with France, which you requested that I would execute personally at Paris....Directly after this I proceeded to Paris. I did not, however, act there...in a public capacity, but as a private individual....As I had no other terms to offer on the part of your Majesty but those of a free trade with France and neutrality in the case of war, I am sure that I should have been dismissed by the French Government in the very beginning of the negotiations if I had been known there as your Envoy. By acting there in a private capacity I have offended no one...[and] I have learnt what would have been at that time the terms of a French treaty with Hayti, without pledging you to anything or without ever discovering that you were even anxious for it.

The three great points to which I directed my attention during my residence at Paris were these: 1st. Will France ever fit out an expedition for the conquest of Hayti? 2nd. Will France ever acknowledge the Independence of Hayti? 3rd. Upon what terms...will France consent to acknowledge such Independence?

I come to the first question. Will France ever fit out an expedition *expressly for the purpose of conquering Hayti?* The universal answer to this in France is—No—Any French Ministers collecting an armament solely French, and solely for such a purpose, would be considered to be mad.... Ridicule has generally accompanied the mention of any expedition to Hayti....It is a proverb among the Military—"as hopeless and disastrous as the Expedition of Leclerc." It is, therefore, almost universally believed in France that no French regiment would go there....It seems also to be a universal opinion in France that the subjugation of Hayti...*is impossible,*...[and] that the French Cabinet have abandoned all thoughts of employing an armament against Hayti, *either now* or at *any future time.*...

But though the French Cabinet have given up the idea of regaining Hayti by force of arms, it does not follow that your Majesty will be allowed to remain forever in the undisturbed possession of your rights. It will be a long time before the French Cabinet will forget that the sovereignty of Hayti once belonged to France, and so long as they remember this, they may either try to distress you in order to bring you to terms, or they may watch for opportunities of destroying you by other means.... Two circumstances may arise, which may enable them to try to gratify their wishes in this respect.

First, if there should ever be unhappily a quarrel between your Majesty and General Boyer, it is supposed that ... [the French] would interfere by sending an armed force to Hayti. They have their eye constantly upon Hayti with this intention, and I believe they indulge the hope of being able to realize it one day or other. This hope is founded upon the hatred which is said to subsist between your Majesty and General Boyer, but principally upon those pages in the Almanach Royal d'Hayti, where your Majesty still retains the names of Port-au-Prince, Jacmel, Les Cayes, Jérémie, and other places occupied by General Boyer, as if they were now under your own Government, or as if you intended some time or other to make them your own. They consider this latter as an unequivocal proof that you have it in contemplation to try to subjugate General Boyer.... In case of an open rupture they would undoubtedly assist General Boyer with as large a naval and military force as they could collect,... for it is my duty *not* to conceal from you that the French Cabinet are far better disposed towards General Boyer than towards yourself.

Second, if your Majesty or General Boyer should do anything which should have the appearance of meddling with European concerns, or with the present state of the slave colonies belonging to the different maritime powers of Europe,... it is supposed that the French Cabinet would do their utmost to engage every Power in Europe to make a common cause with France in the entire subjugation of Hayti, that is, in the entire annihilation both of your Majesty and of General Boyer also....

It would appear, then, ... that so long as your Majesty and General Boyer should live in peace and harmony with each other, and so long as you should afford to Europe no cause of suspicion that you intended to interfere with the condition of the slaves in the different Islands in your neighbourhood, you would have nothing to fear from the French Cabinet....

I come now to the second point. Will France ever acknowledge the Independence of Hayti? ... The present Minister of the Marine and Colonies ... has no objection to make a treaty with your Majesty and General Boyer on very favourable terms, provided you would acknowledge the King of France as your nominal Sovereign; nor would he refuse, I believe, even to acknowledge the Independence of Hayti, but then he would *make you pay very dearly for it.* ...

I come now to the third point. Upon what terms ... would France consent to acknowledge the Independence of Hayti? ... I shall now lay before you [first] the terms ... which, I am told, would be required of you ... [by] the *present,* or any other *Ultra Royal* Administration, [and second by an Administration of the Liberaux].

1. No foreigner would be allowed to make a treaty between France and Hayti. It must be made directly ... by a minister of the King of France and a minister of your Majesty. ...

2. No treaty would be allowed to be made with your Majesty *as King of Hayti,* because if the King of France were to allow your present title at [the] opening of the negotiation, he would be to all intents and purposes acknowledging your Independence. He would, therefore, insist upon making [a] treaty *not with you but with General Christophe* ... upon the principle that the King of France knows no such person at present as the King of Hayti, and that to receive any credentials so signed would be to acknowledge your Majesty's Independence. Thus the negotiation would be stopped and your Envoy would be sent home. ...

3. The guarantee of England would be rejected. The person who should propose such a suspicion of French honour would be dismissed from all further negotiation, if not insulted.

4. France would bind your Majesty never to stir up ... any insurrections of the slaves in the French or other Islands.

5. France would demand of your Majesty an exclusive trade to herself for at least fifty years, if not forever.

6. France would demand from your Majesty and also from General Boyer an indemnification for the losses of the ex-colonists. ... The indemnification in question would not be calculated upon the present pensions (which the ex-colonists receive from the French Government to the amount of 1,000,000 francs annually and which are only *alimentaires*), but upon the land which they had lost in Hayti. A certain sum of money would be fixed upon the land lost by the ex-colonists equal to what would be thought a proper annual rent for the same, and twenty-two times this rent, or this

rent at twenty-two years' purchase, would be the amount of the indemnification required.

These are the terms which, I believe, would be required of your Majesty by the present French Cabinet, or by any other French Cabinet which should go under the name of Ultra Royalist. One of my friends, the venerable Deputy for the lower Rhine . . . [Baron de Turckheim], took upon himself the trouble, at my request, of having frequent conversations with Mons. the Baron Portal, the French Minister of Marine and Colonies, . . . on this subject; and it was from my venerable friend that I became acquainted with the conditions which I have now mentioned. I never saw the Baron Portal himself, but he . . . [said] that he should be happy to see me as a private gentleman, for whose name he had a great esteem, but that he could not talk with me on the affairs of Hayti. At another time he said that he had no objection to see me on that subject, if I would make proposals to him from the proper authority. I declined, however, his invitation; for what would have been the use of accepting it, when I knew that my proposals would have irritated him against your Majesty? when I knew the ignominious terms . . . which he himself had resolved upon? when I knew that as soon as ever he should see my Credentials signed by the Duc de Limonade, as the Minister for Foreign Affairs *of the King of Hayti,* our conference would immediately cease? Indeed, I was informed beforehand that if I entered into conversation with any of the French Cabinet on your Majesty's affairs, I should excite displeasure, if I mentioned you under any other name than that of General Christophe. By refusing, therefore, an interview with the Baron Portal, I have not prejudiced or irritated him or any of the French Ministry against your Majesty. . . . You stand now on as high ground as you did before, but with this important difference, that Monsieur the Baron Portal and the French Ministry know . . . through the means of my venerable friend, the Deputy for the lower Rhine, that you are disposed to make a treaty with France upon honourable conditions, the first of which is an acknowledgement on their part of the Independence of Hayti. . . .

The terms which would be required of your Majesty by a French Cabinet of the *Liberaux* . . . would be more in your favour than [those of the Ultra Royalists]. . . .

1. I believe that no foreigner would be allowed . . . to make a treaty between France and Hayti, but I believe that a foreigner would be allowed not only to bring the parties together, but to introduce, arrange, and even

settle the preliminaries, and that this favour would be especially granted to myself.

2. The same difficulty would occur ... [concerning] the reception of any credentials from your Majesty, *as King of Hayti*, ... [but] the name of *Chef du Gouvernement* might be used instead of that of General Christophe; or if they would permit ... a foreigner to arrange the preliminaries, the treaty might follow in the direct names of the King of France and the King of Hayti.

3. The guarantee of England would be rejected as before. ...

4. It might be asked of your Majesty to bind yourself not to interfere with the condition of the slaves in the French Colonies. ...

5. It might probably be asked again of your Majesty to grant to France an exclusive trade to Hayti, but this would not, I believe, be insisted upon. ...

6. Indemnification for the ex-colonists would certainly be demanded, ... and this seems to be the only serious difficulty. ... It is supposed, however, that the indemnification would not amount to that enormous sum which at the first sight might be expected. ... The land and the land only would be valued. Great reductions also would be made here [for marsh lands and for lands not now under cultivation]. ...

I have now laid before your Majesty the ... conditions which would be required of you by the two different Cabinets of Ultra Royalists and *Liberaux* in making a treaty with France. ... The question resolves itself into three cases. Will you make a treaty with the former? or would you prefer a treaty with the latter? or would you prefer making no treaty at all and abide by the consequences?

With respect to the first question, ... the conditions are too degrading and too burthensome to be submitted to.

With respect to the second, the ... conditions are not dishonourable. ... I see no very great difficulty here but that of indemnification. ... If the acknowledgement of the Independence of Hayti by France (which would be followed by England and other Powers) be a matter so near and dear to your Majesty's heart that you would be willing to make *pecuniary sacrifices* to obtain it, you must wait ... till a new administration consisting of the *Liberaux* be formed. ...

With respect to the third question, that is, would you prefer making *no treaty at all* and abide by the consequences? ... I will suppose ... that your Majesty is inclined to follow this course, [and] ... I will take the liberty of stating what I think you ought to do.

1. I should advise you to keep yourself in such a state of preparation that, while you should be enabled to defend yourself against any attack, you would not be under the necessity of relaxing in any of your plans, either of agriculture or of any other system for the improvement of your Dominions. This might be done by adopting, as I recommended in a former letter, the plan of the Militia of England, but to a greater extent....

2. I should advise you to increase your population by all the means in your power. And here permit me to observe that no opportunity can ever present itself for this purpose equal to that of receiving the free people of colour from the United States....

3. I should advise your Majesty to do everything in your power to prevent any misunderstanding between yourself and General Boyer, so that no opportunity may be afforded to the French Government for an armament to Hayti.

4. To avoid even the appearance of any interference with any of the European slave islands for the same reason.

5. To endeavour to know everything that passes in the two Chambers of France relative to Hayti, in order that you may have intelligence of every hostile movement on the part either of the French Cabinet or of any of the ex-colonists ... who may be in those Assemblies. This knowledge might be obtained by purchasing the *Moniteur* or the *Constitutionnel,* or some other approved French Journal....

6. It might be advisable for some one of your Majesty's friends to go over to Paris once a year for three or four years, to come during the sitting of the two Chambers, to cultivate an interest with the liberal members ... in your Majesty's favour....

7. When I was in France five years ago, I had the mortification to hear your Majesty's Government ridiculed and your private character stigmatized. During my last journey, however, I had the satisfaction of observing that a considerable change had taken place in the public opinion on that subject, but particularly as to your character.... You are now no longer the cruel monster which the ex-colonists had represented you to be. This happy change has been effected by your Majesty's friends, who have circulated ... many facts relative to your political regulations, of which almost all had been before ignorant. It is, therefore, ... absolutely necessary that the French Nation should become better acquainted with your Majesty's true character, ... both as an individual and [as] a legislator.... I would advise, therefore, that the Baron de Vastey should directly compose a little work of about 40 or 50 pages only, for this purpose....

He might ... describe the political state of Hayti as it was when your Majesty [came to power] ... and paint in true colours the disorganized state of society as it was [at] that moment. He should ... state that your Majesty determined to put a stop to these disorders and to lay the foundation of a wise, liberal, just, and virtuous Government. ... The Baron would have here a fine opportunity of observing that ... your Majesty found yourself obliged, contrary to your natural disposition, to make many severe examples by severe punishments for the public good; and that it was this very circumstance which occasioned all the heavy charges against you which have been invented, exaggerated, and sounded all over Europe. ... The Baron should ... begin with the first public act which your Majesty ordered ... and then enumerate all the others as they took place successively, ... —in short, every act done by your Majesty to improve the condition of your subjects. ... He should then take a view of the present state of the inhabitants of Hayti and contrast it with the former, in order to show the changes. ...

After having done this he should say a few words relative to your Majesty's Government, as a Government. ... I have already told you that the French Cabinet are much better disposed to General Boyer than to yourself ... [and] that they give the preference to General Boyer, ... [because] they prefer the nature of his Government to the nature of yours. They told me without any hesitation that "yours was no Government, it was a mere Despotism." ... I should advise, therefore, that the Baron de Vastey should say a few words on this subject in the little work now mentioned. He might state that the system of education which your Majesty was giving to your subjects was intended as a foundation on which to build with safety a political constitution which should embrace the rational liberty and happiness of all your people. I am sure that an avowal like this would please many of your Majesty's friends and disarm many of your enemies.

Permit me to say a few words more concerning this little work. ... Nothing of a political nature should appear in it. No reflection should be made upon France: indeed it would be better not to mention France at all except in a respectful manner. ... About 100 copies ... should be sent to England. ... They should be directed to some one of your Majesty's friends who should be desired to take them to Paris and to distribute them personally to the most distinguished of the Peers and Deputies. A few copies should be reserved to be sent to the most illustrious potentates of Europe. ... One copy should be sent to the editor of the "Revue Encyclopédique," and some interest should be made with him to reprint it in that celebrated work, which is read in France, Italy, Germany, Poland, Prussia, and parts of the Russian Empire. Should it be found to produce an effect, your Majesty's friend should have power to reprint it in France... to give it a wider circulation. But here permit me to observe that the *censeurs* of the French are so very vigilant... that it would not be allowed to be circulated if there was anything in it the least offensive to the French Government.

8. The last thing which I have to recommend to your Majesty is this. If, contrary to all human reason and if contrary to all human expectation, the French Government should ever meditate an attack upon Hayti, your Majesty's friends in England should be authorized by you to dispatch a light and quick sailing vessel to Hayti to make known to you such intention.

I have now given your Majesty the best advice in my power.... If I can be useful to you and to your Country at any other time or on any other occasion, you may command my services; for I should think my life well spent if I could become an instrument under Providence of contributing towards the security, the Independence, and the happiness of Hayti.

I have the honour to be with great esteem and regard,

Your Majesty's friend,

THOMAS CLARKSON[102]

P.S. Messrs. Reid and Irving would have advanced me the £6000 which you sent me, but I drew upon them only for £300, and this covered the expenses of my journey, so that £5700 still remains at your Majesty's disposal.

---

[102] "This letter was sent to Christophe; but, alas! he was not living at the time it arrived,... so that my labours for him and the people of Hayti were all in vain, as relates to this treaty." [Note by Thomas Clarkson.]

[*The preceding letter marks the close of the correspondence between Clarkson and King Henry. The letters which follow are mainly concerned with events after Christophe's death; but since recognition of Haitian independence has been so frequently discussed, it will not be amiss briefly to recount the subsequent story of Franco-Haitian relations. As long as Christophe was alive, his uncompromising attitude discouraged French aggression, but five years after his death, France imposed harsh terms upon Haiti. In July, 1825, after much unsuccessful negotiation, President Boyer, who had absorbed Christophe's territory into his own on the King's death in 1820, and who had gained control over the Spanish part of the island in 1822,*[103] *was forced, under the guns of a French fleet, to accept an ignominious royal ordonnance. This edict acknowledged the independence of Haiti but demanded (1) that France be granted a fifty per cent reduction of the duties required in Haitian ports and (2) that Haiti pay, in five installments, the first due on December 31, 1825, an indemnification of one hundred and fifty million francs. It was impossible for the Haitians to pay the enormous sum which France had imposed upon them. Only one payment of thirty million francs was made, and that by means of a loan floated at Paris in November, 1825, amounting to twenty-four million francs. Franco-Haitian relations grew worse under the agreement, until finally, in 1838, a treaty was signed by the two countries, giving unqualified recognition of Haitian independence and reducing the indemnity to sixty million francs.*[104] *Haiti was not formally recognized by Great Britain until 1838, nor by the United States until 1862.*]

---

[103] In 1821 Spanish Santo Domingo revolted against the sovereignty of Spain and early in 1822 joined the Republic of Haiti. The whole island of Hispaniola, for the first time since the administration of Toussaint, now came under Boyer's government, and the union lasted for twenty-two years.

[104] J. N. Léger, *op. cit.*, pp. 182–189.

LETTER

42

William Wilson to his Father

Cape Henry, Haiti, October 1st, 1820

Dear Father

Just risen from a bed of sickness, from which I did not expect to rise, I write to you with a trembling hand....

The King, I regret to say, has for more than two months been indisposed; but he is now convalescent and attends as before to the affairs of his government, in which he is assisted by the Prince, my pupil. The latter I have not yet seen since my illness, but I expect him daily. I continue to receive the King's approbation, and am in favour with his son, who makes great progress and now speaks English so well as to procure me a great deal of praise....

You will excuse, dear Father, the shortness of a letter written, as this is, by a person who hardly knows how to hold his pen....

Your dutiful and affectionate Son,

WILLIAM WILSON

LETTER
43
George Clarke to Thomas Clarkson

Au Cap, Nov. 4, 1820

Dear Sir

The news of the revolution which has taken place at Hayti will, in all probability, reach the public papers of Europe before I shall find an opportunity of getting this letter conveyed to you. But as I know the interest you feel for the country, I shall presume to send an *aperçu* of the events which have happened here, imperfect as it must be in a letter.

In August the King issued from the Capital to pass as usual the hot season in the country, and to visit the towns and forts of the kingdom. The *fête* of the Queen was held in the palace at Belle-Vue, when he was seized with a fit of apoplexy in the chapel. He was copiously blooded, and in two or three days in some measure recovered, but not sufficiently to leave his bed. In this state he continued all [till?] October, (only being removed to Sans Souci) and the chiefs, no longer awed by his presence and activity, began to express their abhorrence of the restraint in which they were held. The disaffection quickly spread through all ranks, and the soldiers at Saint-Marc, a frontier town, openly revolted. The garrison here at the Cape received orders to march against them. This was on the evening of the sixth of October—Friday. About eleven at night the *tambour* was beaten, and the troops drawn up, when they declared they would no longer bear a king, but be entirely free. The Duc de la Marmelade took off his cross[105] and decorations, and proclaimed himself no longer Duke, but simply General Richard.[106] The Count de Gros Morne did the same, and the various nobles present followed their examples.

---

[105] "The Haitian nobility were elected members of the *Royal and Military Order of St. Henry;* an order of Knighthood created by Christophe shortly after his coronation. . . . The cross of the order was of gold, enamelled with the *lapis lazuli;* and had, on one side, the image of St. Henry, with this inscription: *Henri, Fondateur,* 1811; and on the other, a crown of laurels with a star, and the following motto: *Prix de la valeur."* W. W. Harvey, *op. cit.,* p. 147.

[106] General Richard, Duke of Marmelade, the military governor of the capital of Cape Henry and a member of the Privy Council and of the Royal and Military Order of St. Henry. There are many evidences of friction between Christophe and Richard.

The troops marched out next morning, and encamped at Haut-du-Cap, a village about three miles from this place and nine from Sans Souci. The news was communicated to the King on the Saturday evening. He ordered out his bodyguard and gave the command to the Duke of Fort Royal.[107] They marched on the Sunday. Towards evening they reached Haut-du-Cap and a few shots were exchanged, but a white flag was hoisted, and the republicans exhorted them to join in the cause of freedom. An immediate desertion took place. The commander alone remained faithful to his King. He turned and fled to bear the news to Sans Souci. Henry, being informed of the revolt of his guards, requested to be left that he might reflect on the measures most proper to be pursued. He arose, placed a pistol to his mouth, and before his attendants, who were alarmed by the report, could rush into the room he was dead.

These events passed with the rapidity of a dream. The superb palace at Sans Souci, the centre of all the magnificence of Hayti, was pillaged the same night; and the Queen and Princesses, who a few hours before were the richest individuals perhaps in the world, were reduced to walk nearly barefooted over the hard rocks to the Citadel.

On the 18th the two sons of the King (the Prince Royal and his natural son, Prince Eugène) with the Duke de l'Artibonite, the Duke of Fort Royal, and Baron Dessalines were bayoneted in the prison yard. This was at midnight, at about 200 yards from the college. I was so oppressed by fear that I was unable to sleep, and was walking about my chamber with the windows open. The shrieks I heard made me shudder, though I was at that time ignorant of the cause. On the 19th at the same hour, the Baron de Vastey and six other nobles suffered in the same manner.

With the exception of this, everything has been conducted tranquilly and without bloodshed; but this cold-blooded, useless murder excited a sickening sensation which has scarcely left me.

On the 21st General Boyer was declared President of the North and South. On the 28th he entered here with a numerous army of apparently quiet, well-disposed men. I was introduced a few days after his arrival. He inquired into the state of the college, and expressed great satisfaction. Since that time he has sent to request me to remain unoccupied till he has made the tour of the Northern part. Upon his return it is his intention to reëstablish the college; for from the beginning of the revolution, it has been

---

[107] This was Prince Joachim. Till the moment of his massacre by the insurgents, he "affirmed with unwavering constancy, that so long as there remained to him a single soldier he would maintain the cause of his king." J. Brown, *op. cit.*, Vol. II, p. 243.

closed. In what manner the new government will proceed is uncertain. I shall feel regret if I leave Hayti, after the sacrifices I have made and the prospect I have had of being useful.

Believe me, dear Sir, wherever I may be placed, the recollection of your kindnesses will always impress me with feelings of respect and gratitude.

GEO. CLARKE

I am afraid, Sir, you have thought me negligent in not writing. You honoured me by desiring me to do so whenever I had anything to communicate. My close and continued occupation with sixty pupils left me very little leisure, and in retiring from my employment I have frequently sunk in a seat exhausted by the exertion in such a climate. In answer to your kind inquiries, I was desirous of giving you pleasing information, and but for the late unfortunate events, I should certainly have done so. I was becoming gradually acclimated. In a few years, I should have conducted two or three young men so far in classical and general knowledge as to have left them without hesitation as my successors. Mr. Moore would have done the same in mathematics and chemistry; and Dr. Stewart's medical class was rapidly advancing. Must all these pleasing prospects be closed? I trust not, but the event is very uncertain.

L E T T E R

44

William Wilson to Thomas Clarkson

Cape Haytian,[108] *Dec. 5, 1820*

Dear Sir

Late events in this country have rendered early communication with you so likely a mode of conduct that it appears quite necessary to account for my neglect of it. My first feeling, indeed, prompted me to write daily my observations, ... but the afterthought that many errors might mingle in the account, from too hasty and unjustifiable conclusions, deterred me from the work. The end of this is that ... my facts are curiously confused with traits of character and stories difficult to be believed; and I have always found it necessary to delay the task to be able to execute it with a feeling of satisfaction. . . .

The King passed the first seven months of this year almost entirely at the Cape, occupied in directing the repairs. Never, as those observe who have long known him, was he more active. Rising early, passing many hours on horseback, attending closely, during his more sedentary moments, to the regulation of domestic affairs and foreign correspondence, and retiring late; he was seen and felt everywhere and at all times. His meanest subject was as much under his surveillance as his great officers of state. No exemptions from obscurity.

Every eye was on him and his eye was on everyone.

In the middle of August, he at length left the Cape where he was incommoded by the excessive heat; and, accompanied by the Queen, the Princesses, and his son, the Prince Royal, went to Belle-Vue le Roi, a royal residence in Limonade, about fifteen miles off. It was here that, whilst celebrating the fête of the Queen, and attending divine services surrounded by his family and a crowd of officers and ladies of the palace, a crowd as splendid and as well-regulated as any in Europe—amidst all his greatness—and the satisfaction of pride with which he looked about upon *all* men—he

---

[108] After Christophe's death Cap Henry again became Cap Haïtien and is so called today.

was attacked by an apoplectic fit, which spread in a moment terror over every countenance, and opened—to his enemies, a prospect of his destruction and their freedom—to his friends, the overthrow of all his institutions, and their probable ruin.

This was not, however, the immediate effect of the accident. His surgeon, who happened to be present, succeeded in restoring animation, and thus saved to Haïti a scene of horrors which alone was wanting to its entire destruction. But it was the immediate danger only which was past. This terrible attack was followed by a paralysis, which affecting all his right side, rendered him incapable of all affairs and of any kind of bodily exertion. It is not to be supposed that men, early accustomed to boundless liberty, licentiousness, and brigandage, who had long groaned under, and cursed the yoke which restrained them, would now that it lay loosely on them, neglect to shake it off. Many of them possessed courage to undertake any enterprise, and fortitude to execute it; although they had long trembled before Christophe, because none could resist singly and none could confide the thought of resistance to another. But now that their dreaded superior was apparently impotent to punish, these men became daring; and it was not long before some of them began to consult privately on the safest means of destroying the King and changing the government. The most moderate proposed to effect this by instituting a milder and more liberal institution, without, however, using violence against their present ruler and his partisans, who, they rightly judged, could not now be numerous; others, found mostly among the military, thought it now advisable at once to take up arms and finish the tyranny by the death of Henry and all his adherents. Meantime, the most profound secrecy was observed. Here was seen the superior cunning of the Negro. No thought of opposition to the King's will was observed in any countenance. Not one was there who would not have fallen over and worshipped him to prove his obedience and his devotion.

Those among the King's friends who happened to recollect how large a space he occupied in the "machine of government" foresaw disorder; and a few, the most zealous, with rare temerity ventured to advise the formation of a provisional government, at the head of which, as President of the Council, they proposed to place the Prince Royal. I need not observe that the proposal was violently rejected by the King. Every order, every disposition emanated as before from his proper person. His son was deputed only to preside over its execution.

It was not without a colour of justice that these men determined to resist the authority of the King. It must be acknowledged that they had much reason to complain. They owed him much, it is true, as the chief to whom they were principally indebted for their liberation from French pretensions. They owed him all that they had. As the founder of their most beneficial institutions, he had done everything for them. When he began to command, he found a reign of anarchy, of pillage, of murder, of lawless force, for which he substituted one of order, strict police, and public safety. Under him few crimes were committed. The people derived from him habits of industry and temperance. He restrained unlawful sexual intercourse. He encouraged, authorized, and advanced public education; and to his exertions the next generation will be indebted if they are less barbarous than the present. But, on the other hand, they had rewarded him by a distinction which might have sufficed for the greatest sacrifices, for unbounded efforts— they made him the most absolute monarch in the world. If he made good laws, he was the first to violate them. If he prevented robbery in others, it was to enjoy himself the exclusive privilege of robbing. His punishments were severe, not to say cruel, and his wars and his oppression have cost the country full one-half of its population. He was excessive in his demand for labour, and he never paid those who passed [their] existence in his service. If he discountenanced and severely punished adultery and loose conversation, no woman in his court was free from his libidinous advances. In a word, he was a *philosopher,* according to the modern use of the term. No object was sacred. Man's physical properties were his *material,* which he endeavoured to direct and combine, so as to produce to himself the largest share of enjoyment. He knew how to govern others, but he rarely made an effort to control himself. From long yielding to his passions, it had become with him a principle to indulge them.

In this my endeavour to account for the disposition of the people on this occasion, I have ... unintentionally run into a description of Henry's character. The features of the picture will, I fear, from your long cherished opinion of him, appear distorted. He had a plan for everything. One great end of his was the attainment of a high rank in the estimation of Europe— to raise himself in their idea from the petty chief of *one part* of a revolted colony (the colour of which had been long looked upon as degraded) to the place of the great ones of the earth—to exhibit himself as an exception, an anomaly to the body of his race—to redeem himself, if not his race, back to the mass of humanity. His endeavours for this effect formed a province in his occupations. He had his exhibitions of good, and his concealments, studious concealments of evil. Before the white man in his dominions he was affable, mild, generous, and magnificent, just to a fault, and almost anxious to conciliate. In his foreign correspondence he breathed nothing but a spirit of philanthropy. The happiness of his people, . . . the promulgation of sound religious doctrine, . . . the . . . strict adherence to moral law: these were to constitute the crown, the reward of his exertions. All this appears but too plainly to have been a mask—a mask with which he successfully covered the deformity of his heart and his actions.

But it is time to return to the course of events. The health of the King gradually became better, and the court removed to Sans Souci. Still it was believed by all that he would never be so completely re-established as to regain his wonted activity, and even his guard clearly evinced a disposition to revolt. His illness, too, sharpened his expressions of anger, and no one approached him without real danger. . . . His family and his confidential servants and secretaries were particularly exposed to the effects of his malignant temper.

A number of superior officers, therefore, who remained at the Cape, in concert with some officers of his horse guard, availed themselves of an event common enough in itself, but fatal to the King on this occasion, to excite the soldiers to revolt. The colonel of a regiment in garrison at Saint-Marc was arrested by his general officer and sent, after a slight examination, to the King, who condemned him to imprisonment in irons. On the first notice of this at Saint-Marc, the regiment ran to arms, cut off the head of the general who had denounced their officer, and began to fortify themselves, with the determination to resist the King to the last. This first act of rebellion authorized others. Six thousand men were sent to Saint-Marc to reduce the insurgents; but the general officers dreaded so much the defection of their troops that they attempted nothing, and the spirit of insurrection spread rapidly.

It was on Friday evening, the sixth of October, that, as I was returning home from the house of a friend, my attention was roused by the appearance of many soldiers hastening from every quarter, with arms in their hands, to the *Place d'armes* before the palace, shouting *Vive la Liberté! Vive l'Indépendance! A bas le Tyran! A bas Christophe!* To your houses! To your houses! And suddenly every door was closed; while the assembled military passed the night, some in consultation, others in dancing and riot, and many in mad efforts to excite their comrades to plunder. That night no one slept in the Cape.

It was not till ten o'clock on Saturday, the following morning, that the news reached the King of the Cape troops having risen in revolt under the Duke de la Marmelade, Gen. Richard; and it was not till four that he was convinced of the truth of the report. At the Cape the insurgents were joined by many of the inhabitants, the students from the College, and many criminals who were liberated. Everyone went about armed, and the town was made subject to military law. Every means was employed to rouse and excite the inhabitants: [such] as the report of an order from the King to massacre the whites and the people of colour; many improbable stories of cruelties practiced by the King; and a pretended narrative of his death. In the morning his Majesty's *Aide-de-Camp* came as usual with orders, and was sent back with a reply that there was no longer a King of Haïti. During the forenoon the insurgents marched out to Haut-du-Cap, a hamlet four miles off, on the road to Sans Souci, and there encamped themselves with a river in front and lofty mountains behind, throwing up such fortifications as the haste of the moment would permit. No more than seven chiefs at first appeared in the conspiracy. Of these Marmelade was, as I before observed, the head, with his old name of Richard. The cry was, "Down with the King! No Nobility! No Tyranny!" and every chief tore from his breast the cross of St. Henry, which he trampled under his feet. Every mouth was opened against the King.

Henry, who was still so weak as scarcely to be able to stand, commanded Prince Joachim, the chief officer of his guards, to march with 1200 infantry and four pieces of cannon against the troops at the bridge of Haut-du-Cap; but he first reviewed this detachment before his palace. His right side was supported on this occasion by one of his domestics, and in his left hand he held his pistol. In this situation he harangued the troops, and for the first time during many years, he caused four dollars to be given to each man, promising that if they beat the rebels, they should be allowed to plunder the treasury of the Cape. His exhortation was received as usual with apparent enthusiasm by the soldiery, who, nevertheless, had scarcely entered on their march before they clearly evinced their intention to desert him.

Prince Joachim was the bearer of a letter to the insurgents, which as soon as he arrived at the bridge, he caused to be delivered, and [he] immediately drew up his small force in form of battle. The rebels were four thousand in number, and among them were some of the Chevaux-Légers of the King's household troops commanded by Prophète, a man as brave as he is destitute of principle and humanity. The verbal answer of the revolted troops was that "the people demanded their liberty, that they had broken the chains of slavery, and that they would no longer have a king."

Joachim, having received the insurgents' fire, commanded his men to make the attack, but the latter, instead of obeying the order, threw away their arms, and joining the opposing force, cried out *Vive la Liberté! brisons les chaines de l'Esclavage!* This affair took place on Sunday, the 8th of October, and it was at half past eight that evening that the King received the news of the defection of his household troops. He appeared deeply affected and said, "Since the confidence which the Haytians once reposed in me is no more, I well know what I have to do." He called his children, spoke to them for a few moments, and then motioned them to retire. A few moments after he shot himself through the heart.

The Queen and the Princesses[100] caused the body to be immediately placed on the shoulders of a few faithful domestics and set out on foot to accompany it to the Citadel. That journey more than six miles in length must have been terrible. The road, which makes an angle of at least thirty-five degrees in the ascent, is composed almost entirely of loose stones, so sharp that in going up many feet have been cut through soles half an inch in thickness. The King was interred in the *bastion Henri,* no doubt by his own desire.

A terrible scene of pillage took place at the palace. I have visited this splendid edifice. Its riches, to judge of their traces, must have been prodigious. Their estimate amounts to six millions of dollars (1,350,000 £ sterling) in money, jewels, and precious furniture. More than an equal sum is said to have [been] taken from the Citadel during the reign of disorder which succeeded.

The Prince Royal,[110] my amiable and unfortunate pupil, with Eugène, an illegitimate son of the King's, and the officers who had remained faithful, immediately gave themselves up to the army. The revolution was thus at an end. The unhappy widow, followed by her daughters, came to the Cape, amid the scoffs and the injurious insults of their enemies.

I saw the Prince led into the town, his most interesting figure covered with dust and sweat, suffering under regret for the death of his father, his mother's misfortune, and his own; and in a few days he was conducted from

---

[100] The *Almanach Royal d'Hayti* lists these members of the royal family as: Her Majesty Marie-Louise, Queen of Hayti, born May 8, 1778, married July 16, 1793; Her Royal Highness Frances-Améthiste-Henry, born May 9, 1798; and Her Royal Highness Ann-Athénaïre-Henry, born July 7, 1800.

[110] Jacques-Victor-Henry, born March 3, 1804.

his own house to a loathsome prison, where on the 18th at midnight he was assassinated by Richard, Prophète, and other chiefs, to their eternal disgrace and the degradation of the whole people, who received the news with savage shouts of exultation. His body, with those of others who died with him, was afterwards thrown upon a dunghill, and there exposed till it began to be decomposed. Finally, by common consent of the people and the chiefs of the army, the President of the Republic was acknowledged and proclaimed through the whole country.

Thus finished a course of events unforeseen by all. If in this relation I have been able to clear up one point to your satisfaction, I shall be more than repaid.

I have the honour to be, dear Sir,

Your faithful and obliged Servant,

WILLIAM WILSON

LETTER

45

William Wilson to his Father

Cape Haytian, 5th December, 1820

My dear Father

I received your most affectionate and welcome letters at a moment when they were most acceptable....

I have seen in the short space of ten days a powerful and most absolute monarch shaken from the throne on which he had had the peculiar merit of placing himself....I have seen his son dragged to prison and there assassinated; and I have seen his family, who but a few days—nay, hours—before knew not the extent of their own riches and power of enjoyment, condemned to comparative poverty. Murder and robbery have not only been tolerated, but applauded; no kind of injustice was too flagrant to be committed.

I had but just escaped from an attack of illness,...when the revolution broke out, which has, for the present at least, dimmed my prospect of fortune. The danger was great, especially for one who was known to be attached to the Prince, but I escaped with the loss of about 200 dollars (50£) which my servant ran away with in the night. My clothes, horse, books, furniture, all went untouched. The history of all the events, as they concern me personally, is much too long to be recounted in the short time I have to prepare my letters in....My unfortunate pupil was murdered in prison, ten days after the death of his father. This, dear Father, is the outline of events. My first leisure shall be occupied in giving you as good an account as I am able of the whole. My attention is now sufficiently engaged by plans for the future and, above all, to get justice in England, where the King has large sums of money. For this purpose I write by this conveyance to Mr. Clarkson and A. Biddell, who, having my power of attorney, can act for me without my presence being necessary. I have arrears due to the amount of 170 £ and I shall instruct my friends to demand six years' salary on the rest of the estate, agreeably with the letter of my engagement, which, as well as my service, I can prove. I do not wish you to suppose that I expect to obtain the full compensation of 4050 £; but I have a right to consider myself entitled to a very large remuneration for the sacrifices I have made of time, health, country, and friends, not to mention the expenses of equipment, which as you well know, were large.

As for myself, I think it right to avail myself of the seasoning I have had to remain some years longer in a climate where it seems that alone money is to be made; and for this end, I shall go to the Island of St. Thomas, which, being under [the] British Government and inhabited mostly by foreigners, will afford me both safe protection and employment. There I intend, with all my advantages of character and education, to receive a few pupils of the better class at a high rate, and I have the hope that I may succeed tolerably.

So much for this great change and its effects. I have seen it all; and an instructive lesson it has been. . . .

My aunt has written me a most affectionate . . . letter to induce me to return to England. It is a little singular that she should have expressed some notions about the "nasty black folks" not very erroneous. I have found them most savage and ferocious, fearless and merciless. The King himself, with all his goodness to me individually, was a most tyrannical and a most cruel man. I have seen few but his son who showed good and humane feeling. That young man was most attached to me [and never,] I believe, did harm to any one. . . .

It is probable that in a month I shall find myself at St. Thomas; where if I do not succeed, I shall try Jamaica. . . .

Always believe me, dear Father,

Your dutiful and affectionate Son,

WILLIAM WILSON

LETTER
46
Duncan Stewart to Thomas Clarkson

Cape Haitian, Dec. 8, 1820

Dear Sir

I had written in answer to your letter and had given you as satisfactory answers to your queries as I could, when the change in the affairs of Haiti, by the death of the King and the change in the Government, took place. The state of this part of the country at present is very unsettled, and it is very uncertain whether the republican form of Government which the President, Boyer, has attempted to establish, will last. Accustomed for a series of years to be governed with severity and energy, the people of this side cannot be retained in proper order by the lax system of Government under which they are now placed. The greatest confusion and disorder has [existed] and still exists since the King's death.

The President, Boyer, seems indifferent to all establishments for the moral and intellectual improvement of his people. He has dismissed all the Professors and Schoolmasters who were employed by King Henry, and is unwilling to pay up the arrears of salaries due them. He has taken possession of all the treasure private and public belonging to the late King, and has carried it away with him to Port-au-Prince.

He has left here General Maunay [Magny] as Commandant of the Arrondissement, who is exerting himself to establish order. This he at present finds very difficult.

King Henry died by his own hands; finding himself reduced to a helpless state by paralytics and deserted by all his troops, he shot himself through the heart. During the two last months of his life I attended him by night and by day. He suffered much in body but very much in mind, and his impatience became quite insupportable to all about him. He was, however, at all times quite collected to the last, and sometimes cheerful.

I used often to converse with him for hours. He seemed sensible that he had used his people harshly and that he ought to have been more liberal to his soldiers, but he had a very correct knowledge of the character of the people he governed and how necessary occasional severities were. He, however, went much too far and was often even barbarously cruel. In the latter part of his life he became very avaricious, and what is uncommon in a man of his age, he became very licentious and prostituted the wives of most of his nobility. Indeed, the two or three last years of his life, altho' marked by his displaying in his external policy much good sense and liberality, were sadly stained by acts of oppressive cruelty and dreadful injustice towards his people, and even if the hand of God had not laid him in a sick bed, the vengeance of his people would not long have been delayed. They had a long account to settle with him and they were prepared for it. About 15 of his chiefs, who were very active in carrying his oppressive orders into execution, together with both his sons, suffered in the revolution. The Queen and her daughters are taken care of by the President and have gone to Port-au-Prince. At his death King Henry was due me three months' salary, besides about $20,000 for attendance on his family and nobility. This he promised to pay me and three days before his death told the Baron de Dupuy that he intended to give me $40,000. I understand from the Baron that you have some of the late King Henry's money in your hands. I hope you will do me the kindness not to pay it away until I can prove to you that my claims are just, as the new Government absolutely refuses to pay any of the late King's debts. If your philanthropic views towards this country still continue, I will at all times be happy to communicate any information in my power.

> With every sentiment of esteem,
>
> I am respectfully your most obedient servant,
>
> *DUNCAN STEWART*

LETTER

47

Thomas Clarkson to Jean-Pierre Boyer

To President Boyer

May 25, 1825 [*1821?*][111]

Sir

About three months ago I wrote to General Dupuy,[112] to desire him to inform you that when I corresponded with the late King Henry, I had no other object in view than to serve the Haytian people, and that, as the King was then dead and as the same object continued to interest me, it would give me pleasure to be useful to his successor. Having had no answer from Monsieur Dupuy, I have determined to write to you myself.

Many years ago I received a letter from the late King inviting me to assist him with my advice. Having devoted my life from the twenty-fourth year of my age to the cause of the unhappy Africans and their descendants, it was with extraordinary pleasure that I accepted his proposal, and I began accordingly a correspondence with him, which continued till the day of his death.

The reason . . . I have not corresponded with General Pétion or with yourself is . . . [that] you never asked me to do it. I have never received a letter either from him or from you. Had he or you solicited my good offices, I should have most cheerfully given them to you because the Haytians under your Government were as dear to me as those under the Government of your predecessor.

In my letters to the late King for the first three years, it was my constant endeavour to prevail upon him to cultivate habits of friendship with General Pétion, not only because such friendship would prevent animosities between two neighbouring States allied to each other by ties of blood and many reciprocal sympathies, but because it would unite them against the attacks of France, which could have no other object than the restoration of

---

[111] The date of this letter, 1825, must be erroneous, since Boyer's answer was written on July 30, 1821. See Letter 49, p. 229.

[112] Clarkson's letter to Dupuy is missing from this collection.

slavery. My hope, my earnest desire, now is that the Revolution which has taken place in Hayti may terminate in the Independence and happiness of its people.

With respect to France, it becomes you to be upon your guard. When I was at Paris last year, I understood that the French Government had given up all idea of trying to conquer Hayti by force of arms, but that they had not given up the idea of trying to obtain it *by intrigue.* Is Monseigneur, l'Eveque de Macri, (Monsieur Pierre de Glory) arrived at Port-au-Prince? Have you ever read "Notice sur les singularités d'une Lettre pastorale imprimée tres récemment"? I sent this little brochure lately to Monsieur Dupuy and desired him to communicate it to you.

But though the French Government had given up the idea, when I was last at Paris, of sending an expedition against Hayti, yet I am not sure that these continue to be their sentiments *at the present moment.* Opinions often change with circumstances. Your Revolution in Hayti has changed the face of things there; and, no doubt, this Revolution will frequently force itself upon the consideration of the French Government, with a view of inquiring whether it may not afford them new pretenses or new opportunities for completing their wishes in that quarter. It becomes you, therefore, to be upon your guard, and more particularly when I inform you that the French Journals speak of Hayti more frequently than ever, and in such a way as to excite very unpleasant feelings among the friends of the African race. There is also other reason for alarm. . . . The French Government are now carrying on the Slave Trade . . . to an alarming extent. Had the Abolition of the Slave Trade been resolved upon as an *irrevocable* measure by the French Government, Hayti would have had nothing to fear; but so long as the Slave Trade is allowed to be carried on by French subjects, so long the French planters will have an idea that if Hayti be subdued they will be able to *repeople their plantations.*

I hope that the widow and daughters of the late King Henry, who are now under your care, feel themselves comfortable and happy. Many people in England are interested in their fate.

I am, Sir, with every good wish,

Yours

THOMAS CLARKSON

LETTER

48

Prince Saunders[113] to Thomas Clarkson

Philadelphia, July 14th, 1821

Dear Sir

I have just arrived here from Hayti, where I have been ... since the 22nd of August, 1820. I reached the Cape on the 7th day after the King was first attacked with the apoplexy. You probably have heard the particulars of his indisposition: that it happened ... while the court were at Church, at a place about 8 miles distant from the Cape, called at that time the pleasant prospect of the King.[114]

On my arrival at the Cape ... a messenger from one of the King's Secretaries was sent to ... assure me that his Majesty would be happy to see me as soon as his health would permit. ...

I was the bearer of letters from some of the most respectable people of colour in this City and its neighbourhood upon the subject of their immigrating to that part of the world. ... They vested me with full authority to make every arrangement for them and ... instructed me to act for them as their representative in Hayti.

I had finished a treaty with the King on the 3rd of October [1820], which was to have been ratified on the 5th at the Palace of Sans Souci; it was founded upon principles similar to what he had previously communicated to you. He was to have signed the agreement with his own hand; a vessel was to have been employed at the expense of this Government, and he would have given 25,000 dollars as a first donation towards incidental expenses. So near was I to leaving the country at the time the revolt took place that a vessel bound to Philadelphia was stopped one day after she was ready for sea and my passage engaged. But the disturbance broke out in the night and everything was thrown into the utmost confusion. The disordered state of things continued to increase until Sunday evening the 8th, when the

---

[113] Also spelled Sanders. See p. 45.
[114] Sanders alludes to the royal chapel, Belle-Vue le Roi.

King, finding out that the revolters had prevailed upon his guards to desert him, put a period to his existence, which I am sorry to be obliged to say, I fear put a period to the existence of that people as a nation ... in the eyes of civilized Europe.

Boyer makes great professions, but his sincerity, I fear, is much to be doubted, for every movement of his seems to demonstrate to me that he is completely in the French interest. I was introduced to him the first afternoon after he entered the Cape, and he professed to have the greatest respect for me, but did nothing for me, although I made him fully acquainted with the objects I had in view.

You undoubtedly heard of the assassination ... of the King's sons ... and also ... of a number of the bravest and best men in the country.... You are not ignorant of the unsettled state of the country and the absolute state of brigandage in which everything is.... There is very little respect either for persons of property.... All the gradations of society are done away, and ... the meanest miscreant in the street puts himself upon a par with the first and most respectable man in the land. And it really appears to be the object of Boyer and his party to destroy the influence of all those who were men of consequence in the time of the King and to elevate the mob for his support. . . . There are no means used for their improvement, and there are constantly plans ... to kill off all those who are dissatisfied with the present state of things.

It is evident that Boyer is very much prejudiced against the blacks, as well as many of them to him.... There appears to be but very little ability to govern at present among those who are at the head of affairs. The French are now permitted to go all through the country, and many of those mulattoes and blacks who deserted their brethren and went off with the whites are now placed in some of the highest civil and military offices. These things have excited great alarm in the minds of many of the chiefs and have given rise to much of the uneasiness which has hitherto [prevailed] and does still prevail in that distracted country since the death of the King.

Mr. Clarkson, I have been at very great expense in going to that part of the world and lost everything but my life. I was robbed of all my clothes in the revolution. I got nothing for it, but received the same answer from Boyer that all others did, that he had nothing to do with the affairs of those who were in the services of Christophe.... I am happy to learn that there were means in the hands of yourself and others, so that some of those who were great losers have had their losses and demands settled.

Are there not some funds in England from which I can receive some remuneration? I had the book reprinted in this country which I published in London and there were but very few copies of it sold.[115] I have, since I returned, had a bill presented to me to pay 175 dollars for it, which in addition to my other expenses amounts to nearly one thousand dollars, ... including my voyage there and back again within the last two years, in the service of that people. But had the King lived, I should have been amply rewarded. If you can assist me, I am sure you will do it now.

General Dupuy requested me to say to you that he should send his two oldest sons to be educated under your direction in England.[116] He said he would send them by the first good opportunity.... His lady and three children returned to this City with me. The two boys are to stay here two years and then go to England to be educated. His lady is on a visit to her mother, who has been in this City for fifteen years.

Do write to me immediately after you receive this, ... and believe me to be with distinguished respect,

Yours most truly,

PRINCE SAUNDERS

---

[115] The American edition of *Haytian Papers* was published in Boston in 1818.

[116] With his usual conscientiousness, Clarkson was quick to serve Dupuy. See p. 232.

L E T T E R
49
President Boyer to Thomas Clarkson
{ENGLISH TRANSLATION}

REPUBLIC OF HAITI

At Port-au-Prince, July 30th, 1821,
in the 18th year of our Independence

JEAN-PIERRE BOYER,
President of Haiti,

to Mr. Clarkson in London

I acknowledge receipt, Sir, of the letter of the 24th[117] of last May which you wrote to me. I shall always receive and read with interest your observations concerning what you may learn of the intentions of France toward this country. You say that when you were in Paris the French Government had abandoned all idea of conquering Haiti by force of arms, but still entertained the hope of achieving that end by intrigue. It is certainly possible that France may insist on failing to recognize her own best interests and refuse to profit by the lessons of experience, but I can assure you that any attempt she may make to enslave us would fail when directed against the strength of this government, which is built upon the solidarity and affection of all Haitians. A long series of misfortunes has taught us that only we can guarantee our rights, and that we must be always on guard against the perfidious machinations of our enemies and the pitfalls they place along our route. Haitians, in their pride at having raised themselves from the depths of misery to an independent political existence, will never turn back along the path on which their steps were set by the horrible injustice of their oppressors and their own love of liberty. My countrymen will always find it possible, as they have already demonstrated, to reconcile their need for security with their duty toward mankind.

Monsignor de Glory, Bishop of Macri, whom you mention in your letter,

---

[117] See Letter 47, which is dated May 25.

was sent on an apostolic mission to this country by the Holy See. We received him with all the respect due a person in his position. Since he will of necessity limit his activities to the exercise of his spiritual functions, his presence among us can in no way constitute a danger for the country. This government must protect religion as the cornerstone of all morality and sound social institutions, but if the ministers of religion attempt to make of it merely an instrument for attaining ends other than the salvation of souls, then this government will take all necessary measures to put an end to such maneuvers.

Madame Christophe and her daughters received, after the fall of the government of the North, all the protection to which their great misfortune entitled them. When they expressed a desire to go and spend some time in England for the sake of their health, I gave them permission to do so. They will have the privilege of delivering this letter to you. As you seem to take a great interest in their welfare, I have no doubt you will do what you can to be of service to them.[118]

I have the honor of saluting you with highest esteem.

BOYER

---

[118] Madame Christophe and her two daughters arrived in England in September, 1821, and became the guests of the Clarksons at Playford Hall, near Ipswich, where they remained for nearly a year.

LETTER

50

William Wilson to Thomas Clarkson

Harlow [England], Nov. 3, 1821

Dear Sir

At the time of the Revolution, Dr. Stewart had two months' salary due, which had been drawn from the Treasury and was in M. Dupuy's hands; but this was, in reality, the same as if Dr. Stewart had received it; for I think I can venture to say that M. Dupuy accounted to him for the money. This is not, on my part, bare supposition, for I recollect that a payment was actually made (to my certain knowledge) to the Doctor after his arrival at the Cape from Sans Souci, *i.e.*, after the King's death. I cannot pretend to say that he was paid up to the termination of his engagement, that is, to the day of the King's death, because I do not know on what particular day of the month his engagement commenced. A month's salary could not be drawn from the Treasury before it was fully due; it is, therefore, probable that Stewart had, like me, some trifling arrears (less than a month) due to him at the King's death.

He often expressed his right to be paid for medical attendance on his Majesty and the rest of the Court, which attendance, he said, was not stipulated for on the King's part in the original agreement, but he forgot to mention that he had accepted from his Majesty the honorary ... office of his principal Physician—that he wore the national uniform and was, therefore, subject to any dispositions of the King.

I believe that he rendered great services to the King, and that if there be an employee of the late King's government who for attachment to him and for real service merits a reward, it is Dr. Stewart. Tho' I do not respect or esteem the Doctor, I can never forget the good feeling and conduct which he displayed on the 8th of October, when he exposed himself, without being compelled by ... any apparent prospect of convenience or gain to himself, to imminent dangers in the service of the surviving Royal Family.

I am convinced that it is for your tranquillity and for that of Madame Christophe that I should be wholly silent on the subject of my affairs, and

I do not hesitate a moment in promising silence; but, besides this compliance, I owe you many thanks for your injunction; partly because, without it, I might have incurred the reproach of my own mind by an act of injustice to you, and partly that it will make me circumspect for the sake of my own pecuniary concerns. I must observe, by the way, that, when in Town last Sunday, I met the elder Fowlerton, to whose questions about my affairs I answered that Madame Christophe had "behaved well," without mentioning one particular. There was, however, no merit in this reserve, as without your renewed caution, I might have mentioned the business openly.

In answer to your obliging inquiries about Mr. Birt's bill, I have to observe that the demand of £37–18–6 is for a week's medical attendance and for medicine. He never advanced me one dollar by way of loan. I have, now that my ideas of the value of money are altered by a change of climate, begun to question the equity of his demand. I am, however, willing to compound the matter with Mr. Birt by giving him any sum which *you* may judge proper. But my funds are already so reduced by such disbursements that I have very little to give, and can only make myself answerable for future payment, if the decision should be for a considerable sum.

The terms on which I can, with a due regard to my own interest, undertake the charge of educating and boarding Mr. Dupuy's two sons are . . . 60 Guineas (about 300 Gourdes) per annum cash, for less than which I do not think Mr. Dupuy could have them educated in England. . . . I think about 1500 Gourdes would be a proper sum for Mr. Dupuy to deposit.

Thus, Sir, I have endeavoured to answer your several inquiries (the greater part prompted by concern for my interest); and though I have continually new cause to feel the value of your benevolence, I can still, as ever, only subscribe myself,

Your faithful and humble Servant,

WILLIAM WILSON

Harlow, Nov. 12, 1821

Dear Madam

I hastily seize the first interval of leisure to answer, as well as I can, your interesting inquiries. . . . I feel truly happy that I can return what I am sure will be to you the most pleasing reply, unqualified by one doubt. In the northern districts of Hayti, none—not even the bitterest enemies of the Christophe family—ever accused Madame Christophe of connivance at the unworthy acts of her husband. I must, in justice to her, repeat what I heard from the lips of the rebel Richard, (Marmelade) during the few days of the *Soulèvement* which overthrew Henry's Government. "If," said he, speaking of the sanguinary disposition of the King and adducing his own case in proof of Henry's wish to destroy all the inhabitants of the Cape on the first news of the revolt, "if Madame Christophe had not interposed, I should have before now made three visits to the *Fossette* (the ordinary place for military executions), I should not now be here to make the Tyrant tremble. For her sake, I will not permit one of her family to be hurt." This was heard by at least twelve whites, who, interested for the fate of Madame Christophe and her family, had gone like me to learn if possible his intention towards them.

On another occasion I was returning home from an execution, prompted only by curiosity, and was overtaken by two chiefs. . . . These were Prophète, a man who fought under Dessalines and has since been always about the King's person, and Nord-Alexis, who like the other had made his apprenticeship of war under Toussaint and Dessalines. Both, though they poured forth loud invectives against Henry and my unfortunate pupil, refrained from any expression of reproach against Madame Christophe, and it is remarkable that it was these very men who with Richard presided two days after at the assassination of the Prince. Now, men who were so utterly careless of the Queen's peace of mind as to murder her son, would certainly not have withheld the accusation. I may even add, would not have refrained from revenge, if cause had been.

Madame Christophe, in common with all Haytian females, is distinguished by a *douceur,* an humanity, which shudders at violence. It is the men only who are sanguinary. Madame St. Martin, a *religieuse* of the Cape ... who was perhaps more in the secrets of the Palace than any other person, except M. Dupuy and a few necessary officers, was my particular friend, and though having, even during the King's life, to blame his bad deeds, never failed to make a glorious distinction between his conduct and that of the rest of the Royal Family. The Princesses, she said, were incessant in their acts of humanity, ... remitting through her to the wretched inmates of the prisons, the means of comfort, and relieving misery wherever they found it. ... So many valuable acts could not have been performed without the existence of a certain tenderness of heart, quite incompatible with that indifference to scenes of cruelty with which, it seems, they are charged.

With respect to Henry himself, we must recollect in what a school his character was formed: the best perhaps for the cultivation of military talents, the worst for the improvement of his better feelings. This, you will remember, Madam, was the philosophist school, which had been so largely established in France before the Revolution; which had, even before that great effect of its influence, spread far over America and the Islands; and with the opinions of which, not the military only, stationed in St. Domingo, but also the inhabitants of that colony were intimately possessed. That this was not altogether incapable of producing a heathenish sort of virtue was seen in the character of Kléber, Pichegru, Moreau, and others—all, if I mistake not, formed in it. But that it presented no formidable barrier to the inroads of the vices might be seen, not only in the character of our Henry, but in those of most of the personages deeply imbued with its precepts, who have acted in the great drama of French public events during the last thirty years. Before Henry arrived at Cape François, it is very likely that he had no settled principles; indeed, it is more than probable that he continued to act during the whole of his long public existence from the strong impulse of personal interest alone;[119] and from his admiration of the leading men then in the Cape and his known intimacy with them, we may fairly infer that he could not remain altogether untainted by their bad example.

I do believe that he had a natural greatness of mind, which tended to despise petty or insecure advantages (perhaps ... from that effect, better

---

[119] A marginal note in Clarkson's hand reads: "I do not believe this."

called *le talent de saisir le point*) and that he did not, therefore, grasp at the government, immediately it became vacant: one source, I remember, of your admiration; but then we are to remember the evident danger of the post, which, in the short space of a year, had been filled by two unfortunate individuals;[120] and all the difficulties of which would lie open to his penetrating eye. No wonder, he would not take so important a step, in a hasty manner.[121] But let us look at his conduct, after he had, a short time, as President, felt the pulse of the people he aspired to govern, and we shall see, with what rapacious eagerness he laid hold on the kingly honours.[122] I have had this story from more than one credible person at the Cape. No one had the least notice of his intention to render his own authority absolute and permanent till a very short time before it was executed. This enthrallment of the liberties of his fellow citizens (for such it was, however salutary in its immediate effects) induced, to complete or to continue it, acts of severity, devoid at first of those flagrant features which now that the veil is torn suddenly from the last of the series create in us so much astonishment; but still flagitious enough to open the way and indurate his temper for the perpetration of more atrocious crimes.[123] He encouraged the observances of religion, I should think, from motives of policy. He imagined that they were a powerful instrument, in skillful hands, for the direction of public feeling. He loved his children and was particularly careful of their education, and that not only in recent times, but even in their earliest infancy. I have original letters of his now before me, which afford the strongest evidence of both these facts; and I will enclose two or three of them to serve as a new proof to you of his singular merit in this particular.[124]

[120] Wilson is in error; Dessalines alone was in power from January, 1804, until his death in October, 1806.

[121] Wilson's statement is misleading. There was no hesitation on Christophe's part. On the death of Dessalines, Christophe as provisional leader ordered the election of a Constituent Assembly for the purpose of establishing a republican government and was elected President on December 28, 1806. Through the machinations of Pétion, however, the position was denuded of all authority, and Christophe spurned the honor. The resultant friction divided the country into two parts, one government being under Pétion, the other under Christophe, who was elected President for life by his adherents.

[122] Actually four years elapsed. Christophe delayed the assumption of kingship until 1811 in the vain hope of reuniting the country.

[123] It is worth remarking that Wilson did not reach Haiti until the middle of April, 1820, and that, therefore, his knowledge of Christophe's character and activities before that date was based on hearsay. Moreover, since both Christophe's illness and the revolution occurred shortly after his arrival, Wilson was dependent upon informants inimical to the King. Note in this letter Wilson's references to Prophète and Nord-Alexis, who "poured forth loud invectives against Henry," and to "more than one credible person at the Cape," who told him about Christophe's assumption of absolute authority.

[124] See the first four letters in this volume, pp. 87–90.

I would say a few words of Boyer, but the picture presents so many disgusting features of weakness and cowardice, allied to presumption and tyranny, so many proofs both of stupidity and licentiousness, that I turn from it, as I am sure you would, with abhorrence.

I have the honour to be, dear Madam,

Your faithful and obedient Servant,

WILLIAM WILSON

LETTER

52[125]

Thomas Clarkson to Zachary Macaulay

Playford [Hall], November 19, 1821

Dear Sir

I sit down to write you a letter which I have had upon my mind for some time, and which I trust only to your eyes and those of Mr. Wilberforce, to whom I wish you to send it when you have perused it.

I invited our amiable friends the Christophes, as you know, to spend three weeks or a month at my house, with a view of taking them from expensive lodgings as well as of showing my respect to the widow and the fatherless, and of giving Captain Sutherland time to be looking out for a proper situation for them on leaving me. Whether the report of the ladies to him, after having been some time at our house, was too favourable, as it related to our kind treatment of them or their comforts under our roof, I cannot say, but Captain Sutherland made a proposition to me at which I was astonished, namely, to take the family into my house to board for four or five months. I told him I thought he had mistaken both my situation and character, and besides, other difficulties stood in the way.

By having so large a family in our house, we should be hindered from continuing our hospitality to our friends. Besides, to take such a family for such a length of time could not but derange my finances, and I revolted at the idea of taking money from my friends. These reasons, however, did not satisfy Captain Sutherland, and he renewed his application again and again. He urged that money was no object to them, and that if I would consent to take them and suffer a remuneration, he would consider it as an act of charity in me, and so would the ladies themselves. At length I consented to mention the matter to Mrs. Clarkson. She gave it a full consideration, and the pity for them which was first excited in her when I put the question to her increased on the further consideration of it. Besides, in their melancholy situation ... society seemed to her to be necessary. ...

---

[125] The originals of Letters 52 and 55 are not among the Clarkson papers in the British Museum.

These and many other considerations, and particularly an expression of the ladies that they should be nowhere so happy, and let me add the belief that Mr. Wilberforce and yourself would be more satisfied that they should be under our quiet roof than elsewhere, so operated upon my wife that . . . at length she gave her consent, and mine followed. . . . The hateful idea of taking money on such an occasion was in some degree got rid of by my proposing that Captain Sutherland should, on the departure of the family from us, leave with us what he thought to be only a reimbursement of the additional expenses incurred by us after the first month. . . . A more delightful family never entered a person's house. Their dispositions are so amiable, their tempers under such complete subjugation, and their minds so enlightened, that it is a pleasure to live with such people. . . . They will probably be provided for here till April next. . . .

I come now to other parts of the story . . . [to enable] you to form some judgment about Captain Sutherland. About two days after the matter had been agreed upon, he informed me that he had ordered a black maidservant to come from London to wait upon them at Playford. I thought this extremely strange, as nothing had been said before about such a person, . . . but understanding that this female had accompanied them from the Cape to Port-au-Prince and from Port-au-Prince to England, and believing she might be essential to the comfort of the ladies, I did not say one word in opposition, but received her, though it was doubtful whether my servants would harmonize with a person of this description.

In the course of about two days after this, Captain Sutherland informed me that he should return to London in three or four days, and that on his arrival there he should send down a manservant, and a young lady as a companion for the ladies and to teach them drawing and other accomplishments: in fact, he wished them to have a separate establishment in our house. Observe, he did not ask my permission, but said he meant to do it! . . . I cannot express to you the indignation which I felt at the authority usurped on this occasion, though I hope I commanded my temper. I refused the proposition, however, in the most determined manner. . . .

I have reason, however, to suppose that this was only a part of a more expensive plan intended, for the next day a horse dealer from Ipswich brought him a fine horse to look at; and on questioning him about it, it appeared that he was actually going to buy two carriage horses, and to hire, if not buy, a coach for the ladies. This, of course, implied the hiring of a coachman also. Thus, whether I liked it or not, I was to be driven out of my own peaceable way of living, and to take within my premises the three ladies, the black maidservant, a governess, a coachman, and a footman.... Being, however, invincibly resolute, I turned the whole system topsy-turvy, and compromised with him that we would keep entirely as we now are, *i.e.*, the three ladies and the black maidservant; that I would hire for them a carriage and a pair of horses at Ipswich sometimes once and sometimes twice a week; that I would hire them musical instruments at two guineas a month; and that I would get a drawing master to attend them from Ipswich....

I fear that when they leave our house ... [Captain Sutherland] will be dashing into unnecessary expenses. He talks of buying them a coach when they go to London in the spring, and keeping horses and servants. He proposes in the summer to take them to his own friends to Sutherland in Scotland, the most remote county in it, to ship them and the carriage in a Leith smack, and to travel in the carriage from Edinburgh to Sutherland, and so back to London. He proposes also, when he has sold all the jewels, to provide for the mother and the girls separately, and to get the two latter married when they go back to Port-au-Prince. But I trust the ladies have too much good sense to follow all that he has in design for them.

With respect to Captain Sutherland himself, I know not what to make of him. At times I am much pleased with him. I am always pleased with the deep interest which he seems to have in the welfare of the ladies, and the attachment which he seems to bear them. At other times I have no patience with him. He says one thing today and another thing tomorrow. When he was here last, he made them uneasy by lecturing them on their expenditure; and the next day, finding they were uneasy, he sent for a carriage and took them to Ipswich, and ordered a carriage three times besides in the same week, and once besides for himself, thus giving them an example of extravagance. These facts will enable both you and Mr. Wilberforce to assist me in forming an opinion concerning Captain Sutherland, who is but twenty-six years of age, and giving me your advice both as to my future conduct with respect to these ladies and as to the captain himself.... That he has done much for them in preserving their jewels, and bringing them [the ladies] to England and in putting them in the way of being served by Mr. Wilberforce and others, cannot be doubted, but they do not owe their lives to him as he has once asserted. They owe them to their own exemplary and benevolent conduct. They had more than a hundred orphans, whom they brought up, educated, fed, and clothed, and the whole country knew this. They spent their time in visiting the sick and aged, and relieving the poor.... When the ladies went to the Cape [after Christophe's death], people from town and country flocked in with poultry, vegetables, and money for their daily support. At this time some officers of Christophe, supposing they had jewels, entered their house to murder them for the sake of plunder. They debated the matter, ... and when they had resolved upon the deed, the soldiers and sentinels ... said: "You can get nothing there, for they are daily fed upon charity. Besides, what evil have they done? Have they not always been doing good? You shall not murder them while we are here, and the very attempt to do it will be followed by the revolt of all our regiments in their favour." Thus was the design frustrated.... A report being afterwards spread that the enemies [of the royal family] had engaged a pirate vessel to take and murder them on their way to Port-au-Prince, several persons joined in hiring a proper vessel at their own expense to carry ... [the ladies] thither, in which fifty young men, all armed, volunteered to accompany them.

Yours truly,

THOMAS CLARKSON

LETTER

53

B. Sutherland to Thomas Clarkson

London, 22nd Nov., 1821

My dear Sir

... I have been waiting to ascertain more clearly the merits of the claim of ... Campbell, Bowden and Co. The circumstances are exactly these. Christophe had ordered dresses for the Queen and Princesses, with sets of harness for the Royal Family, and after they had been prepared according to Baron Dupuy's order and sent out to the Cape, part were taken and ... part rejected. Those that were taken were paid for, but those that were rejected were not, and hence arises the claim of £3700 brought now against the King's personal estate. It appears that Baron Dupuy since the King's death has given a certificate to Mr. Thompson (agent of Campbell and Bowden at the Cape) specifying that the articles in question were ordered by the King; consequently, it would appear that the King's estate becomes liable for the debt, but there are circumstances that will prevent these gentlemen from succeeding against us, as they expect, and the worst that can happen will be a compromise by giving perhaps a third of the amount. I have put the affair into Mr. Stephen's hands, and there is little doubt but the wisest steps will be taken to prevent wrong. ... I and Mr. Stephen have not yet been furnished with the documents which *they* pretend will prove their claim. As soon as we are I shall let you know all particulars. The delay you'll observe is on the other side not on ours.

Remember me to Mrs. Clarkson and her charges and believe me,

Sincerely yours,

B. SUTHERLAND

L E T T E R

54

William Wilson to Mrs. Clarkson

30 Jan., 1822

Dear Madam

I write this . . . to accompany a few letters and memoranda concerning Hayti. . . . The latter were supplied by M. Grégoire at my request, I having told him that you were anxious to collect materials for a right estimate of the character of the late ruler of it. The letters are part of a large packet which I gleaned from the floors of the Prince's Palace at Sans Souci, a week after the pillage. (In several rooms the papers were lying two feet deep, as well as in all the *Bureaux* of the Government and in the neighbouring courtyards.) They mark the extreme solicitude of the King for the improvement of his son, and exhibit one of the best points of his character. I am sorry that I am unable to add, in contrast, Boyer's proclamation. I gave away my copies of these documents at St. Thomas. . . .

I am almost afraid to enter upon the consideration of Boyer's character. He has proved himself so willing to injure me in the tender point—*interest,* that I may hardly be called an impartial judge. I believe him to be so great a coward as to be capable of any injustice to relieve his fears. I do not, indeed, believe that he has the least disposition to encourage justice, either from a natural love of order or from a perception of the benefits which it furnishes to mankind. I believe him to be a sensualist and nothing else, with all the vices, active and passive, of the character.

With respect to the question whether he was accessory to the assassination of poor Victor, it is possible . . . that he authorized it, and it is also possible that he knew nothing of it till after its commission. . . . I cannot cease to believe him capable of such a crime, even if the insurgents had not spared him the trouble. The only mode which I can suggest for the discovery of the truth is Mr. Sutherland's account of the time and way in which the accounts of the murders were received in the camp of the President—to find out from him how it was first published, whether he had ever heard it hinted at before the actual notification of the event, whether it excited surprise, and whether he saw the President ... at the time. If these points could be made out unobscured by S.'s peculiar opinions and prejudices, some one of them might guide to the truth. The Prince was murdered in the night of the eighteenth, when Boyer could not have advanced further than Gonaïves. If S. had heard the circumstance mentioned by way of anticipation before Boyer reached Plaisance, I think it will be enough to criminate Boyer. His proclamation, in which he disavowed and reprobated the deed, was got up with a great deal of art. Indeed, I think nothing is lost by the absence of these papers in forming one's opinion, because they are as little to be relied upon as any French bulletin whatever. It is my earnest belief that it was one of the first instructions given by Boyer in his first embassy to his new subjects—that they should *extirpate* the old government....

One word I must say on Dupuy's character, who seems to have fallen under heavy suspicion. On all occasions Dupuy treated me extremely well. I am obliged to him for his interference in my behalf during Henry's life, and since that time for the exercise of ... hospitality.... I have the best opinion of Dupuy.... I never heard Dupuy accused by any person at the Cape of participating in the plot against Henry. He had many enemies, mortal enemies, among the insurgents by whom his life was almost sure to be sacrificed during the disorders. Various attempts were made, and he was obliged to fortify himself in his house at the Cape, till he was relieved by Prophète, to whom he had rendered services in the King's time. He does not appear to possess any property. He has not bettered his condition since Henry's death. In his lifetime, he was next to himself. In a time of public commotion he was exposed as a prominently obnoxious character to the enmity of every individual. At the time when he is said to have voted for the murders, he did not go to the council at all, being shut up in his house. As to poor Belliard, who is certainly the most humane person I ever met in Hayti, he was personally devoted to the King and his family. He accepted no service under the new government; he continues to *praise* Henry's character; and he has so little influence that his plantations have been pillaged to the last stick. I know how justifiable the Queen's suspicions are, from the perfidy with which she has generally been treated, but I think that in these two cases, especially the latter, she is deceived. I cannot perceive how it could further Dupuy's interest to overthrow Henry's Government. He may, indeed, have had some notice of the plot, but if he did not make it known, it was through his firm conviction that no measures of the King's could change his destiny. He knew, if he knew anything, that Prophète and Richard would not leave the Cape and that any movement about the court would be the signal to begin. He may have attempted to conciliate the black chief, Prophète, to insure his own safety; but we must remember with admiration that he did not desert the Queen and her family, that he attended them in that distressing march to the Citadel, [and] that he suffered himself to be carried a prisoner to the Cape, where hundreds were insisting upon his destruction.

Two points of inquiry in your letter remain unanswered, relating to Sutherland and Dr. Stewart. My acquaintance ... with the former is very slight. He possesses, I dare say, some good qualities, but I think they are such as are least likely to be seen in his present situation. I know nothing definite concerning his character or his past history. He had the reputation at the Cape of being imprudent; but that was all. Still I think that his residence with Madame Christophe and her daughters is not advisable, and even improper. Dr. Stewart is, I think, much entitled to the Queen's respect and gratitude, as nothing could exceed his care and attention to the King, or his assiduity to her after the King's death. I never heard the imputation which you mention. Mrs. Stewart has no personal and few mental attractions. I have no hesitation in declaring my belief of the legality of this connection....

I am, dear Madam,

Your faithful and humble Servant,

WILLIAM WILSON

LETTER

55

Thomas Clarkson to Zachary Macaulay

Playford [Hall], January 31, 1822

Dear Sir

I trouble you with a few lines on the subject of the affairs of our poor ladies, who are well in health and cheerful in spirits, and whose amiable dispositions and gentle and correct manners occasion them daily to grow in our love and esteem. I am persuaded that there is nothing which the Christophes desire so much as to be respectable. There is nothing to do but to show them all possible kindness as opportunities occur, and not to appear to wish to influence them. If they themselves feel something of shyness respecting abolitionists, it arises from their fear of being confounded with Africans. I can pity their weakness. I have observed that very few persons can bear to be reminded of any circumstances in their history which may be thought degrading. Even Lafayette appeared not quite well pleased with an allusion to the dungeons of Olmütz.

You gentlemen who live in London know, I fear, but little of the distressed state of the country. How the Government will be able to collect their taxes in the ensuing year nobody can divine, and if the taxes are not to be collected, how is the interest of the Funds to be paid? This [state of things has affected my mind] as it relates to our poor ladies, and I therefore earnestly recommend it to you to take into your serious consideration what would be the safest investment for the money which will come from the sale of their jewels this very day, as well as whether it would not be prudent to remove some of the money which has been already invested in our Funds into others. The great question after all is the comparative security between the English and Foreign Funds, and I am free to confess that I think almost any foreign Funds more secure than our own at this moment. . . .

Sutherland has acted with great propriety of late. He tells me he will abide by your judgment as to the placing out of the money, and also that he is desirous of adding your name to his own in any investment that he may make. . . .

Yours truly,

THOMAS CLARKSON

LETTER

56

William Wilberforce to Mrs. Clarkson

Near London
March 11ᵗʰ, 1822

My dear Madam

...I am persuaded for the benefit of the ladies it is much to be desired that you should accompany them to town.... It is obviously of great importance to females so entirely unacquainted with our manners, characters, etc., to have with them a friend of their own sex, who will give them the benefit of her experience in forming new acquaintances, and therefore, I hope you will not suffer any motives of feeling or of delicacy ... to obstruct your rendering our Haytian friends the solid service they would doubtless receive from your accompanying them. I am sure I·should be cordially glad to render them any benefit, and so would Mrs. W. also. But I have no time to spare, and she has not at present spirits to undertake an office which would require a considerable share of them.[126] Let me not forget to ask you, was Capt. Sutherland at Playford Hall when Madame Christophe wrote me word that their pecuniary affairs were settled to her satisfaction, or was it by his suggestion that she sent me that intelligence? ...

I remain ever,

My dear Madam,

very sincerely yours

W. WILBERFORCE

---

[126] Years later Clarkson confided to Benjamin Haydon that "when Christophe's wife and daughters, all accomplished women, were brought or introduced by him to Wilberforce, and others in high life, there was a sort of shrink at admitting them into high society." Earl Leslie Griggs, *Thomas Clarkson, the Friend of Slaves* (London, 1936), p. 147.

L E T T E R

57

Athénaïre Christophe to Mrs. Clarkson

{ENGLISH TRANSLATION}

Exmouth Cottage
West Hill
Hastings
Saturday evening, October 26ᵗʰ, 1822

My dear Madame Clarkson

Your letter was an agreeable surprise, and the good news it brought of your state of health fulfilled both our hopes and our wishes. It was also a pleasure to learn that your daughter is again well; please remember us to her and to her family. We should like, too, to be remembered to Mr. Montague, Mrs. Alexander, Mrs. Shaw, and to all your neighbors. We should indeed be grateful if you would offer our compliments to Mr. Mallet.

We all appreciated deeply your expressions of interest in our own welfare. Understanding the sincerity of your sentiments toward us, I cannot refrain from begging you to accept, along with our thanks, the compliments of our family and friends in Haiti. They are indeed sorry that it is impossible for them to pay you their respects in person, and have requested that we should speak for them to you and to Mr. Clarkson.

Mother's health has greatly improved since we have been at Hastings. We hope that she will soon be completely free from her rheumatism, since the climate here is much milder than at Blackstone. My sister and I are both quite well. She joins me in reiterating both to you and to Mr. Clarkson the gratitude with which we declare ourselves your devoted servants.

The daughters of the Thornton family have been here for several weeks, so we have been enjoying the pleasure of their company. Really, madame, Hastings is just now the rival of Spa; with the Fontaines de Geronatère, etc., etc., and a Count L. to amuse the ladies with his extravagances, I believe the comparison would be altogether exact. Adieu, madame. With best regards, I am your devoted

ATHÉNAÏRE HENRY C.

I hope you will excuse my scribbling. I cannot rewrite this letter without losing my chance to have it delivered to you immediately.

LETTER
58
Prince Saunders to Thomas Clarkson

Philadelphia, May 2, 1823
Dear Sir

I now take up my pen to address you upon a subject which . . . lies near your heart. I mean . . . the establishment of a regular and well-balanced government in the Island of Hayti. You are undoubtedly aware of the unsettled state of things in that country since the death of his late Majesty King Henry . . . and of the alarming torrent of licentiousness and disorder which pervades the greatest portion of every class in society. It has, in fact, seemed to be the object of the present rulers to level all those distinctions which the government of the late King very necessarily . . . established. . . . The most depraved and debased characters in the community, by their vehement declamations in favor of liberty and equality, mislead the un-enlightened multitude. . . . We now see in those very families who under the late government of the King were remarkable for their decency of manners . . . an almost entire relinquishment of those virtues and that regu-larity . . . and industry which were then so conspicuous. . . . But blessed be God, I believe there is yet a redeeming spirit among some of the people. . . . They now say, "During the reign of the King our children were instructed, our property and persons were respected, the arts and sciences of older and more improved states were introduced and successfully cultivated among us, and we were making rapid advancements on the way towards a rank among the enlightened nations of Europe. But alas, where are we now! In the horrible vortex of licentiousness, and on the high road to destruction!"

I arrived here from Hayti but a few weeks since, after a residence there of six months, and can assure you that I have an accurate knowledge of . . . the sentiments of the best and most enlightened men in that country. One of the . . . best informed officers . . . said to me that Gen. Boyer, . . . since his first having taken the Presidency in the South, had never performed one act which was in the least advantageous to the country, but that everything that was done seemed to tend to its ruin.... In the first place, President Boyer ... by his own example sets at nought the solemn obligations of the marriage vows, and ... promiscuous intercourse is fast extending its harmful influences over the late Kingdom.... All those incentives which were formerly given to the bringing up of legitimate children are fast subsiding, and the children ... in the North ... are now left ... to follow the multitude to do evil. The numerous schools and academies which were established throughout the King's dominions are abolished, and most of the buildings themselves have been defaced or entirely torn down by these unprincipled barbarians. I, in fact, have heard it asserted by some of the principal officers from the South that education must not be too general; if it is, ... there will be nobody to work. But the present state of things there shows the fallacy of that argument.... The King was endeavouring to make instruction universal, and there was no difficulty in procuring faithful domestics ... and labourers of every description.... Since the extension of the government of what is called the Republic, all confidence is destroyed ... and is substituted by an almost unparalleled state of anarchy and disorder....

During my last visit to Hayti I received an interesting letter ... from an association of black people in the State of North Carolina, informing me that there were 14,000 free people of colour in that state alone, who were desirous of going to Hayti with all possible dispatch, in case I would give them encouragement.... You have for some time been aware that there are many thousands in Philadelphia ... and in different sections of the United States, who were upon the eve of going to Hayti under very favourable circumstances, when the death of the King took place, and blasted all their prospects. These same persons *are waiting, anxiously waiting*.... If there could be an interval of tranquillity and good government of sufficient duration for them to remove and get a little established, they would soon be so numerous, that in conjunction with the friends of order who are now there, they would have a favourable influence in producing a salutary change upon the whole state of things there.

In order to effect these ... objects ... the first effort should be the adoption of that invaluable constitutional law which was promulgated in 1811 ... and was ... [the origin of] the Code Henry.... The superior and acknowledged excellence of the Code Henry was very strikingly exemplified during the ten years' reign of King Henry, when put in competition with the lax and heterogeneous system of what is called the laws of the Republic. It is an affecting consideration ... that the people in the South part of Hayti, who had lived under the governments of Pétion and Boyer, were at the least calculation twenty years behind the people of the Kingdom in their habits of industry and their improvements in the arts, sciences, and manners of civilized society.

That there were errors, and many very great errors, committed during the reign of King Henry everyone acquainted with the transactions of his late government and court must acknowledge with deep regret. But I give it to you and will declare it to the world ... that so far as he himself was concerned in the commission of any of those excesses or enormities which were sometimes perpetrated (and uniformly alleged against the King) *they proceeded from his head and not his heart;* for he did indeed wish to be a friend and a father to his subjects and a benefactor ... to the descendants of Africa throughout the world. King Henry was destroyed by a treacherous, deceitful, and intriguing set of advisers who were desirous of his overthrow that they might elevate themselves. ... It pleased the Sovereign disposer of events to affect him with severe indisposition, and his intriguing enemies and false friends, under the pretext of proclaiming his son (who was a favorite with the army and the people) Regent and changing the ministry, ... succeeded in bringing about the revolution which destroyed him and overthrew his whole family. ... It is the opinion of the ... best men among the Haytians that the female part of the former Royal Family are the best qualified and truly deserving of being restored to that elevated ... situation which they lately filled with so much grace and real dignity. ...

President Boyer and his Britannic Majesty's Government are not upon very good terms; neither does he appear to be with any of the governments holding possessions among the Islands of the Archipelago. That kind attention and respect which was formerly shown to his Britannic Majesty's naval and military officers who were in the habit of rendering us frequent visits in the King's time, is entirely at an end; so that now we but very seldom see any of them.

I have engaged to make you acquainted with the views and feelings of a very large majority of the best and most enlightened people of Hayti relative to the restoration of the Constitution and Code ... and with them the surviving members of the Royal Family. ... The present appears to us to be an auspicious moment for us to raise our voice in favour of the restoration of an orderly government. ... Is it possible for any men of feeling to remain idle spectators while they see what has cost themselves and others so great a price all lost and overwhelmed by the licentiousness and mismanagement of an unprincipled military mob? ...

Therefore, Sir, I now beseech you ... to come over and help us by your excellent counsel and by your influence with the courts of Europe, England and Russia in particular, whose friendship for the late Kingdom is universally known by all the best instructed Haytians. It is for the interest of all the powers who have possessions in the West Indies that there should be a well-balanced government in Hayti. ...

Yours faithfully,

PRINCE SAUNDERS

Prince Saunders to Thomas Clarkson

Philadelphia, May 19, 1823

My dear Sir

Since I last wrote to you it has occurred to me that it might be proper to apprise you that some of the ministers and officers who were near the person of the late King cannot be implicitly confided in, because they were the betrayers and destroyers of the King, and that amiable, intelligent, and accomplished youth, the Prince Royal of Hayti. He was, indeed, the darling and the hope of all good Haytians. Mr. Wilson, his late preceptor, has undoubtedly told you that this excellent young man bid fair to be a lasting blessing to his country, and of extensive utility to the world. But he was cruelly butchered by those for whom he had [done] nothing but the most disinterested acts of kindness. The only crime of this innocent and illustrious victim was that he was too well beloved by the people and the army. and that he accordingly was a hindrance to the promotion of their unprincipled ambition—that by intrigue and perfidy they might overthrow the government and get hold of the purse strings of the Treasury....

There were many in official situations during the King's reign who did many things without the knowledge or consent of the King, which caused the people to complain; and then these very same base and deceitful men would use every artifice in their power to prevent the individual so injured and oppressed from obtaining access to his Majesty to make him acquainted with their grievances; although it was his uniform command that the humblest individual should be permitted to approach him, saying that he was the father, the protector, and friend of all the Haytians, and all had an equal claim upon his kind attentions. The Queen was for some time apprehensive of the intrigues which some individuals were practicing at the Court, but she had no idea of the alarming extent to which they had arrived, until it was too late.

Baron Dupuy and the Duke of Limonade have much to reproach themselves with, if they ever reflect upon the past. Dupuy to my certain knowledge was acquainted with the plot against the King for more than a month before it was developed by revolution and all its subsequent evils, and he constantly affected the greatest sincerity and fidelity for his Majesty, and until the last he was in attendance upon his person. These individuals are as much opposed to the present licentious state of things as any persons in the country, but the people will never trust them in any important situations again. I heard when I was in Hayti that Dupuy had been trying to obtain some property which had been put into the hands of Reid, Irving and Company in London by the late King, and that Dupuy had so managed as to have it . . . deposited in his name. Is that true or not? The Duchess of Valier, sister to the Queen, told me that she had heard so and was desirous of knowing the truth of it.

I have written the Queen a very long and particular letter which I have desired her to show you and you only. I have also advised her to make you her counsellor. . . .

I have the honor to be with distinguished consideration yours,

PRINCE SAUNDERS

LETTER

60

The Christophes to Mrs. Clarkson

Weymouth, Dorset
13 Sept., 1824

My dearest Madam

It is with sincere regret that we now find ourselves obliged thus to take our affectionate leave of you, as we had hoped to have had the pleasure of seeing you before our departure from London. As that we now find to be impossible, we avail ourselves of the present of wishing you health, every species of pleasure, and much happiness including of course Mr. C., to whom we also beg our best respects. We therefore once more very respectfully bid you *Adieu* and most sincerely are,

My dearest Madam,

most faithfully yours

M. L. H. Christophe
Améthiste H. Christophe
A. Athénaïre H. C.[127]

---

[127] The widow and daughters of King Henry, after visiting three years in England, finally settled in Pisa and spent the rest of their lives there.

DOCUMENTS

*issued by King Henry and sent
to Thomas Clarkson*

DOCUMENT
1
Ordonnance of King Henry
{ENGLISH TRANSLATION}

[November 20, 1818]

LIBERTY, INDEPENDENCE OR DEATH

[Published in the]
ROYAL HAITIAN GAZETTE
of the 28ᵗʰ of December, 1818, the 15ᵗʰ year of Independence

FROM UNION, STRENGTH
Sans Souci, the 25ᵗʰ of December

ORDONNANCE OF THE KING

Henry, by the grace of God and the constitutional law of the State, King of Haiti, etc., etc., etc., to all those present and to come, greetings;

Acting upon the report of our Minister of Finance and of the Interior;

Persuaded that the greatest benefit which we can secure for our faithful subjects is an education appropriate to their condition in life; that this education—especially when it is founded on the true principles necessary for the maintenance of the liberty, independence, religion, and morality of the Haitian people—is not only one of the most fertile sources of general prosperity, but that it contributes to the good order of society, encourages obedience to the laws, and the accomplishment of duties of every sort;

Wishing, so far as is within our power, to impart a uniform organization to this important branch of the administration of the state, and to systematize by means of suitable regulations and surveillance all efforts made toward the attainment of so desirable an end;

Having consulted our Grand Council:

ARTICLE ONE

We have created and do create a Royal Chamber of Public Instruction, composed of the following persons: the Dukes of Marmelade and Dondon;

257

the Counts of Saint-Louis, Terrier-Rouge, Ouanaminthe, Limonade, Mont-Rouis; Barons Joseph Dessalines, Vastey, Louis Dessalines, Dupuy; Chevaliers Jean-Joseph, Prézeau, Dupin, Cincinatus Leconte; and Lieutenant Jean-Charles, Jr., aide-de-camp of His Majesty.

2. Our Minister of Finance and of the Interior shall preside over the Royal Chamber of Public Instruction, and the latter shall choose from among its own members a vice-president and secretaries.

3. The ranks of the members of the Chamber shall correspond to the order of their appointment; persons appointed the same day shall rank according to their age.

4. The Chamber shall be divided into as many sections as it may deem desirable, shall distribute the work to be done among its members, and shall draw up its own rules of procedure.

5. The Chamber is especially charged with the direction and supervision of the primary schools, academies, secondary schools, and other national institutions of public instruction; with the maintenance of order, morality, and the quality of teaching. It requests and suggests to the King such measures as it may judge to be necessary for the upkeep of the afore-mentioned educational institutions, or for their order and discipline.

6. Public instruction is under our direct and especial protection.

7. The Chamber is especially charged with encouraging the progress of public instruction, with establishing primary schools in the parishes where none exist and academies and secondary schools throughout the Kingdom, wherever they may be needed.

8. Every schoolmaster and professor, in order to be entitled to exercise his functions, must have a certificate of good behavior; he must furthermore be examined by the inspectors appointed by the Royal Chamber of Public Instruction in order to obtain a license, if he be judged worthy of it.

9. To have the right to exercise his functions, a teacher must also secure, in addition to his license, a special permit from the Chamber authorizing him to teach in a given locality.

10. Only those schoolmasters and professors who have been chosen and appointed by the Royal Chamber of Public Instruction shall be paid by the Government.

11. In national primary schools, academies, and secondary schools, instruction shall be free of cost; the Government shall pay the teachers, and furnish the books and other objects necessary to the functioning of such institutions.

12. The Royal Chamber of Public Instruction shall appoint, for each school and academy, three special supervisors, chosen from among the officials and substantial citizens of the place where the school or academy is situated.

13. The special supervisors shall be responsible to the Royal Chamber of Public Instruction in all matters pertaining to their functions.

14. In addition to the special supervisors appointed for each school and academy, the Chamber shall choose from among its own members inspectors whose duty it shall be to make frequent tours for the purpose of visiting the schools and academies and requesting of the special supervisors, schoolmasters, and professors, a report on the progress of instruction.

15. Should the special supervisors or the inspectors with good reason so request, the Royal Chamber of Public Instruction may transfer a schoolmaster or professor from one school to another, and if there is great urgency, in the case of scandal or abuse of position, may suspend him in the exercise of his functions or dismiss him, revoking his license and his permit.

16. Private schools which are already in existence must submit to regulation by the Royal Chamber of Public Instruction, and are under the special supervision of the latter.

17. Any person or group of persons who so desire shall be allowed to found a school or academy, on condition that the teacher be provided with a license and permit from the Royal Chamber of Public Instruction.

18. If a person shall found a school, either through a direct gift of money or by means of a legacy, he may reserve for his heirs, in whatever order he may designate, the right to nominate a teacher.

19. If an individual who possesses a license shall wish to set up a school in a parish, in order to obtain a permit to do so he must present his request to the Royal Chamber of Public Instruction along with his license and certificates of good conduct.

20. Children of opposite sexes shall never be brought together in the same school to receive instruction.

21. The Royal Chamber of Public Instruction shall take particular care to see that the classes in all the schools and academies are based on sound principles, religion, respect of law, and love of sovereign. The Chamber shall proceed immediately to draw up rules for the regulation of the schools, and to indicate the methods and texts which the teachers shall use.

22. The Royal Chamber of Public Instruction may order that texts suitable for the use of the schools be prepared and printed.

23. A librarian, appointed by the Chamber, shall be placed in charge of the books and other objects necessary for the work of the schools.

24. The Chamber shall strive to determine which are the methods by which the students in the schools make greatest progress, in order to establish subsequently model schools throughout the Kingdom.

25. Every six months, the Chamber shall inform the King concerning the general progress of public instruction, the masters and teachers who have most distinguished themselves, and the scholars who have achieved most and shown the greatest zeal for knowledge.

Given in our Palace of Sans Souci, the 20th of November, 1818, in the 15th year of Independence, and the 8th of our reign.

Signed, *HENRY*

Signed, *COUNT LIMONADE,*
Secretary of State, Minister of Foreign Affairs

At Sans Souci, from the Royal Presses.

DOCUMENT
2
Ordonnance of King Henry
{ENGLISH TRANSLATION}

[January 1, 1819]

ORDONNANCE OF THE KING

Henry, by the grace of God and the constitutional law of the State, King of Haiti, etc., etc., etc., to all those present and to come, greetings;

Acting upon the report of our Royal Chamber of Public Instruction of the 1st of December concerning the organization of the national schools and academies;

We have ordered and do order as follows:

TITLE ONE
Organization of the National Schools

CHAPTER ONE
Concerning Pupils and the Conditions for their Admission

ARTICLE 1. In order to be admitted to the schools a pupil must:

1st. Be between 6 and 15 years of age.

2nd. Present a doctor's certificate to the effect that he has no chronic or contagious disease.

2. The parents are expected to lodge, nourish, and clothe children placed in the national schools; the government assumes responsibility only for instruction and the upkeep of the school.

3. Those parents who live at a distance from the cities or towns where a school is situated are required to indicate to the special supervisors a person whose domicile is near the site of the school, so that the residence of the pupil and the person responsible for his board and room shall be known.

4. The special supervisors assigned to each school shall present each month to the Royal Chamber of Public Instruction a list of the names of the pupils who were sent by their parents and who have fulfilled the conditions of admission to the national schools, so that the Chamber may approve them and admit them definitively.

5. Pupils may be absent from their classes only on days of rest: on Sundays and the holidays enumerated in the following article.

6. Thursday and Sunday of each week, the national holidays decreed by law, and Corpus Christi, Easter, Christmas, Palm Sunday, and All Saints' Day shall be celebrated.

7. A pupil may not be absent from his class for as much as an entire day or several days without obtaining from the special supervisors a written permit which makes mention of the duration of the absence and the reasons for it.

8. The special supervisors shall be very sparing in the issuance of permits of this type, which should be granted only in cases of urgency and absolute necessity.

CHAPTER TWO

Concerning the Instruction of the Pupils

9. On Sundays and holidays there shall be prayers and a discourse within the comprehension of the pupils; attendance on the part of the latter shall be obligatory.

10. Instruction shall be given in both English and French.

11. Pupils shall be taught, according to the English system, to read, to write, and to figure; there shall be lessons in grammar and arithmetic.

12. Any pupil who has not completed his primary instruction at the end of three years shall be dismissed from the school.

CHAPTER THREE

Concerning the Order and Discipline of the National Schools

DUTIES OF THE MONITORS AND PUPILS

13. The schools shall open and close their doors at the hours hereinafter mentioned, that is:

14. On the long days of the year, morning classes shall be in session from six o'clock until eleven o'clock, and afternoon classes from two o'clock to six; on short days the hours shall be from seven to eleven, and from two until five.

15. Monitors are expected to arrive at the school one-half hour earlier than the time indicated above, in order to open the doors, be present when the pupils reach the building, and see that the classes begin precisely at the proper moment.

16. Each class is entrusted to a monitor, who is responsible to the master for the quality of his instruction.

17. The monitors shall call the roll of their respective classes as the master may order and at the moment of the beginning of the day's work; the names of absent pupils shall be inscribed in a general list.

18. Any pupil who arrives at school after the calling of the roll shall be considered absent.

19. The classes owe obedience to their respective monitors during school hours, and the monitors to the masters.

20. The monitors shall be responsible for gathering up books, slates, writing materials, etc., at the end of the day, and putting them away in cupboards in good order.

21. Every Saturday, the montitors shall render to the master an accounting of the books, slates, etc., which they have received from him, in order that he may see in what condition they have been left.

22. The monitors shall be distinguished by medals, according to their rank.

23. The monitors are authorized to mete out only the punishments specified in the regulations.

24. A monitor who is appointed to carry out a punishment may not refuse to do so, under penalty of being himself doubly punished.

25. Pupils are expressly forbidden to wear a handkerchief on their heads,[1] unless it be by reason of illness.

26. All monitors are required to remove the handkerchief from the head of any pupil who may be found wearing one during school hours.

27. The monitors are also expected to see that the pupils come to school cleanly and properly dressed; throughout the schools the greatest cleanliness, good order, and decency must be observed.

28. The monitors shall see to it the pupils leave their classes properly and in the strictest order; pupils must not loiter in the streets, but proceed directly to their homes.

---

[1] During the French colonial period, a madras handkerchief used as a headdress had become a part of every Haitian Negro's costume and is still the mark of the French West Indian. This quaint regulation would indicate that Christophe had come to regard that article of attire as a symbol of slavery.

Concerning Recompenses

29. Every monitor who has behaved himself well and who at the end of the year obtains from the master a certificate of good conduct shall receive a prize.

30. Every pupil who by examinations shall be recognized as first in his class shall receive a medal.

Concerning Punishments

31. Discipline shall be inculcated among the pupils by means of the rod or whip, or, in serious cases, by imprisonment on bread and water, as follows:

For arriving after roll call,

For leaving one's seat,

For failure to learn one's lessons because of laziness,

For tearing or ruining one's book,

For making noises during a class,

For disputes, quarrels, or fighting,

For insults, lies, or deception,

From six to twelve blows with the rod or whip, according to the gravity of the case;

For not attending Sunday devotions, the pupil shall be deprived of his free hours and free weekday, and shall spend this time at school;

For being absent without permission,

For disobedience to the master,

For disobedience to the monitor,

For taking the holy name of God in vain,

The pupil shall be imprisoned, on bread and water, for a period of from one to two weeks, according to the gravity of the case.

There shall be double punishment for a repeated offense and double punishment for monitors who fail to fulfill their duties.

32. A pupil may complain to the master of the punishment meted out to him, if the monitor has acted without good reason.

DUTIES OF THE MASTERS

33. Except on the occasions provided by law, the work of the school should suffer no interruption; in case of illness, the teacher shall have himself replaced by the first monitor, and shall advise the special supervisors of his action.

34. Masters are forbidden to give to the pupils any other hours and days of recreation than those mentioned in Article 6.

35. Masters are expressly forbidden to give pupils permission to be absent, to send them away from the school on errands, and to employ them in matters not related to their studies; in short, pupils are not to be distracted for any cause or under any pretext during the precious time which they should devote to instruction.

36. Masters are expressly forbidden to use other textbooks than those authorized by the Royal Chamber of Public Instruction.

37. Each time they may be so requested, the master shall render to the special supervisors an exact account of the situation of their respective schools, and shall acquaint them with the names of the pupils who have missed attending class, so that the causes of all absences may be ascertained.

38. In addition to the quarterly reports which must be made out according to the model supplied, the schoolmasters shall deliver to the supervisors each month a detailed report of the state of instruction and the progress of their schools, class by class. Mention should be made of any changes which have occurred, and it is especially necessary to include the names of pupils who have completed their primary education.

39. Schoolmasters are expected to observe and to insist religiously upon the observance of all regulations relating to public instruction; the teachers must take the lead in furnishing their pupils with good examples as well as sound precepts.

DUTIES OF THE SPECIAL SUPERVISORS

40. The special supervisors are required to visit the school entrusted to their case at least three times per week, taking turns in the performance of this duty.

41. During their visits they shall request of the masters an account of the condition of the school; they shall inquire as to what pupils are absent, in order to investigate the explanations given for non-attendance; they shall make certain that the regulations concerning discipline are well enforced; they shall have the pupils repeat their lessons; they shall make a report of what they have seen to the Royal Chamber of Public Instruction.

42. The special supervisors are responsible to the Chamber for any abuses or negligence which may exist in the schools.

DUTIES OF THE INSPECTORS OF THE ROYAL CHAMBER OF PUBLIC INSTRUCTION

43. The inspectors, in their tours of duty, shall visit carefully schools and academies, shall assure themselves that discipline is well administered, and shall inquire of supervisors and schoolmasters concerning the condition of the institutions.

44. The inspectors shall communicate to the Chamber, in the form of written reports, the results of their visits, so that the Chamber may form an idea of the progress of instruction, the improvements of which the system stands in need, and the defects which may exist.

TITLE TWO
Organization of the Royal Academies

CHAPTER FOUR
Concerning Students and the Conditions for Their Admission

45. Every three months, the special supervisors appointed to the national schools, acting upon the report of the masters of these schools, shall draw up an exact list of the pupils who have completed their primary education.

46. These pupils shall be presented by the special supervisors to the academy inspectors, who shall examine those so recommended.

47. The inspectors, guided by the results of the examination, shall present to the Chamber a list of qualified pupils, who may then be admitted definitively to the academies by the Chamber.

48. The parents of students in the academies shall have toward their children the same obligations as those prescribed in the case of the national schools, with respect to lodging, food, and clothing; the government shall assume responsibility only for the instruction of the students.

49. Students may be absent from the academy only on days of rest, Sundays, and holidays; students may not remain away from school for as much as an entire day without having obtained from the special supervisors a written permit, such as is described in Articles 6, 7, and 8, Title One, Chapter One.

CHAPTER FIVE
Concerning the Instruction of the Students

50. The instruction shall be based on religion, morality, and love of country, sovereign, and liberty.

51. On Sundays and holidays there shall be prayers and a discourse, which students in the academies are required to attend.

52. Instruction shall be given, according to the methods of the English system, in grammar, history, geography, arithmetic, and the Latin, English, and French languages.

53. The special supervisors in each academy shall indicate to the professors a certain number of superior students, who shall be encouraged to do extra work in the arts and sciences.

54. The academy professors shall strive to understand the character, gifts, and inclinations of each student, so as to discover his vocation and prepare him to receive professional training in the royal colleges.

CHAPTER SIX
Concerning the Order and Discipline of the Academies

55. The duties of the monitors and students, the recompenses, the punishments, the duties of the professors, of the special supervisors, and of the inspectors in the academies are the same as those prescribed for the national schools in Title One.

56. The Royal Chamber of Public Instruction shall have the present ordonnance printed and displayed in all the schools and academies, so that no one may pretend ignorance of it. His Majesty further charges the Chamber with the execution of the ordonnance.

Given in our Royal Palace of Sans Souci, the 1st of January, 1819, in the 16th year of Independence, and the 8th of our reign.

Signed, *HENRY*

Signed, *COUNT LIMONADE,*
Secretary of State, Minister of Foreign Affairs

At Sans Souci, from the Royal Presses.

DOCUMENT

3

Edict of King Henry

{ENGLISH TRANSLATION}

[July 14, 1819]

EDICT OF THE KING

Providing for concessions of land to the soldiers, subalterns and officers of
the army who have not yet received a portion of the public domain
HENRY, by the grace of God and the constitutional law of the State,
KING OF HAITI, etc., etc., to all those present and to come, greetings;

After having increased the financial resources of the state by the sale of
portions of the public domain and thus made it possible for all Haitians to
acquire such property, we are none the less grieved to find that a great many
soldiers, because of lack of means, have not yet been able to share in the
benefits arising from the sale of public land.

Ever mindful of the need for improving the lot of the brave defenders of
our country, wishing to aid effectively this group of soldiers, who are among
the champions to whom the nation owes a debt of gratitude, and to help
them to find at the end of their days, amidst their infirmities, an honored
security which they may pass on to their descendants;

Considering, moreover, that this public domain, which is the fruit of the
conquests of the entire nation, could be put to no better use than to concede
it to those to whom we owe such a debt of gratitude;

Having consulted the opinions of our Grand Council of State and our
Privy Council, we have willed and do will, have decreed and do decree as
follows:

ARTICLE FIRST

Those officers, subalterns, and soldiers who do not yet possess any part
of the public domain will have and shall receive concessions of land,
granted from the unsold portions of the aforesaid domain, irrevocably,
as follows:

To each colonel	20 units of land,
	each of 100 square yards,
	the yard of three and one-half feet
To each lieutenant colonel	15
To each captain	10
To each lieutenant	8
To each second lieutenant	6
To each sergeant-major	4
To each sergeant	3
To each corporal	2
To each soldier of any branch of the service	1

2. Those who receive land may sell the latter or dispose of it in any way they see fit.

3. These plots of land shall be chosen in the neighborhood of regimental barracks or in the most suitable locations.

4. All who receive concessions will be expected to produce various food-stuffs on their land, according to the nature or the soil, and to observe all present and future laws governing the possession of property.

5. Two commissions, each of twenty-one members, one for the Province of the North, and the other for the Province of the West, chosen and appointed by us, shall carry out the distribution of concessions and the delivery of the corresponding deeds.

6. In addition to the duties described in the above article, the commissions shall see that the land is surveyed and laid out with squared markers of durable wood; on each marker shall appear the number of the concession and the initials of its new owner. When the latter enters into possession of his property, the fact shall be formally reported.

7. Immediately upon the publication of the present edict and the setting up of the two commissions, our Minister of Finance and of the Interior will supply the commissioners with a list of the unsold portions of the public domain; this list shall include the former name of the property, section by section.

8. The Inspector General of the Army shall immediately examine the muster rolls, name by name, rank by rank, regiment by regiment, battalion by battalion, company by company, designating the location of the barracks of each regiment, in order that the identity of those soldiers who have not yet received land from the public domain may be known.

9. A list of the names of those soldiers who have not received public land, and their rank, shall be drawn up by the afore-mentioned Inspector

General and delivered to the two commissions; one list shall be prepared for the northern commission and another for the western commission.

10. The commissions, upon receiving these lists, shall draw up an exact report, arranged name by name and rank by rank, which will show: (1) the soldiers who are entitled to receive concessions of land; (2) the quantity of land which should be granted them; and (3) the location of the land to be granted. They shall present this report to our Minister of Finance and of the Interior, who will make his recommendations to us.

11. When we have granted the concessions, the titles will be given to our Minister of Finance and of the Interior, who will in turn deliver them to the two commissions.

12. The commissions shall inform the generals who command a division or a province of the date set for the entry of the new landowners; said entries shall always be made following the order of the number of each regiment, in the presence of the military chiefs and of the King's Lieutenant of the parish in which the property is located.

13. The commissions shall, in so far as may be possible, consult the preferences of the new owner when land is being assigned.

14. No fee shall be charged by the commission for delivering the title of the land to its owner and for the latter's entry upon the land.

15. The members of the two commissions shall be paid by the government for their work.

16. The commissions will be directly responsible to our Minister of Finance and of the Interior in all matters relating to their work.

17. As soon as a regiment has entered into possession of its land, the commissions shall inform our Minister of Finance and of the Interior, who will in turn report the fact to us, after he has verified the completion of the work according to the list provided for in Article 10.

18. At the end of each month, the commissions shall send our Minister of Finance and of the Interior a report of their activities and extracts of the report of the entry of each new landowner.

19. The commissions shall hear all claims which may be made, either by soldiers having a right to obtain concessions, or by those who have some difficulty in entering into possession of their lands. They shall pass on the validity of these diverse claims and shall report to our Minister of Finance and of the Interior all claims which have been accepted, so that justice may be done in all cases.

20. We will draw up regulations governing the period of service of the soldiers and the time which they may devote to the cultivation of their land.
21. Our Minister of Finance and of the Interior, the Inspector General of the Army, and the commanding generals of each division or province are charged with the execution of the present edict in so far as its provisions concern each of them.

We order and command that the present, sealed by our hand, shall be addressed to all courts, tribunals, and administrative authorities, that they may transcribe it in their registers, observe it, and have it observed throughout the Kingdom. The Minister of Justice is charged with its promulgation.

Given in our Royal Palace of the Citadel, this 14th of July, 1819, in the 16th year of our Independnece and the 9th of our reign.

Signed, *HENRY*

Signed, *COUNT LIMONADE,*
Secretary of State, Minister of Foreign Affairs

At Sans Souci, from the Royal Presses.

APPENDIX

[February 15, 1817]

Mr. Davidson came to my office on January 20, 1816, with several letters to be sent by messenger overland to Port Plate. As usual, he asked my help in arranging that these letters should cross the frontier without being read by any official. I was very busy at the moment, so told him to leave them with the messenger who was to carry them, and that I would shortly approve them. He came back a few minutes later and declared he absolutely must start the mesenger on his way with the letters. I took them and found three of them unsealed. These I signed without reading them. However, he had a fourth letter in his hand, which he presented to me sealed. I thought it my duty to open this letter; it aroused my suspicions since it alone was sealed. The following passage is what I found in it:

King Henry has had no success against Pétion in the South. His ships have returned with only one prize, a sloop; they were several times routed by Pétion's ships. His troops have all been captured. In view of these facts, if you find it necessary to visit the South, you can do so with confidence. In Port-au-Prince mahogany is worth from 20 to 25 francs a ton. I hope to see you here soon.

JAMES DAVIDSON

Since the expedition against Jérémie had left three weeks earlier and we had as yet received no news of it, and since three foreign ships had arrived during the day—from Saint Thomas, the United States, and the Spanish part of the Island—, I was anxious to learn from Mr. Davidson the source of the news he was repeating with such assurance. I therefore asked him. He answered gruffly that he would name no names, but that he had heard about it in a public café. I pointed out that, in his letter, he didn't say "I have heard that," but instead made positive assertions. I demanded full informa-

273

tion. He absolutely refused, saying that he owed me no accounting. Thereupon I had him brought before the governor, who was ill and received him in his bedroom. Again Davidson refused to tell how he had learned the news.

The governor stated that he had learned there were agents from Port-au-Prince hidden in the city, who were circulating false rumors and trying to spread alarm among the people. He suggested that perhaps Mr. Davidson had been in communication with them. Two of these agents, who had come from the Spanish part of the Island, had already been arrested.

I then said to Mr. Davidson: "If you refuse to tell me who informed you that the expedition was a failure, I shall ask the governor to put you in jail until you identify the person who gave you the news." When he once more refused absolutely, I requested the governor to imprison him, hoping in that way to get to the bottom of the affair.

The governor sent Davidson to the prison, guarded by a lieutenant. The latter turned him over to the warden. I have heard that the lieutenant told the warden that Davidson was suspected of espionage, and the jailer applied thumbscrews; but the governor assured me that that was out of the question.[1] The governor didn't even know whether or not there were thumbscrews at the jail.

When I reported the matter to Your Majesty, you wrote me to call the foreign residents together and to read them your letter. At the same time I was to tell them that, if Mr. Davidson did not reveal the source of his news, he would be brought to trial. In conformity with your orders, I made known to these gentlemen the contents of Your Majesty's letter. I also read Mr. Davidson's letter. Of the 50 or 60 foreigners present, not one attempted to

---

[1] Despite Dupuy's report, the following letter from Christophe, written at the time Davidson was imprisoned, shows that the thumbscrewing was not only known to Christophe, but had been ordered by him.

At the Palace of Sans Souci, the 28th of January, 1816,
  in the 13th year of our Independence

THE KING
to Baron de Dupuy, Secretary Interpreter of the King

I give my fullest approval, Baron, to your course of action with regard to Mr. Davidson. You did well to put him in solitary confinement. I am ordering the governor to keep him there, in thumbscrews and in irons, where he will be subject to my orders and will not be allowed to communicate with anyone. He shall eat exactly the same food that is given to the prisoners, for he is a real spy taken in espionage. If you continue with your active surveillance, you will catch others. We must get to the bottom of this affair. You will keep Davidson's letter carefully at hand, as a convincing proof of his crime. . . .

                                             DE LIMONADE
                                             For the King

argue Davidson's case. Only one, Mr. Strafford, an English merchant in business here, spoke to me privately, and asked permission to go to see Your Majesty at Sans Souci. This was granted without difficulty, and Mr. Strafford brought the order ... to the governor.

Since leaving prison, Mr. Davidson has never mentioned to me having had thumbscrews applied during his detention. He has come to my office several times to ask for favors with regard to certain unpaid debts because of which he was threatened with imprisonment. He owed 6000 francs to Mr. Bourne, among others, and hasn't yet repaid them. Davidson has only a room in this city, and is not really a merchant, as is commonly said.

Messrs. Bradock, Masson, and Richardson came to see me, asking me to give this same Davidson a permit to return to England. They suggested that I see to it that he leave, because he was going to be arrested on account of the debts he had contracted here. I did as they requested, since it seemed there was no way for Davidson to pay what he owed; I thought that the imprisonment his creditors would have inflicted on him could not make him pay, and consequently that it was better to approve his departure for home.

Such are the circumstances, in detail, of all that has happened with respect to Mr. Davidson.

Cape Henry, the 15ᵗʰ of February, 1817,
14ᵗʰ year of Independence[2]

---

[2] Cf. Charles Mackenzie, *Notes on Haiti,* ... 2 vols. (London, 1830), Appendix.

FRENCH ORIGINAL OF

LETTER

7

King Henry to Thomas Clarkson

Au Palais de Sans Soucy ce 18. 9ᵇʳᵉ, 1816,
l'an 13 de l'indépendance

LE ROI,

A Monsieur Thomas Clarckson &c, &c, &c

Monsieur & Ami,

J'ai lu et médité avec toute l'Attention dont je suis Capable, les Communications que vous m'avez faite, par la lettre que vous m'avez écrite le Cinq août dernier.

Infiniment Sensible et touché de tout l'intérêt que vous prenez à la cause des Affricains et de leurs descendants, à la prospérité du Royaume d'haïty, et à ma gloire particulière, Je vous répondrai avec la même Franchise et la même Sincérité qui doivent exister dans nos relations, et je me flatte que vous apprendrez à m'apprécier & à me Connaître, comme je connais et apprécie mes honorables Amis.

Tout Entier a mon projet d'Etablir l'Instruction, de donner la plus grande latitude à la morale, et de concourrir aux vues grandes & généreuses de nos Amis, J'ai reçu avec reconnaissance les maitres et professeurs qu'ils m'ont Envoyés; J'ai fait Etablir à leur arrivée Mˢˢʳˢ Gulliver & Sanders dans la Capitale, pour y enseigner Selon la méthode de Lancaster, et leur ai fait procurer des Eleves; Je suis Emerveillé de Cette Méthode & de l'Intelligence précoce que montre les Eleves, et Je regarde, en effet, comme le plus grand Présent que mes amis m'ait fait, que l'Envoy de ces Maitres et professeurs.

Mʳ. Evans professeur de dessein & de peinture a été établi à Sans Soucy, et son école est en activité.

J'attends les autres maitres et professeurs que mes amis doivent m'Envoyer, pour les placer dans différentes villes du Royaume, étendre les Bienfaits de l'instruction et monter le Collège Royal.

Je suis trop jaloux de mériter l'Estime et l'amitié que me Témoignent nos Estimables Amis, pour ne point Faire Tous les efforts qui sont en mon pouvoir pour répondre à leur Attente.

Depuis la proclamation de Notre Indépendance, la maxime du gouvernement qui m'a précédé, et qui est aussi la mienne, a été de ne jamais nous mêler des affaires intérieures de nos voisins; nous en avons fait un article fondamental de nos Constitutions; Nous avons Toujours pensé que nous devions nous borner seulement à défendre notre Territoire, établir le règne des lois à la place de la licence, qui est naturellement la suite de toute révolution; que nous avions à faire reprendre et prospérer la Culture et le Commerce, enfin à jouir paisiblement chez Nous, de la liberté, de la paix, que nous avons acquises au prix de Notre Sang; cette vérité est si evidente, que jamais l'on a entendu dire même, que chez nos plus proches voisins, les Espagnols, où l'Esclavage règne de l'autre Côté de nos limites, nous ayons Cherché à Troubler en aucune manière la paix & la Tranquillité dont ils jouissent, ni à nous immiscer dans le régime suivi chez Eux; Ils sont avec nous dans les relations du Bon voisinage & du Commerce; Je leur ai Fourni gratuitement, dans le Temps, et d'après leurs sollicitations, des armes et des munitions pour les aider à Chasser les français qui occupaient leur Capitale; mon plan s'accordait alors parfaitement avec celui du gouvernement Anglais, qui leur avait Fourni des forces et des moyens pour Coopérer au même But.

Depuis longtemps mes Bâtiments de guerre ne sont Employés qu'au Cabotage, et ne s'Eloignent pas de la côte; le gouvernement de S.M.B. n'ignore pas ces faits, j'en suis persuadé; il n'ajoute Surement pas foi aux allégations mensongères des planteurs; Il se pourrait peut être que la Connaissance de ces faits ne soit pas assez répandue parmi la nation Britannique; cependant il n'est pas possible que la vérité ne soit pas connue, elle finit Toujours à la longue par Triompher de l'imposture.

Pourquoi donc voudrait-on que nous déviassions des principes que nous avons toujours professés? Comment peut on nous faire l'Injure de penser, que nous, qui avons tant de Sujets de nous louer du gouvernement & du peuple Britannique, par l'Intérêt qu'ils nous ont toujours montré, nous Chercherions à troubler le régime de leurs Colonies? Est-ce parce que ces mêmes Colonies ont éprouvé des Troubles et des agitations intérieures? mais ceci n'a rien, et ne peut rien avoir de Commun avec la cause que nous défendons depuis plus de 27 ans.

La Cause des Espagnols ne nous est pas moins Etrangère; Il est vrai, cependant, et ce n'est pas un des moindres sujets de nos Chagrins, que dans la partie sous le Commandement du général Pétion, l'on reçoit les Corsaires des patriotes Espagnols, qu'ils s'y ravitaillent, y font leurs armements, y complettent leurs équipages, et y vendent leurs Prises, et que les Bâtiments haïtiens de cette partie du territoire, naviguent avec ceux des Indépendants; c'est ce qui a pu donner lieu aux bruits qui ont Courus, mais il Serait injuste de Confondre cette partie où règne la licence, avec notre gouvernement, et nous attribuer des faits qui Sont bien Eloignés de nos principes.

J'ai déploré avec Tous les bons haïtiens, et nos Estimables amis d'Angleterre, la Cruelle nécessité dans laquelle je me suis trouvé de prendre les armes pour repousser l'agression du général Pétion; mon existence en péril et celle de mes Compagnons d'Armes, m'en Faisaient une impérieuse Loi; mais que n'ai-je pas fait pour diminuer autant qu'il dépendait de moi, les fléaux de notre Guerre civile! Instruit par l'Expérience que nos démêlés faisaient la joie de nos Ennemis, Je me suis uniquement borné à la deffensive, laissant au Temps, à calmer les passions, et à ramener les Esprits; Je n'ai cessé de faire les premiers pas, pour ramener le Général Pétion à des Sentiments plus Justes de ses devoirs, et de ce qu'il se doit à lui même et à son pays, parce que si mes démarches pacifiques pouvaient coûter quelque chose à mon amour propre, les grands Intérêts de mon pays, obligeaient que j'en fisse le Sacrifice pour le bonheur de mes Concitoyens, c'est ce que j'ai Fait, et je dis avec orgueil, je l'ai Fait avec Toute l'aisance et la sincérité qui me Caractérisent; Qu'en est-il résulté? Toujours des refus Formels de se réunir à moi, pour la défense de notre pays menacé, toujours des injures, des menaces, des outrages, ont accueillies les propositions les plus Justes, les plus honorables qu'il m'était permis de lui Faire.

Le Général Pétion est entrainé dans une Cause qui n'est pas la sienne; c'est en vain qu'il voudrait y entrainer les haïtiens sous son Commandement; Ils ne sont pas plus disposés que ceux du Nord, de l'Est et de la partie de l'Ouest du Royaume, à reprendre les Chaines de l'Esclavage. Il est consolant pour moi, de voir que la généralité des haïtiens s'est Entendue, et que d'un bout de l'Isle à l'autre, le Danger Commun nous a tacitement réuni, car nous Abhorrons Tous les Français et leur gouvernement Oppresseur.

Le Général Pétion, par son refus de faire Cause Commune avec moi, par les intelligences qu'il entretient avec les Ennemis de l'Etat, auxquels il s'est vendu, par l'azile et la protection qu'il donne aux Ex- Colons français, a donné de Justes méfiances à la partie du peuple qu'il a égaré; il est Surveillé, il Court Inévitablement à sa perte; Les Rapports que je reçois de Cette partie sont des plus Satisfaisants. L'arrivée d'une Force Française quelconque ne ferait que hâter la réunion Complette des haïtiens.

Je Goûte parfaitement, Monsieur & ami, Toutes les raisons que vous m'avez Exposées; Il n'est peut être aucune des réflexions justes et Pensées que vous m'avez Communiquées que je n'aie Faites moi-même, mais que puis-je de plus? Ma Conscience m'en rend le Consolant Témoignage.

Malgré les mensonges & les Calomnies, que le Général Pétion et ses agents ont Continuellement Cherché à répandre Sur ma personne et mon gouvernement, Fort de la droiture de mes Intentions, prenant toujours Dieu & les hommes à témoin de mes Actions, Je laisse à mes amis, à mes Concitoyens, à mes Contemporains & à l'histoire à prononcer.

Ça été une bien grande Satisfaction pour moi, d'apprendre Toute la part que le Magnanime Empereur de Russie, les principales puissances de l'Europe, & l'Illustre Général Wellington, ont prise à l'Abolition de la Traite; Je Connais Toutes les peines & les soins que vous vous êtes donnés à cet Effet, et je vous en Témoigne toute ma Reconnaissance.

Je ne saurais mieux vous remercier de vos sages et bons avis, qu'en vous priant de me les Continuer, et de me faire toujours part de vos lumières, de votre grande Expérience de la politique des Cabinets Européens, et des machinations que nos Ennemis pourraient Trâmer contre Nous. Je recevrai Toujours vos avis avec plaisir pour le bien de mon pays.

Nous ne pouvons plus être Trompé par le Gouvernement Français; Nous savons que ce gouvernement influencé par les Ex-Colons, ne reviendra jamais à des principes plus Justes à notre Egard, et que s'il avait l'air de Consentir à quelques Concessions, ce ne serait que pour mieux nous Tromper; Le Commerce Exclusif qu'il pourrait demander, serait une Atteinte portée à notre Indépendance, de quel droit, à quel Titre le demanderait-il?

La France ne Serait pas plus heureuse en rappelant auprès des puissances alliées le principe de sa possession légitime. Cet argument Tournerait contre elle-même, par L'Exemple qu'elle a déja donné envers les Etats Unis d'amérique.

Est-ce bien après avoir Cherché à massacrer Toute une population, et n'avoir pu y réussir, qu'Elle pourrait donner l'assurance qu'Elle ne Régnerait à haïty, que Comme Sur un peuple libre?

Indépendance Absolue, tant en matières de gouvern^t. que de Commerce, voila Ce que nous voulons, voila Ce que nous prétendons, voila ce que nous sommes déterminés à vouloir où à Cesser d'Etre.[2]

Le Cabinet Français vient encore, de Faire une Nouvelle Tentative, et d'Insulter le peuple haïtien par l'Envoy de Trois Commissaires, Ex-Colons, tous des hommes Tarés et Flétris dans l'opinion des haïtiens; Vous verrez dans nos papiers publics que je vous addresse, de quelle manière Inconvenante & ridicule Ils se sont présentés pour Communiquer avec Nous.

Pour faire cesser les outrages des Français, et pour leur ôter Tout espoir de nous abuser, de nous diviser, d'Intriguer Pour parvenir à leurs fins criminelles, J'ai Cru devoir rendre la Déclaration que je vous addresse sous ce pli, vous y verrez par l'Exposé des Faits, la véritable Situation des Choses à haïty.

Je Recommande Toujours à vos soins, à votre Zèle, à votre humanité, de ne point perdre de Vue la grande Cause des Affricains nos Frères & des haïtiens leurs descendants; vous qui avez défendu Cette Cause Sublime, ne pouvez être Indifférent à mes sollicitations.

Croyez moi, Monsieur, avec la plus haute Considération & l'amitié la plus Cordiale

HENRY

---

[2] In the last part of this sentence, "voila ce que nous sommes déterminés à *vouloir* où à Cesser d'Etre": instead of "vouloir," read "avoir."

SELECTED BILIOGRAPHY

Aubin, Eugène, *En Haïti*, Paris, 1910.

Basket, Sir James, *History of the Island of St. Domingo from Its First Discovery by Columbus to the Present Period*, New York, 1824.

Brown, J., M.D., *The History and Present Condition of St. Domingo*, 2 vols., Philadelphia, 1837.

Coupland, R., *Wilberforce, a Narrative*, Oxford, 1923.

Davis, H. P., *Black Democracy. The Story of Haiti*, New York, 1928.

Dorsainvil, Dr. J.-C., *Manuel d'histoire d'Haïti*, Port-au-Prince, 1925.

Franklin, James, *The Present State of Hayti (Saint Domingo)*, London, 1828.

Griggs, Earl Leslie, *Thomas Clarkson, the Friend of Slaves*, London, 1936.

Harvey, W. W., *Sketches of Hayti; from the Expulsion of the French, to the Death of Christophe*, London, 1827.

[Hassal, Mary], *Secret History; or the Horrors of St. Domingo, in a Series of Letters, Written by a Lady at Cape François to Colonel Burr, Late Vice-President of the United States,...* Philadelphia, 1808. (Published anonymously.)

Hazard, Samuel, *Santo Domingo, Past and Present; with a Glance at Hayti*, New York, 1873.

Knutsford, Viscountess, *The Life and Letters of Zachary Macaulay*, London, 1900.

Korngold, Ralph, *Citizen Toussaint*, Boston, 1945.

Leconte, Vergniaud, *Henri Christophe dans l'histoire d'Haïti*, Paris, 1931.

Léger, J. N., *Haiti: Her History and Her Detractors*, New York, 1907.

Leyburn, James G., *The Haitian People*, New Haven, 1941.

Loederer, Richard A., *Voodoo Fire in Haiti*, New York, 1935.

Logan, R. W., *The Diplomatic Relations of the United States with Haiti, 1776–1891*, Chapel Hill, North Carolina, 1941.

Mackenzie, Charles, *Notes on Haiti, Made During a Residence in That Republic*, 2 vols., London, 1830.

Madiou, Thomas, *Histoire d'Haïti*, 3 vols., Port-au-Prince, 1923.

Montague, Ludwell Lee, *Haiti and the United States, 1714–1938*, Durham, North Carolina, 1940.

Niles, Blair, *Black Haiti*, New York, 1926.

Sanders, Prince, *Haytian Papers*, London, 1816, and Boston, 1818.

Sannon, H. Pauléus, *Histoire de Toussaint-Louverture*, 3 vols., Port-au-Prince, 1920.

Stoddard, T. Lothrop, *The French Revolution in San Domingo*, Boston and New York, 1914.

Vandercook, John W., *Black Majesty*, New York, 1928.

Vastey, Baron de, *An Essay on the Causes of the Revolution and Civil Wars of Hayti*, ... Translated from the French by W. H. M. B., Exeter, 1823.

Wilberforce, Robert Isaac and Samuel, *The Life of William Wilberforce*, 5 vols., London, 1838.

INDEX

Alexander I (Emperor of Russia), 70–71, 92, 94, 97 n., 101, 105, 110, 117, 120–122, 129 n., 131–135, 140, 147, 164, 279
Alexander, Mrs., 247
Allen, William, 117, 166, 190
Artibonite, Duke of the, 211
Aury, Commodore, 99 n.

Banks, Sir Joseph, 45, 62
Basket, Sir James, 52 n., 165 n.
Belair, Charles, 30
Belliard, 243
Berry, Duke of, 107 n., 197
Biddell, A., 220
Birt, 136, 140, 149, 154, 159, 161, 164, 178, 181, 189, 194, 200, 232
Bolívar, Simón, 99 n.
Bonaparte, Joseph, 98 n.
Bonaparte, Napoleon. *See* Napoleon I
Boudet, General, 27
Boukman, 13
Bourne, 275
Boyer, Jean-Pierre: successor of Pétion, 69, 115; Popham's negotiations for treaty with, 69; rebels establish contact with, 74; assumes power in north, 76–78, 208, 211–212, 219; Clarkson recommends understanding with, 115–116, 123, 201–202, 205; France proposes treaty with, 121, 143; Christophe's account of relations with, 130; immigration of American Negroes proposed to, 141; moves against Gomar, 151–152; rumor he is negotiating with France, 160; Christophe's policy toward, 177; preferred to Christophe by France, 206; gains control of entire island of Hispaniola, 208; forced to sign treaty with France, 208; arrival at Cape, 211; faults of his government, 222; protects Christophe's widow and daughters, 223; letter from Clarkson to, 224–225; judged by Prince Sanders, 227, 248–250;

letter to Clarkson, 229–230; judged by William Wilson, 236, 242–243
Bradock, 275
Brown, J., 16 n., 30 n., 109 n., 211 n.
Burr, Aaron, 32

Castlereagh, Viscount, 62, 120, 122, 131
Cazes. *See* Decazes, Elie
Chavannes, Jean-Baptiste, 12
Christophe, Ann-Athénaïre-Henry and Frances-Améthiste-Henry (Princesses of Haiti), 42, 48–49, 74–76, 78–79, 211, 213, 218, 223, 230, 234, 237–241, 244–247, 254
Christophe, Ferdinand (Prince of Haiti), 27
Christophe, Henry (King of Haiti): character and personality, 4, 38–39, 43, 79–80, 183, 214–216, 222–223, 234–235, 242, character compared with that of Pétion, 79–80, contrasted with that of Clarkson, 64; accomplishments and failures, general summary of, 4, 55, 77, 79–80, 173–174, 183–184, 215 (*see also* Sanders, Prince; Stewart, Duncan; Wilson, William), chief aspirations for his subjects, 39, 46, 91–92, 134, treatment of his subjects in general, 43, 46–47, 54, 73, 213, 222–223, 252, 264, treatment of his officials, 43, 54, 74, 210, 213–214, 216, 223, 252–253, attitude toward white visitors, 43, 53, 150, 216, treatment of foreign residents, 53–54, 146, 165 (*see also* Davidson, James), accomplishments contrasted with those of Boyer, 77–78, 222–223, 227, 235–236, 242, 248–250; his campaigns under Toussaint, 19, 22–24; relation to Dessalines, 19, 27–28, 30–31, 35; surrender to Leclerc, 24–26, 28, 30; family, 27, 38, 42, 87–90, 233–234, son Ferdinand in France, 27, wife, 38, fate of heir to throne of, 76, 211, 218–220, 242–243, 252 (*see also* other entries beginning with the name Christophe); signer of Act of Independence

283

Christophe, Henry—*Continued*
of 1804, 33; early life, 38; authorizes assembly to form government for all Haiti (1806), 40; declines presidency of all Haiti and causes division, 40–41; President of State of Haiti (1807), 41; relations with Republic of Haiti, 41–42, 52, 57–59, 68–69, 99–100, 130, 151–152, 169, 177 (*see also* Boyer, Jean-Pierre; Clarkson, Thomas; Gomar, Count of Jérémie; Pétion, Alexandre); proclaimed King Henry the First and establishes Kingdom of Haiti (1811), 42–43; sets up hereditary nobility, 42–43; Royal and Military Order of St. Henry, 43, 210; principal Haitian advisers, 43–45, 184 (*see also* Dupuy, Baron; Limonade, Julien Prévost, Count of; Vastey, Baron Pompée Valentin); Code Henry, 45, 249, Code Rural, 45–46, 67–68; steps to increase number of property owners, 46, 67, 107, 268–271; court life, 43, 48–49, orders cathedral built for coronation, 43, Palace of Sans Souci, 47, 211, 218; military arrangements in Kingdom of Haiti, 49–50, Royal Dahomet bodyguard, 50, 75, Citadel Henry, 50–51, 54, 75–77, 118–119, 218, plan to use militia in place of large standing army, 68, 108–109, 129, 150–151; efforts to increase commerce, 51–52; relations with Santo Domingo, 52, 98, 104–105, 128; relations with England, 52, 61–63, 70, 106–107, nonintervention in British colonies, 52, 98–99, plan for British recognition of Haitian independence, 70, 108–109, 113, 128–129, 169–170; relations with the United States, 52–53, 68, 125, 163, 180; friendship with Duncan Stewart, 53–54, 183–185, 222–223, 231, 244; relations with France after his rise to power, 56, 71–73, 101, 132–135, 173–174, fears of new French invasion, 56–57, 72, 107, plans for French recognition of Haitian independence, 56–57, 60, 71–73, 175, first French commission to Haiti, 57–59, second French commission to Haiti, 60–61, 101, French abolition of slave trade, 61, 92, 111–113, views on indemnification of ex-colonists, 71, 175–176, overtures made by De Vincent, 126–127, 138–139, 195, authorizes Clarkson to be ambassador to France (1819), 168–177, 194–195, attitude on trade relations with France, 175–177 (*see also* Clarkson, Thomas); establishes public instruction, 62, 64–66, 91–93, 97–98, 257–267, later progress of schools and Royal College, 97, 129–130, 137, 151,

157–158, 181, 192–193, 212; efforts to improve agriculture, 62, 108, 150–151, 184, 193, 268–271; begins correspondence with Wilberforce (1814), 62 (*see also* Wilberforce, William); begins correspondence with Clarkson (1815), 63, summary of results of correspondence with Clarkson, 68–73; plans to settle American Negroes in Haiti, 68, 149, 165, 226; seeks aid of Emperor Alexander of Russia, 70–71, 105, 131–135, 140; financial arrangements with Clarkson, 71, 78, 167, 194; illness, 73, 209–210, 213–214, 226, rebellion against, 73–75, 210–211, 214–220, 226–227, death, 75, 211, 218, 222; fate of kingdom established by, 76–77, 208, 211–212, 222, 248–249; interest in South American revolutionists, 99; relations with Spain, 105–106, 108, 110, 114, 124–125, 128; information and comment on the Davidson affair, 105–106, 273–275

Christophe, Jacques-Victor-Henry (Prince Royal of Haiti), 42, 48, 67, 74, 76, 87–90, 192, 209, 211, 213–214, 218–220, 233, 242, 252

Christophe, Marie-Louise (Queen of Haiti): marriage, 38; relations with ladies from Philadelphia, 48–49; at time of Christophe's death, 73–76, 210–211, 218; takes refuge in England, 78–79; treatment at hands of Boyer, 230; William Wilson keeps her secret, 231–232; judged by Wilson, 233–234; dealings with Sutherland, 237–241; her suspicions of Dupuy and others, 243–244, 252; guest of the Clarksons, 245–246; letters of thanks, 247, 254

Clarke, George, 67, 186–187, 192, 196, 210–212

Clarkson, Thomas: birth and early life, 63; character and personality, 63–64; receives first letter from Christophe (1815), 63, summary of results of correspondence with Christophe, 69–73; sends teachers to Haiti, 64, 66–67, 91–93, 97–98, 117, 157–158, 186–187; general role in Haitian affairs compared with role of Wilberforce, 67, relations with Wilberforce, 72, 78–79, 125, 146, 156, 196, 237–240, 246, relations with other English abolitionists (*see* Macaulay, Zachary; Stephen); advice on Haitian education, 67, 185 n.; views on Haitian militia, 67, 114; advocates friendly relations with Republic of Haiti, 68–69, 116, 123, 201, 224; correspondence with American abolitionists, 68, 141–142 (*see also* San-